P9-EDE-796

ALSO BY DANIEL BURSTEIN

Euroquake
Yen!

TURNING THE *TABLES*

A Machiavellian Strategy for Dealing with Japan

DANIEL BURSTEIN

SIMON & SCHUSTER

New York   London   Toronto   Sydney   Tokyo   Singapore

SIMON & SCHUSTER
Simon & Schuster Building
Rockefeller Center
1230 Avenue of the Americas
New York, New York 10020

Designed by Irving Perkins Associates, Inc.
Manufactured in the United States of America

10 9 8 7 6 5 4 3 2 1

Library of Congress Cataloging-in-Publication Data
Burstein, Daniel.
    Turning the tables : a Machiavellian strategy for dealing with Japan / Daniel
Burstein.
        p. cm.
    Includes bibliographical references and index.
    1. United States—Foreign economic relations—Japan. 2. Japan—Foreign
economic relations—United States. 3. Japan—Economic conditions—1945-
4. Strategic alliances (Business)—United States. 5. Industrial promotion—
United States. I. Title.
HF1456.5.J3B78   1993
337.73052—dc20   92-41869
                                                                       CIP

ISBN: 0-671-78953-8

In loving memory of my mother and father,
Dorothy T. Burstein and Leon B. Burstein,
global citizens ahead of their time

Contents

Introduction: Machiavellianism for a New Age   **11**

Part I: Premises   **19**

1. *After the Bubble: The Changing U.S.-Japan Equation*   **21**
   A Bible Story
   The Hallelujah Chorus
   The Bubble Bursts
   What Has Changed—And What Has Not

2. *The Coming U.S.-Japan "Detente"*   **47**
   The Coming War Isn't Coming
   Japan as Metaphor
   Revising "Revisionism"

3. *The Portents of Peace*   **68**
   Fifty Years After Pearl Harbor
   The New "Japan Question"
      1. You Won't Have Japan to Kick Around Anymore
      2. The Empire Matures
      3. Who Is Us?
      4. Buy American?
      5. When Picking Up a Rock, Be Careful of Your Feet
      6. A Hot Political Issue Keeps Turning into a Nonstarter
      7. Money Talks—And Silences
      8. The Attraction of a $50 Billion Growth Market
      9. The Children Are the Future

10. The Complex Macro Environment
U.S.-Japan Relations in the 1990s

Part II: Problems and Challenges   **89**

4. *Continuous Improvement: The Dawn of a New*
   Business Order   **91**
   The Lexus Factor
   The Ten Core Competencies of Japanese Capitalism
       1. Continuous Improvement
       2. Total Quality and Zero Defects
       3. R&D: Tomorrow's Competitive Battles Today
       4. Process Innovation
       5. The Robot Explosion and Flexible Manufacturing
       6. Critical Technologies
       7. Relationship Capitalism: The *Keiretsu* System of
          Business Alliances
       8. Capital Formation
       9. The Ultimate Capital—Human Capital
      10. Strategic Globalization
   Productivity, Productivity, Productivity

5. *Paradigm Shift*   **139**
   Premonitions of the Bubble
   Making a Virtue of Necessity
   A High-Stakes Debate About the Future

6. *Heading Toward the Millennium: The Next Japan*   **160**
   The Crash as a Rite of Passage
   The Consumer Society
   The Profit-Making Society
   The Creative Society
   The Leading Society of the Pacific Rim
   The Global Society

7. *Heading Toward the Millennium: The Next America*   **186**
   The Real Reason Why Johnny Can't Compete
   American Assets—Use Them or Lose Them
   The Strategy Gap

Contents

Part III: Solutions and Conclusions **211**

8. *Turning the Tables: Toward a Japan Strategy
   for the Future* **213**
   Getting Started: Practical Proposals for the Mid-'90s
   1. Shift Gears on the Auto Sector
   2. Go Digital!
   3. Time to Invest in Japan
   4. Time to Invest *with* Japan
   5. Internationalize the *Keiretsu* System
   6. Resist the Temptation to Raise Prices
   7. Don't Backslide on Product Development Times
   8. Turn the Guns of Japanese Industrial Policy Around
   9. Maximize the Advantage of Low-Cost U.S. Capital
   10. Help Japan Do the Right Thing on Burden Sharing
   Reich's Dilemma
   The Next Step: Aikido Thinking
   In Search of a Bold Vision
   A Postindustrial Organization
   U.S.-Japan, Inc.: The Deal of the Next Century

Notes **249**

Acknowledgments **259**

Index **261**

Introduction: Machiavellianism for a New Age

Taking everything into account, [the wise prince] will find that some of the things that appear to be virtues will, if he practices them, ruin him, and some of the things that appear to be vices will bring him security and prosperity.

—NICCOLÒ MACHIAVELLI, *The Prince*[1]

WHEN THE FLORENTINE STATESMAN Niccolò Machiavelli retreated in poverty and political isolation to his family's countryside villa in 1513 and set about writing *The Prince,* he obviously knew nothing about automobiles, semiconductors, dollar-yen exchange rates, or any of the other issues that have come to characterize the late-twentieth-century economic conflict between the United States and Japan. Why, then, should the name of Machiavelli be invoked at the beginning of a book about U.S.-Japan relations on the cusp of the twenty-first century?

The new geoeconomics I envision draws inspiration from Machiavelli's brutally frank assessments of power relationships and from his crisply formulated strategies for how leaders should go about obtaining, wielding, and maintaining the power of their state.

Despite the high-minded rhetoric that is often heard in public forums where U.S.-Japan relations are discussed—hoary clichés about "the principles of free trade" or the importance of "friendship" between nations—the fact is that the U.S.-Japan relationship is principally about economic power and economic interests. These interests are often in conflict, or at least perceived to be so. The Japanese side has always understood this. The American side, however, has not.

For more than three decades Japan has followed a conscious strategy of maximizing its economic growth and international competitiveness. Meanwhile, the United States, once the wealthiest and most competitive economy the world had ever known, placed its priorities elsewhere. Especially in the Reagan-Bush years, American leaders maintained an open ideological *opposition* to developing any sort of conscious national strategy to maximize competitiveness.

In the years after World War II, Japan was prohibited from developing as a great military or political power on the world stage. Its growth had to turn, like a tropism, toward the economic realm. Virtually all of its impulses to strategic thought, all the best and brightest minds among its leadership, and all its national energies have been directed down the economic track—with enormously satisfying results. America's recent history has been much the opposite. Our propensity for strategic thought, our best and brightest, and our national energies have responded to the military-political demands of the Cold War. Yet with the Cold War over, we are discovering that we Americans must learn to do what the Japanese already do so well. We must develop a geo-economic strategy and a means to implement it if America is to remain a high-wage, high-productivity, high-growth, high-quality, and highly competitive society.

People can and do debate the merits of economic growth relative to less materialistic benchmarks of the quality of life. But without it, there will be no solutions to any of the vexing problems the United States faces as a society. Continuation of present trends will polarize American society and eat away at the fabric of what is best (and least materialistic) in the American tradition: our personal freedom, our sense of opportunity and possibility, and our pursuit of happiness.

We are already witnessing some of the painful effects of a society in which the overall economy ceases to expand: the spread of homelessness, gang violence and the structural unemployment of the underclass; the squeezing of the middle class; the intensifying animosities between black and white citizens, and the generalized phenomena of downward mobility and public cynicism toward the political process. The weaker the American economy becomes from decline within as well as intensified competition from without, the more likely it is that the American Dream will be denied to future generations.

Fluctuations always occur within history's trend lines, and we have recently witnessed some dramatic ones. The Japanese, who appeared economically invincible in the second half of the 1980s, began the 1990s with three years of a stock market meltdown, falling real estate values, weakening balance sheets at banks and insurance companies, rising bankruptcies, and numerous accompanying nightmares in their once brilliantly successful financial system. Even the best-managed Japanese industrial companies have been forced to cut back on new capital investment, new products, and expansion in foreign markets. Japan as a whole has been so wrapped up in its domestic economic problems that it has not been able to project the kind of new influence internationally that many observers, myself included, expected to see by now.

The United States, on the other hand, has managed to avoid the financial apocalypse threatened by its accumulation of debt and deficits in the 1980s. Quality has improved in American manufacturing. Some economists argue that American workers have now become the developed world's low-cost producers.

Tempting though it is, it is naive to believe that the "Japan problem" is simply solving itself through a combination of a weaker Japan and a stronger America. We will be better prepared for the future if we understand the high probability that the Japanese will ultimately repair the damage from their tattered financial system, just as they have surmounted the other formidable challenges over the last two decades—the Nixon currency shock of the early 1970s, the oil shocks of the mid and late '70s, the yen shock of the mid-'80s, and the rising protectionist currents in global markets of the late 1980s.

It is my expectation that, by the second half of the 1990s, a restructured Japanese economy will be back on course toward becoming the world's most competitive and dominant force—although perhaps without the accompanying fanfare, arrogance, fear, and emotionalism we witnessed in the 1980s.

The United States, meanwhile, has not yet manifested the desire, let alone the determination, to make the structural changes necessary to restore world-class competitiveness to its own system. Although some of the right issues were finally aired in the 1992 presidential campaign, and while Bill Clinton certainly understands these issues in a way Ronald Reagan and George Bush never did, it is not yet clear that substantive changes will be made in the next four years. The process of American reinvention that is needed will take nothing less than the attention and leadership of several administrations to achieve success, not to mention the support of a newly enlightened and cooperative Congress.

The recent years have demonstrated that our "Japan problem" is, at its core, an "America problem." The reason the Japanese have appeared to be passing us by is *not* primarily that they have treated us unfairly and gotten away with it. Rather, it is because they have continued to do what we once did very well in America—work hard, invest hard, invent hard, and do it all as a cohesive society pulling together.

My guess is that 90 percent of Japanese success is attributable to exemplary economic and social values within their society, and only about 10 percent to practices that might be legitimately classed as "unfair." The 10 percent that *is* unfair is maddening and even outrageous. It is doubly outrageous because the Japanese trumpet the notion that their economic strength derives *only* from the excellence of their business values and because it is so hard to get leading Japanese business figures even to acknowledge the legitimacy of American complaints about fairness.

The truth is that the next year's worth of *60 Minutes* could be filled with nothing but exposés and horror stories concerning egregious instances of Japan, Inc. keeping its markets closed, plotting conspiracies against American competitors, thumbing noses at American law, evading U.S. taxes, attempting to manipulate Washington, and evidencing a smug superiority complex toward Americans if not downright racism. Yet to be realistic—and to maintain our American commitment to fairness—we need to understand that even though these things happen and even though we should use every tool in our arsenal to prevent them from continuing to happen, such cases account for only a small minority of total economic interchanges with Japan.

Why Japanese business and government leaders don't understand that it is in their own interests to change the kinds of behavior that give Japan such a bad reputation in America is yet another maddening dimension of the issue. But when Americans choose to focus on unfairness and related problems—what I quantify as less than 10 percent of the total U.S.-Japan economic experience—we are missing the more important part of the story, no matter how valid our criticisms. Indeed, if American society as a whole were moving forward economically, we would scarcely notice Japanese unfairness.

In 1988, I described my first book about U.S.-Japan issues, *Yen!*, as a "report from the front lines of a war." This book is a second, but very different report from a later stage of that same war. The same combatants are still fighting, but the terrain has changed. So have the weapons and much else. I hope my readers will not be surprised to find that many of my own ideas have changed as conditions have changed.

Machiavelli's thinking resonates with the issues before us. Unlike most of our American political leadership class, Machiavelli recognized that history was characterized by the rise and fall of great empires. He warned that the wealth of a state should never be confused with any sort of permanent birthright to success. But neither did he see the decline of a state as preordained or permanent. In the dialectic between what he termed *fortuna* (fate) and *virtù* (intelligent actions of free will), he believed it possible for leaders—"wise princes," in his parlance—to use the latter to resist the tide of the former. Even a great state that had already descended into the lower depths of decline could reverse the trend. Sometimes, he wrote, the experience of severe decline was a necessary precondition for rebirth.

Suspending the usual (and usually hypocritical) flourishes of accepted ethical, moral, and religious thinking, Machiavelli cut right to the quick of the question: What was in the best interests of his beloved city-state, Florence? And what was the best way of advancing Florentine interests?

Machiavelli's reputation paid a price for offering such blunt pragmatism to his countrymen. For the better part of the last five centuries, his name has been synonymous with amorality, cynicism, and the lust for power. Some vested interests were so threatened by his analysis that they even accused him of "satanism." Yet recent scholarship has begun to uncover a Machiavelli who was actually a liberal and a humanitarian. Much of what he wrote in *The Prince* was not exactly what he believed, but rather, a deliberately overstated and provocative rendition of his beliefs, designed to wake Florence up to the dangers from neighboring city-states, foreign powers, and weak leadership from within.

At the very moment when the first progressive societies of modern times were being born, Machiavelli recognized a truth as old as the clashes between Athens and Sparta—yet one that seems to elude our leaders today. Liberal, humanitarian societies must continue to make tough choices and fight for their own interests as they evolve. Otherwise, no matter how rich and talented they may be, they will not be able to meet the challenges posed by the newer, more disciplined and rising states.

Machiavelli was fond of showing how qualities deemed to be virtues or vices in the abstract conventional wisdom of society could change into their opposite in the world of political interests and power. His reasoning is equally relevant in challenging two opposing camps of conventional wisdom today.

On the one hand, the "competitiveness gap" between the United States and Japan is wider than the conventional laissez-faire wisdom of the Reagan-Bush years could ever imagine. Despite the appearance of serious difficulties in Japan's domestic economy, and despite renewed drives for quality and competitiveness at many American businesses, the reality is that Japan has *already* won the race to dominate many of the key growth sectors and markets of the early twenty-first century.

On the other hand, much conventional wisdom on the part of those who profess to understand the economic challenge posed by Japan is also wrong. The protectionist solutions proposed by this camp may be even worse than blind disregard of the challenge. It is too late for most kinds of protectionism to work to America's advantage. Rather than "getting tough" with the super-competitive Japanese, American policy should be focused on "getting strategic." In *some* cases, that may mean "getting easy"—for example, making it easier for Japanese companies to move their new technology and manufacturing systems to the United States.

The time has come to harness Japan's economic and technological power to help us do what we are currently unable and unwilling to do for ourselves; that is, to help us renew our economy and promote our own long-term interests. This book suggests a number of short- and medium-term ideas and strategies for doing that. It also argues for a new long-term strategy—the creation of a Trans-Pacific Community to formally link Japan and the United States in a more mutually beneficial economic structure than is possible when our interdependence is left to the marketplace.

At this particular historical moment—when Japan's economic weak spots lie most exposed and when the United States still retains controlling positions at critical junctures of the global power structure—a unique window of opportunity has opened. For the entire post–World War II era, Japan has grown from strength to strength with the benefit of witting and unwitting American aid. Now the United States has the chance to turn the tables and begin to gain new strength by leveraging what Japan has to offer.

During Bill Clinton's run for the Presidency, bluntly worded signs were posted in his campaign headquarters declaring,"It's the economy, stupid." The purpose was to remind all concerned that their candidate's most incontestable advantage was George Bush's horrendous record on economic growth. Immediately upon his election, Clinton vowed to focus like a "laser beam" on reviving the U.S. economy.

But as this highly intelligent President Laser Beam enters the White House, he would do well to post a sign that reminds even the intensely sophisticated crew around him, "The economy is global, stupid." In the post–Cold War world, there is no such thing as focusing on the U.S. economy to the exclusion of global issues. And within the realm of international economics, no single country requires such careful strategic consideration as Japan.

Machiavelli reminds us that Asia has no monopoly on strategic thinking. Western cultural history is also imbued with its own rich legacy on this score. Our contemporary American problem is not that we lack the means to think long-term or the traditions to think with vision and plan, or the talents necessary to implement clever strategies in the global competition. We have all these faculties and characteristics. For various reasons, our leaders just haven't seen fit to use them.

This book is a call not to arms but to brains. It is time to stop letting history simply happen to us. It is time that our wise princes—politicians, business leaders, and concerned citizens— employ their *virtù* to resist the direction *fortuna* will otherwise carry us.

It is time to turn the tables in dealing with Japan.

Part I

PREMISES

1

After the Bubble: The Changing U.S.– Japan Equation

A Bible Story

Hollywood: sometime in the near future.

Casting about for a suitable retirement project, Ronald Reagan decides to launch a film production company dedicated to making inspirational movies in support of traditional American values. In the tradition of Cecil B. de Mille, his first project features a plot based on late-twentieth-century events, but told in Bible allegory style. The basic story goes something like this:

Just like Job in ancient times, the American people are tested by one trial after another: trade deficits and budget deficits. Hostile takeovers and dismemberment of once-proud and profitable corporations. Frightening levels of debt, collapsing savings and loans, cratering real estate empires, and unraveling LBOs. Mass layoffs, structural unemployment, and double-dip recessions. Flat productivity, declining quality, and the hollowing out of manufacturing. A foreign buy-up of prime American real estate, industrial companies, and advanced technology. Competitor nations that continually outmaneuver Americans at the negotiating table. A Treasury ever more in debt to foreign investors and beholden to their interests. Decay of the basic education system, runaway health care costs, and declining living standards for all but the richest Americans.

Latter-day Jeremiahs warn the nation to change its ways. These prophets of doom foretell a future in which the American economy is overrun by hordes of Japanese, German, and other assorted Asian and European invaders, unless Americans start working harder and smarter, sacrificing some of their profligate consumption for the sake of future investment, electing more capable leaders, and otherwise renewing their national competitiveness. But the people do not listen.

A famine of the spirit descends upon the land. A majority of perennially optimistic Americans have turned pessimistic. They believe Japan has already surpassed the United States economically and that their children's standard of living will be lower than their own. The American Dream is vanishing.

Just when things can look no worse, God finally hears America's prayers. He forgives Americans for building golden calves to worship the false gods of greed and excess in the 1980s. He forgives them for turning America's metropolises into latter-day Sodoms and Gomorrahs. He forgives them everything, because, just as Ronald Reagan often said, Americans are indeed God's chosen people, destined to live in His shining City on the Hill.

God waves one mighty hand over the Evil Empire of the Soviet Union, which proceeds to crumble just like the ancient Walls of Jericho. Having dismembered America's old foe, He turns His wrath to America's new foe—Japan. He bursts the Tokyo financial bubble and melts down the Japanese miracle economy. As the Japanese prepare their final assault on U.S. markets, God raises His hand to smite the enemy just in time. He closes the passage through the waters of the Pacific and drowns the Japanese charioteers in their Toyotas and Nissans.

In His infinite wisdom, God has delivered Americans from future bondage to giant Japanese corporations and set them free to practice the religion of American-style capitalism once again. In place of the gloomy forecasts made by the prophets of doom, America's future will see many more fat years to come. Hallelujah!

The Hallelujah Chorus

The preceding scenario is obviously not coming to the neighborhood video store any time soon. Yet exaggerated as it is, it bears an uncanny resemblance to what might be called the "New Wisdom," which is beginning to be dispensed by influential voices responsible for shaping public opinion and the U.S. political agenda.

Consider these real-life samplings:

• Karen Elliott House, writing in *The Wall Street Journal,* likens Japan's economy to the "Amazing Shrinkies"—a children's toy made of plastic pieces that "shrink while one watches." The shrinking Japanese, she says, were "never the economic terminators of America's imaginings" and certainly shouldn't be thought of as such now that Japan's "bubble has burst." American experts who see Japan as "an invincible economic engine destined to roll over the world, leaving America a second-rate global power" have always been playing an unnecessary "dirge," which sounds "downright discordant" in light of Japan's recent failings. The United States is now "clearly . . . reasserting its economic primacy over an uncertain Japan." The right music for today, says House, is a "Hallelujah Chorus."[1]

• Or consider this paean to the new competitive prowess of American business from investment manager James J. Cramer in a *New Republic* cover story, entitled, "We're Back! The Unsung Revival of American Manufacturing": "After a decade of gloomy prognostication from economists, journalists and politicians, it may come as a surprise that America now is equal to or better than most of its trading competitors. Our manufacturing companies dominate, not just in mundane fields such as chemicals, wood, paper, and metals, but also in such areas as aerospace, communications, computers and semiconductors."[2]

• Or this view from the cover of *Forbes:* "Tired of gloom and doom in the press and on the tube? Weary of politicians who say that unless you elect them the U.S. will go down the drain?" Then listen to this good news: The United States "is now the world's most competitive economy." In many product categories, the United States has become the world's low-cost producer. "That's why our foreign trade is booming and a trade surplus is within grasp."[3]

• Or this wisdom from stock market pundit A. Gary Shilling: "Japan is in big trouble. I knew it two years ago when suburban matrons cornered me at cocktail parties to worry about those unstoppable giants from the Far East. When a trend becomes cocktail party conversation, it's usually ready to ebb—and the trend of unstoppable Japan is no exception."[4] Soon, says Shilling, the story on the cover of *Time* won't be the Japanese threat, but the fact that Japan's financial structure is "fragile," that its economy is "rigid," and that the Japanese are worried because they can't compete with *us*.[5]

• Or this summary statement from supply-side economist Alan Reynolds: "Japan's economy is clearly sinking. . . . The most serious threat from Japan is that country's economic weakness, not its strength."[6]

Meanwhile, the intellectual arguments about American decline that captivated public attention in the late 1980s—and even made popular best-sellers out of weighty academic works like Paul Kennedy's *The Rise and Fall of the Great Powers*—are now handily dismissed by a new crop of smug voices of the '90s.

The definitive work in the booming field of decline-dismissal is *The Seven Fat Years and How to Do It Again*, by *Wall Street Journal* editorial page director Robert L. Bartley. Owing to his assiduous use of the *Journal*'s editorial pages to promote the ideas of Reaganomics, Bartley has come to be seen by some as the intellectual godfather of the Reagan Revolution. Now, he wants to "do it again"—that is, to create a new Reaganesque belief system capable of understanding that America is on top of the world and will continue to be there—if only the "declinist prophecy" is rejected. To prevent it from becoming self-fulfilling, Bartley wants the "American elite" to stop talking about his "seven fat years" of economic growth between 1983 and mid-1990 as a failure, to stop believing America is in decline, and to muzzle the "gaggle of declinists," led, presumably by Bill Clinton and Al Gore, who are too busy "wallowing neurotically in arcane and ill-understood statistics" to realize how successful the 1980s were.[7]

Japan merits only eight passing references in Bartley's lengthy history of the American economy during the so-called fat years. In his cosmology, if the American economy lost some jobs to Japanese competition during the 1980s, the losses were adequately offset by benefits to American consumers. From his rendition of recent trends, one would not know that Japan, as summarized recently by a leading business magazine, is an economy that was less than 10% the size of America's in 1960 and is now just over 60%; whose trade surplus doubled in seven year despite a 50% increase in the value of its currency; that habitually spends 70% to 100% more of its GDP on capital investment than the U.S., and 33% more on nonmilitary R&D; whose household savings rate is more than three times higher than America's; and . . . compared with the U.S., employs 70,000 more scientists and engineers on R&D in its labs and ten times the number of robots on its assembly lines.[8]

It is interesting to note that Bartley's chief literary device for telling his tale is a "Man from Mars" who lands by chance in Kankakee, Illinois, one day in 1990 and is thereafter continually perplexed at the contradiction between how prosperous everything looks and how much people are bemoaning the decline of their country. Bartley appears to have erred in picking Kankakee out of a hat as a stand-in for "anywhere U.S.A." According to one acerbic reviewer, the real-life Kankakee, like many American towns and cities, "was simply clobbered by the Reagan '80s, losing about two-thirds of its manufacturing jobs when a couple of big appliance manufacturers suddenly moved out and losing a large state mental hospital to budget cuts. The center of the city is boarded up. Crime is a thorny downtown problem, crack is ubiquitous in poor neighborhoods and racial tension is a constant irritant."[9]

Just as Bartley cannot see the real Kankakee through his rose-colored glasses, he cannot see the reality of the 1980s as a time when U.S. manufacturing industries were lost, productivity was stagnant, the average person's living standards fell, the middle class faced a growing squeeze, and the underclass grew exponentially. His "Man from Mars" sees Kankakee only as a town of gleaming air-conditioned shopping malls crammed with consumer goods. In like manner, Bartley sees the last decade as a time when the economy grew robustly, massive new wealth was generated, and U.S. technological, military, and ideological power dominated the world.

For Americans, it is tempting—very tempting—to believe the New Wisdom of Bartley and others whose views may be less extreme but who share major elements of his belief in America's New Dominance and Japan's New Decline. This sunny, confident optimism is very much in keeping with America's national character. Indeed, what was *out* of character was the deep-seated pessimism that developed in recent years about America's ability to compete.

The New Wisdom is also tempting because it sounds new. In our uncertain society, theories that seek to explain what is happening in the economy are virtually always unprovable. A good researcher can find as much data against a proposition as for it. Bartley, for example, praises the 10.6 percent increase in the output-per-hour of American workers that he says took place between 1983 and 1990. The figure may sound positive in the abstract, but not in comparison to the figure Bartley ignores—a 22.6 percent increase in the output-per-hour of the Japanese workers against whom Americans must now compete.

Explanations of economic phenomena are, to an unfortunate degree, more like fashions than their explicators would like to believe. They go in and out of style, the pendulum swings tend to be dramatic, and there is always a craving for something new. America's near-obsession with Japan's economic strength lasted longer than most fashions. But years of discussion, debate, and intense American emotions over the Japan question have exhausted and jaded even the concerned citizenry. The public ear desperately desires a new song.

The New Wisdom seems to be a good song because it resonates well with the surface realities people see around them. What the public mind once perceived as "Japan taking over America"—and even the world—now seems to be a movie running in reverse.

Like Ronald Reagan's vision of "morning again in America," this Hallelujah Chorus now asks us only to believe that which we desperately want to believe anyway. The most tempting—and most dangerous—aspect of their siren song is this: If it is true that Japan has shrunk back down to being just another big economy in an interdependent world, and if the U.S. economy is *not* in decline relative to the most fearsome challenger imaginable, then Americans can dispense with the unappetizing menu of tough political choices, sacrifices, and changes called for by those who believe America's future prosperity *is* in doubt.

Tempting as the New Wisdom may be, it is this book's contention that it is a mirage. The basic economic equation between Japan and the United States has indeed changed, but not as much as might appear from a simple comparison of how the Nikkei

Index has performed relative to the Dow-Jones. It would be se-riously short-sighted, if not downright suicidal, for Americans to think that the competitiveness dragon has been slain or that the long-running showdown between American and Japanese capi-talism has been canceled.

Most important, the relative comedown of Japan and the rel-ative comeback of America should remind us that our biggest economic battle is inside our own borders. Important as it is in a global economy to be internationally competitive in tradeable goods and services, our trade deficit currently represents only about 1 percent of the total American economy. Even at its worst, 1987–88, the U.S. trade deficit was only about 2 percent.

All U.S. import and export activity combined accounts for only about one-seventh of the total economy. To be sure, this foreign trade sector is highly strategic. It involves the lifeblood of several big industries such as automobiles and electronics, which in turn have significant ripple effects through the rest of the economy. It involves flows of vital technologies. It leads to crucial influences on the macroeconomic margins of currency and interest rates. And it will become a greater proportion of the economy as borders blur and barriers fall. But it is still quite a small slice of the current total pie.

How much wealth, opportunity, and social progress we can make in America is still determined overwhelmingly by what goes on in our *domestic* economic activities. The balance of trade is only a rough barometer of what is happening deep below the surface of an economy. The heart of the "competitiveness" issue is not so much whether the U.S. economy can beat the rest of the world at making cars, steel, or software, although those are important considerations. Rather, it is whether we can improve our own productivity, stimulate greater economic growth, and invest more intelligently for the future.

If we make headway in these areas, our goods and services will almost inevitably be competitive on world markets, although we will still need political initiatives to open and expand those mar-kets. If we don't make progress on these critical issues, our real living standards will continue to decline. This will be true even if for any number of anomalous reasons—such as increased pro-tectionism—we are able to hold off a further slide in our trade balance.

Martin Edelston is the publisher of *Boardroom Reports*, a newsletter that has increasingly turned its attention in recent years to practical ways to improve American business performance. He puts an interesting spin on the jargon tossed back and forth between the two sides in this debate. The Hallelujah Chorus likes to refer to the competitiveness camp as "declinists." Ironically, argues Edelston, the reality is just the opposite: "The true 'declinists' are those who say America is *not* in decline. By celebrating the status quo and opposing the changes we need, they hasten decline." Conversely, he says, "Those who acknowledge the uncomfortable reality that America is in decline are the true optimists and builders of America. They are the proponents of the constructive actions needed to revitalize the country."

The Bubble Bursts

For the six years 1986–91, Americans looked on with fear and envy as Japan's economy appeared to grow from strength to srength. The Japanese boom of the late 1980s dwarfed even the best years for the United States under the stimulus of Reaganomics. In Japan, the *average* annual growth in output, productivity, capital investment, and commercial spending on R&D tended to outpace *peak* American performance. Furthermore, *all* the new wealth Japan accumulated was multiplied by a factor of two when it was transferred into international markets. This was the result of the disastrous U.S. policy of devaluing the dollar in a vain attempt to balance the trade books by juggling currencies instead of changing fundamental business practices.

The rest is well-known recent history: Japanese investors bought up New York skyscrapers, California golf courses, Hawaiian and Australian beachfront resorts, luxury hotels in major cities of the world, and French Impressionist paintings—among many other trophies. They opened gleaming new greenfield factories, including a string of what have become the most modern and efficient auto plants in America.

Japanese companies gained powerful new links to the U.S. economy by buying hundreds of American companies whole and acquiring strategic minority positions within others. Bridgestone, the Japanese tire maker, bought Firestone; Kawasaki Steel bought Armco; Dainippon Ink bought Reicchold Chemical; Sony bought

Columbia Pictures and CBS Records; Matsushita bought MCA. The Saison Group bought the Intercontinental Hotel chain and Aoki Corp. bought Westin. Bank of Tokyo bought Union Bank; Sumitomo Bank took a piece of Goldman Sachs; Nippon Life a slice of Shearson; Yasuda Life a chunk of Paine Webber. Between 1985 and 1991, Japanese corporations bought or invested in 180 U.S. companies in the computer industry, 84 financial service firms, 59 chemical operations and another 59 in pharmaceuticals and health care, 43 machinery makers, and 42 enterprises involved in mining and metals.

The list of the ten biggest banks in the world became an exclusive Japanese club. The market capitalization of the Tokyo Stock Exchange soared past New York. The U.S. Treasury became reliant on Japanese bond-buyers to finance ever-larger American deficits. At every turn, Japan, Inc., appeared to be outwitting and outcompeting Americans, as well as everyone else around the globe.

What is more, Japan appeared strong in every area where America was weak. Japan became the world's leading creditor, while the United States surpassed Latin America's basket cases as the world's biggest debtor. Japan had a staggering trade surplus, America had an equally staggering trade deficit. Japanese savings rates were high, American rates were dwindling. The yen was strong, the dollar weak.

Japanese companies had access to low-cost capital, American capital was so expensive as to make investment in new plant and equipment prohibitive. Japan had a rock-solid financial system; America was experiencing the near-anarchy of deregulation, its excesses and its failed financial institutions. The Japanese stock market always went up, the American stock market rode a nervous roller coaster and sometimes even crashed.

Japanese companies were investing prodigiously in plant and equipment, America was disinvesting in manufacturing and infrastructure. Japanese companies were globalizing and gaining market share, American companies were pulling back and losing share. Tokyo used managed trade and industrial policy with great success, Washington disdained such governmental interference in the marketplace.

In those days, it was hard to pick up a daily newspaper without learning of some new way in which Japan was succeeding and

America was faltering. Whether it was the introduction of a new Japanese supercomputer, or the acquisition of another building on Fifth Avenue by a Japanese insurance company, every bit of news about Japan served as another straw in the wind suggesting the economic empire of the rising sun knew no limits.

At several points along the way, all of America seemed to come together in collective anger and panic: The disclosure of a Toshiba subsidiary's sale of submarine-silencing equipment to the Soviet Union in 1987 was one such moment. Another came in 1989 when two unique American icons were acquired almost simultaneously by Japanese investors—Columbia Pictures by Sony and a major interest in Rockefeller Center by Mitsubishi's real estate arm.

By the dawn of the 1990s, the United States was heading into recession, the S&L crisis was cresting, junk bond–backed LBOs had begun to go belly-up, and George Bush found himself unable to smooth jittery national nerves with sweet pablum the way Ronald Reagan once had. In this context, Americans no longer needed any one single news item to focus their attention on Japan's rise and America's fall from grace. Instead, this process had become an article of faith. Democratic presidential candidate Paul Tsongas declared in New Hampshire, "The Cold War is over. Japan won."[10] Voters seemed to agree—Tsongas came out of nowhere to emerge at the head of the pack in that first primary.

A spate of opinion polls indicated just how deep and pervasive pessimism about America's future had become. One of the most interesting was conducted by the Washington-based U.S. Council on Competitiveness. It found that the vast majority of Americans believed Japan had *already* surpassed the United States in terms of global economic strength and living standards—even though the professional economists who are most bullish on Japan don't see that happening for another decade or so. Six out of ten people expressed the view that because of America's failure to compete in the global economy, the living standards of their children would be no better—and probably would be worse—than their own.

Other polls showed that Americans now feared Japan more than the Soviet Union. A CIA-sponsored study entitled *Japan 2000* reinforced this view with its conclusion that Japan is "a fundamentally amoral society that will dominate the world through its economic prowess unless challenged anew by the West."[11] Declared the report: "The Japanese economic strategy is clear. They

are investing virtually all of their profits and energy to commercialize new technologies, develop new markets, improve efficiency and expand investments around the world in preparation
for the next phase in economic domination.''[12]

Perhaps the low point of American self-esteem vis-à-vis Japan
was experienced in January of 1992 during President George
Bush's ill-fated, humiliating visit to Tokyo. The trip took place
in the midst of a bitter U.S. recession and the beginning of another
presidential election session. As such, it was one of the most
media-covered of all U.S.-Japan interchanges.

To offer domestic public opinion the appearance of a president
concerned about the U.S. economy and willing to be tough on
trade, Bush asked the leaders of the auto industry to travel with
him. He was thus surrounded by the CEOs of GM, Ford, and
Chrysler—the three companies that have been most overwhelmingly and consistently outcompeted by their Japanese counterparts ever since the late 1950s when the Japanese first entered
the global race. (Reflect for a moment on this statistic: In 1960,
the United States produced 52 percent of all new cars in the
world, while Japan made just 1 percent. In 1990, Japanese production had soared to 28 percent of the world total, while the
U.S. share had shrunk by two-thirds to 17 percent.)[13]

General Motors had just announced plans to close more than
a dozen plants and lay off some seventy thousand employees.
Similarly sizable cutbacks had already occurred at Ford and Chrysler. Shutting down factories that served as economic cornerstones
in already troubled communities, the Big Three executives were
hardly sympathetic figures.

As news reports proliferated of industry executives' multi-mil-
lion-dollar salaries—and of how those salaries rose even as profits
at the companies fell—the industry's effort to blame its collective
$10 billion in 1991 corporate losses on unfair Japanese trade prac-
tices became less credible. And when Americans realized that
the cars the Big Three had so much trouble selling in Japan relied on left-hand-drive steering wheels rather than offering the
right-hand drive used in Japan, the picture was complete of a
dinosauric industry unwilling to adapt to the new era of global
competition.

Bush's role as an unsuccessful salesman for the most uncompetitive segment of American industry emphasized how far out

of touch he was with the challenge of this new era. The Japanese responded with an alternating mix of pathos and contempt.

"It's so symbolic: The superpower America is tired and everyone around it has to take care of it," said Naohiro Amaya, former deputy chief of Japan's powerful Ministry of International Trade and Industry (MITI).[14] He was referring to the constantly replayed television images of the flu-stricken Bush collapsing at a state dinner in his honor and then throwing up on the trousers of Japanese prime minister Kiichi Miyazawa, who bravely cradled the president's head for several minutes until he was able to stand.

If history were a movie directed by Oliver Stone, critics would complain that the scene where Bush collapses into Miyazawa's arms is too heavy-handed. Yet as reality, it was hard to deny the haunting veracity of the imagery.

Other Japanese were not as compassionate about the sinking superpower's plight. Yoshio Sakurauchi, speaker of the lower house of the Japanese Diet, derided efforts of American companies to get auto parts contracts from Japan, saying that America had become "Japan's subcontractor"—and not a very good one at that. American parts, he said, had too many defects to be acceptable in Japan. The reason for the U.S. trade deficit with Japan was not unfair practices but the "deterioration in quality of U.S. workers," a third of whom, he hissed contemptuously, can't even read.[15]

Shortly thereafter, Prime Minister Miyazawa tried to calm the storm that arose in the United States over Sakurauchi's remarks. But as has become standard practice over the years, the efforts to "clarify" barbed and bashing-type remarks about the United States only revealed more of the Japanese mindset toward America. In this case Miyazawa triggered a second wave of the storm by pointing out that it *was* true, after all, that America had lost its work ethic.

As with other flaps in the past, the reason these comments caused such a stir in the United States was not that they were false, but precisely because they contained uncomfortable elements of truth. Angry Americans launched the most forceful "Buy American" movement ever aimed at Japanese cars and other products. Japan hunkered down for a new wave of bashing, protectionist legislation, and a worsening relationship with the United States.

Suddenly, however, the mood began to change. By the spring of 1992, the American economy had taken its first tentative steps out of the darkness of recession and into the sunlight of moderate growth. The Dow-Jones averages rose to new record highs. But across the Pacific at just the same time, the Nikkei Index of blue-chip Japanese stocks, which had actually been crashing slowly and steadily for over two years, suddenly plunged right through its supposed ultimate floor support level of 20,000. Quickly, it nose-dived all the way into the 14,000s.

By the time the long-running crash abated, the market had fallen 25,000 points from the dizzy record highs set on the last trading days of 1989. It had cannibalized nearly $3 trillion of market value—about equal to the *total* market capitalization of the biggest *one thousand* U.S. corporations. In its final convulsions, the crash wiped out almost all the remaining market gains of the second half of the 1980s.

Japan's "Bubble Economy"—so-called because the hyperinflation of stock and property prices in the late 1980s called to mind one of history's earliest stock market manias, the great South Sea Bubble of 1720 in London—had actually ended two years earlier in Japan. But in 1992, Americans as well as Japanese realized it was definitely over.

As the bubble deflated, Japan's astronomical real estate values plummeted. Osaka property was down 40 percent in 1992 from 1989 levels, Tokyo skidded 30 percent. Some of the swashbuckling Japanese investors who bought American assets at premium prices in the 1980s now tried desperately to unload whatever they could. Minoru Isutani, the controversial tycoon who in 1990 snapped up California's famed Pebble Beach golf course (perhaps the most sought-after of all American trophy properties in golf-crazed Japan), sold it seventeen months later at a reported loss of $341 million (to another Japanese company). A Los Angeles real estate expert described Isutani's experience as the "most disastrous real estate deal known to man."[16]

Falling stock and real estate prices triggered a chain reaction of Japanese bankruptcies—$63 billion in 1991, perhaps over $100 billion in 1992. Depending on who does the estimate and which less-than-explicit Japanese bank reports are used, nonperforming loans at major banks ranged from a worrisome $50 billion to an apocalyptic $385 billion in 1992.[17] Some analysts at foreign securities firms now believe the number may even top $500 billion.

Within those numbers is contained one of the most telling stories of 1980s excess: that of Mrs. Nui Onoue, a wily Osaka restaurateur in her late fifties who came to be known as the "Bubble Lady." A onetime barmaid with reported connections to the Yakuza underworld, Onoue carried out what appears to have been a Ponzi scheme of record proportions. She convinced several leading financial institutions to lend her money, then used the loans to obtain even greater credit, and then managed to rack up stunning gains in the stock and property markets that landed her a spot among the twenty-five richest people in the world. Her success made it even easier to borrow money with no questions asked.

When the markets came tumbling down, however, Mrs. Onoue's empire came unraveled. Big banks and securities firms suddenly realized that in their stampede to ingratiate themselves with the Bubble Lady, they had managed to lend her $3 billion against essentially zero collateral. The collapse of Mrs. Onoue's empire brought down top executives at two of Japan's most formidable banks, IBJ and Fuji, and sent shock waves of red ink across the books of a number of large financial institutions.

As the Nikkei Index fell below 20,000, Japan's rock-stable banking system, which had never countenanced a single actual bank failure in the postwar period, was seriously threatened. In the Japanese system, major banks are also major shareholders of industrial corporations and are allowed to count a portion of their unrealized gains on stocks in their portfolios as part of their capital. But as their huge "unrealized gains" began to evaporate in the crash, the capital adequacy of the banks came into question. With the Basel-based Bank for International Settlements (BIS) requiring 8 percent capital ratios for major global banking institutions as of 1993, each of Tokyo's major city banks danced on thin ice just above the minimum requirements.

According to outside experts, even if the Nikkei Index stabilized at 19,000, the Bank of Tokyo would be underwater on its capital adequacy, while a 15,000 Nikkei might sink such giants as Dai-Ichi Kangyo (the world's largest bank), Fuji, Mitsubishi, Sakura, and Sanwa.

In a desperate search for capital, experts predicted, the big banks would be forced to liquidate shares in the constellation of corporations around them, and the entire *keiretsu* system (long-term stable cross-shareholdings between members of Japan's major corporate families) might come unstuck. While it is not clear there will be a stampede in this direction, some sell-offs have indeed begun, posing new challenges to the historical ways of doing business in Japan.

Meanwhile, the giant industrial corporations at the heart of Japan's global success awoke rudely into a new era where they could no longer borrow money easily and cheaply from their banks and from the public as they had in the 1980s. Through the miracle of "warrant bonds" (a Japanese cousin to American junk bonds), companies had once financed capital investment at home and expansion overseas almost without cost. Japanese investors of the 1980s had snapped up these ridiculously low interest bonds (some actually bore no interest at all) whenever they had been offered. The interest rate was assumed to be immaterial, because the warrants would soon be converted into stock in a constantly appreciating market. Today, not only are companies habituated to such costless financing confronting real costs of capital for the first time in years, they must also cope with a $180 billion stream of bonds, never converted into stock, whose principal payments will be coming due in the next three years.

The bursting of the financial bubble also coincided with the end of the longest economic expansion in Japan's postwar history, and with the onset of a recession in the real economy coupled with slower growth in export markets overseas. Profits dried up at major enterprises. Even Japan's most globally successful industries—autos and electronics—felt the heat. Companies such as Sony, Fujitsu, Nissan, and JVC all announced first-ever losses. Toshiba cut its capital investment budget 30 percent. Matsushita sliced its product-offering menu from 1,369 to 1,065, began to cut its paternalistic and inefficient ties to thousands of retail shops, and refused to allow the American managers of its MCA subsidiary (which it had purchased for over $6 billion in 1991) to go ahead with a planned bid to buy Virgin Records in 1992.

Among the auto companies, the combination of the bursting bubble and the sharpening recession threatened the very existence of the weaker sisters: One small Japanese automaker, Daihatsu, withdrew from the U.S. market completely. Subaru was rumored to be considering a similar move. And, in the ultimate role-reversing irony, Isuzu was said to be looking for a cash in-fusion and possibly managerial expertise from General Motors.

Japan, the world's leading capital exporter of the 1980s, even became a capital-importing nation again. Having maintained an average net capital *outflow* between 1986 and 1989 of more than $100 billion per year, Japan drew in an *inflow* of $30 billion to $40 billion in net long-term capital during 1991–92.

The post-bubble environment allowed business leaders to speak out on the structural weaknesses of Japan's business system in a way that was impossible when everything was going right. "In the bubble economy, Japanese companies lost their way," observed Michio Nakajima, president of Citizen Watch.[18] Accord-ing to NTT Data president Shiro Fujita, the much-touted Japa-nese system of "just-in-time" delivery of parts and supplies is actually responsible for the horrendous traffic in Tokyo and other cities. "Just-in-time is the reason everyone is late. The streets are filled with trucks making just-in-time deliveries. It's ridicu-lous."[19] Honda president Nobuhiko Kawamoto went further still: "Everything we have done in recent years has been 'over'—overproduction, overselling, overkill. We need to compete, yes. But in moderation."[20]

Sony chairman Akio Morita spoke the most daring words of all: "Japan is in desperate need of a new philosophy of management; a new paradigm for competitiveness; a new sense of self."[21]

Dancing on what they think is the grave of the Japanese eco-nomic miracle, the purveyors of the New Wisdom may not realize that Japan's business leaders are now busy applying their talents to the task of creating a new Japan—one that may well emerge stronger, more powerful, and even more competitive.

What Has Changed—And What Has Not

Japan lost much with the deflation of its financial bubble. Its big banks, securities firms, and insurance companies will *not* be the dominant, controlling forces in the global financial services in-dustry during this decade they previously looked to be, although their sheer size will continue to keep them in the front ranks of world institutions.

The export of Japanese capital—including the acquisition of

assets all over the world and the greenfield expansion of Japanese manufacturers to the major markets—will now progress much more cautiously than in the past. With slower growth at home and costlier capital to justify, Japanese industrial companies will not take the same liberties they did before. They will invest somewhat less vigorously in new plant and equipment, introduce fewer new products, keep older products on the market longer in order to milk their maximum profit potential, and buy far fewer foreign companies.

These and many other changes will open doors for excellent, innovative American and other foreign companies to win back market share from their Japanese competitors.

It will take Japanese financial institutions a minimum of five years to rebuild their balance sheets, digest problem loans, and restructure. But this process will eventually bring them to a point where they will again be global lenders, buyers, and investors on a scale comparable to their role in the late 1980s—minus the absurd real estate deals and other excesses of the bubble economy.

Stripped of swollen, Sumo-sized market capitalizations that developed when stocks were at their peak, Japanese businesses look considerably less fearsome. In the 1980s, there was a time when obscure also-ran Japanese companies enjoyed market values double or triple the size of the leading American companies in the same industry. The bursting of the bubble has normalized Japanese market values, although the competitive reversals of the 1980s are still evident in some comparisons: Toyota, for example, with over $20 billion in cash on hand, still has enough money to buy General Motors lock, stock, and stamping plants.

Even stock market analysts who remain bullish on Japan believe it could be the end of the century before the Nikkei rises again toward the 40,000 zone, especially if the market is to do what regulators want: perform more in accordance with corporate earnings and other solid "fundamentals," rather than running on rumor, insider trading, blind hope, and blind faith.

But although the stock market became decoupled from fundamentals in the 1980s, the fundamentals did not disappear from Japanese business. While the effects of America's financially driven excesses have been toxic, Japan has *not* lost the fundamentally sound, excellent, and world-leading features of its real economy. These include its basic education and training systems, its work ethic, its long-term investment time horizons, its social harmony and government-business-labor partnerships, its aptitude for sophisticated engineering and manufacturing, its approach to continuous improvement, cost reduction, flexibility, and quality in manufacturing systems, its corporate commitment to exports and global markets, its national support for critical industries, its special talents at process innovation and the commercialization of new technology, and its dominant market share in key global businesses such as automobiles and electronics.

One can even argue that the factors for excellence in the Japanese economy will be *enhanced* by purging what became, in the 1980s, terribly un-Japanese speculation, financial engineering, and financial anomalies. Indeed, there is a school of thought that maintains that Yasushi Mieno, the governor of the bank of Japan, knew exactly what he was doing in December 1989 when he took office at the very height of the frothy excesses. He did the job for which the Japanese elite had chosen him: He intentionally punctured the bubble through steep increases in the discount rate and suffocation of money supply growth.

Mieno was empowered to run the Japanese speculative economy back down to earth for the sake of the long-term health of the underlying real economy. *Fortune* described the process this way:

> Japan's economic slowdown, including the frightening stock market collapse, is part of a bold strategic stroke that will ultimately render the country an even stronger competitor than it has been. When Japan emerges from this downturn, it will have vanquished a growing inflation threat, doused a speculative fever in the financial markets, improved the quality of workers' lives, and brought runaway real estate prices closer to a level that average people can afford. All this while keeping unemployment under 3%. Did America do as well with its recession?[22]

Some of the supposed economic "carnage" we read about may be more media hype than reality. Yes, Japan, Inc., is shedding a few of its long-standing commitments to permanent job security. Nomura Securities, the world's biggest brokerage house, has announced cuts of two thousand jobs over the next few years. But in typical Japanese fashion, Nomura's explicit plan is to achieve that goal principally by eliminating members of its female work-force, most of whom had little hope of successfully climbing the all-male career ladder anyway. The story is similar at other large companies. Most of those losing jobs are part-time workers (often women) who were never covered by "lifetime employment" guar-antees in the first place. Permanent workers are more likely to see their bonuses cut rather than pink slips. All of this is un-doubtedly painful. But it is still a question of degree. And what has happened in Japan is extremely mild compared to the down-ward mobility faced by workers in Western countries. Even in the period from 1990 to 1991 when central bankers and Ministry of Finance regulators were deliberately trying to burst the bubble, the Japanese economy enjoyed some quarters with double-digit annualized GDP growth, a record $110 billion world trade surplus, a generally strong yen, the lowest inflation rate of any major coun-try, a government budget *surplus*, and some of the highest average real wage increases for any workforce anywhere.

One on-the-spot survey of Japanese public opinion in 1992 concluded, "Economic growth is flat, corporate profits are plung-ing, and the stock market is a disaster. But Japanese consumers, whose spending accounts for 60% of the economy, have hardly noticed. Unlike the U.S., there are no layoffs, let alone bread-lines. . . . 'Recession?' " blurts one Tokyo bar patron. " 'The bubble has burst, that's for sure, but how can you call this a recession?' "23

Among my own friends in New York and Tokyo, it is interesting to contrast the reactions to the end of the eras of excess that gripped both cities in the 1980s. In New York, new values for the '90s are clearly de rigueur, but deep nostalgia remains for the good times of the last decade. In Tokyo, even those whose ex-pense accounts have been cut back, and who must drink now at neighborhood hole-in-the-walls rather than the Ginza's flashy hostess bars, are happy to have the '80s behind them. "Now we can concentrate on business again," says an up-and-coming young Mitsubishi man.

In New York, people speak about the future with fear and a measure of hopeless frustration. In Tokyo, a naive sense of well-being reminiscent of America in the early 1960s still infuses all but the handful of individuals who overextended themselves in the stock and real estate markets. Whereas panels of august intellectuals and experts convene in New York to discuss how to deal with the economic constraints on America's global role, the colloquia in Tokyo focus on what Japan's future role should be, as if it could be almost anything the Japanese choose.

When the Japanese government finally announced its long-awaited $87 billion rescue package for the stumbling post-bubble economy in August 1992, few observers believed the money was enough to do the trick. Yet there is plenty more where that came from. The $87 billion was only a down payment, especially since it looks as if the Japanese financial authorities have now tacitly agreed to rescue the banking system from the onus of massive non-performing loans. But even if $87 billion is insufficient to address Japan's domestic problems, it seemed a bold and dramatic use of fiscal expansion in comparison with Washington's deficit-constrained inability to use any government stimulus at all to awaken the American economy from recession.

Mortimer B. Zuckerman, editor-in-chief of *U.S. News & World Report,* observed in an editorial that Japan's morning-after-the-1980s hangover was superficially similar to America's own experience of waking up to the post-Reagan era. But the similarity extends only up to a point:

> In Japan, unlike America, government runs a net budget surplus that gives policy makers considerable latitude to reflate the economy. Further, Japan's supercompetitive companies, with their state-of-the-art factories, are expanding exports at a record rate to make up for flagging demand. Their work force is not only diligent, educated and highly skilled, it is also fully employed. Most important, the Japanese believe their problems are real and are taking them seriously.[24]

Japan's financial authorities certainly know what they are trying to do. Even in Japan, however, they can't control the process completely. The stock market crash in particular appears to have overshot their targets, and the mess caused by the bursting bubble may prove less containable than they originally thought. A huge mopping-up operation remains.

But as Kenneth Courtis, strategist and senior economist at Deutsche Bank Capital Markets in Tokyo, points out:

> If Mieno and his people succeed in controlling the damage—and I think they will—Japan ends up with a return to the lean, mean

economic disciplines which made its companies so strong in the first place, plus some new and badly needed structural changes. The result is an even more competitive Japan by the mid-'90s. We'll have to petition the Nobel Committee to offer a prize in applied economics to the people responsible for pulling this off.

On the other side of the equation is the U.S. economy and American corporate performance. It is absolutely true that some American companies *have* responded positively to the challenges posed by global competitors in the 1980s. They became leaner, improved quality, and moved closer to their customers. They expanded into global markets and even cushioned America's recent recession with huge export growth. They have emphasized training and experimented with new management practices from "skunk works" to "total quality." Some have even attempted to pursue long-term visions at the expense of short-term profit.

Industries from automobiles to steel to farm equipment have sliced payrolls and management layers, introduced new technology, and regained their ability to compete on cost with the rest of the world. The same trend has taken place at companies that compete in more advanced technologies. Xerox has won back some of the market share it once lost to Japanese competitors like Canon, while Boeing, even in the face of growing competitive pressure from the European Airbus consortium, continues to lead the world in quality and productivity in building commercial aircraft. Merck makes extraordinarily high investments in long-term R&D without shareholder rebellion. Companies that vend the unique products of American consumer culture, such as Coca-Cola, McDonald's, and Disney, have long been leaders in globalization.

The trend lines suggested by achievements in some of the *most* advanced of new industries are more encouraging still. In computer software, biotechnology, and emerging niches of electronics such as digital signal processing chips and interactive media, American entrepreneurs are continuing to make world-leading breakthroughs. In fact, new technological developments, as well as the changes in the overall terms of economic competition, have allowed American companies to rush far ahead of the Japanese competition in these promising fields of the future.

A "U.S. comeback in consumer electronics" is forecast by *Fortune* based on advanced new videophones from AT&T, digital personal communicators from Motorola, digital signal processing chips from a variety of Silicon Valley startups, and multimedia home computers from IBM, Next, Silicon Graphics, and others.[25] *Financial World* foresees a "second chance" for U.S. companies to "outflank Japanese consumer electronic giants" based on breakthroughs achieved by American companies in digital HDTV technology and interactive multimedia devices that marry hardware and software, computer and video technology.[26] And Mark Stahlman, a technology analyst with Alex Brown & Sons, claims the giant Japanese companies have run out of steam and are about to crash. Even the Japanese "semiconductor juggernaut," he says, is "on the rocks."[27]

The bursting of the bubble will slow Japan's effort to catch up in most businesses where the United States currently leads. These include not only esoteric technology sectors, but basic industry segments such as chemicals and pharmaceuticals and advanced services such as financial services, information services, and entertainment.

No longer able to throw cost-free money into R&D, diversification projects, and foreign acquisitions, Japanese business may suffer a widening gap with the United States in these and other select areas of the global economic race. For example, Japan's national TV network, NHK, recently abandoned plans to try to start an "Asia"-based all-news satellite network to compete with CNN. Some NHK executives even criticized the grandiosity of former NHK chief Keiji Shima's plan for a CNN competitor, acknowledging that Japan lacks the human resources for such a venture. In the post-bubble environment, it also lacks the $800 million per year in financial resources needed for the new network's startup.

Such developments should not be confused with permanent American leadership in the new and emerging fields. The architects of Japan's post-bubble economy are interested in finding ways to replicate America's success at "creative" pursuits, basic science, and "software"-type businesses within the framework of the new Japanese system. They may well succeed. But in the mid-'90s it will be slower going than it once looked.

American leadership in key sectors of technology and service businesses will certainly contribute vigorously to the U.S. economy. As we will see in Chapter 8, it may be possible to use these indigenous American strengths as strategic platforms on which to reconstruct the entire U.S.-Japan relationship.

Nevertheless, the prosaic reality is that in the near future, the advanced technology/advanced service economy will be able to add less to the total U.S. economy than will be lost through continued erosion of many manufacturing businesses.

It is therefore important to understand that when it comes to basic manufacturing, even the best among America's corporate stories of recent years is rarely an unqualified success. As a *New York Times* account of the improvements in the U.S. automobile industry observed, "A decade after the Big Three automakers vowed to beat the Japanese on cost and quality, they are still losing market share to their Japanese competitors. American cars look better, drive better, and are more reliable than in the past. But better is not good enough to slow the Japanese."[28]

In the auto industry, as in other areas of heavy manufacturing, cost reductions have been achieved largely by eliminating people and shuttering plants, not through improved efficiency. Layoffs are unsustainable over time as a method for competing with Japanese companies, which are investing in robots and other productivity-enhancing equipment while constantly improving every aspect of the manufacturing process. Moreover, the attempt to improve the corporate bottom line by eliminating people has obvious adverse effects on the "national bottom line" as unemployment increases and the fabric of communities established around industrial sites is torn apart. Increasingly, it is the exploding social cost associated with these kinds of problems that undermines America's long-term competitiveness.

It is also keenly relevant to note that a substantial proportion of America's new industrial competitiveness has been achieved in one way or another as a result of Japanese investment in basic industries. In 1991, fully 25 percent of all passenger cars manufactured in the United States were built in eight Japanese "transplants" and factories that operate as joint ventures between U.S. and Japanese companies. In the steel industry, much of the newfound ability of American plants to compete on price and quality with steel produced elsewhere has resulted from Japanese investments and transfers of technology.

Japan has also made powerful indirect contributions to the U.S. industrial revival by providing a new manufacturing model for

American companies to emulate. The General Motors Saturn operation, for example, is an explicit attempt to recreate in an American context a Japanese-style approach to work. "Continuous improvement" programs at hundreds of U.S. businesses reflect the influence of recent Japanese thinking about quality, customer service, cost reduction, and the manufacturing process itself.

The United States will probably be home to many outstanding, innovative, and competitive corporations into the twenty-*second* century and beyond. But America continues to lose the long-term battle with Japan because of overall problems within its economic and social structure. Even when Japan has a capital investment "recession" as it did in 1992, it is important to keep the numbers in perspective: When the "slashing" of the budgets was finished, the Japanese still outinvested Americans on a per capita basis.

Capital investment is not synonymous with productivity growth, but there is a close correlation. It should be no surprise, then, that Japanese productivity increases have *averaged* a 3 percent annual growth differential over U.S. levels for the last *thirty years*.

Yes, the American worker is still "the most productive in the world," as we are often told. But from Hong Kong to Germany, every workforce in every competitor nation has consistently gained on the American worker throughout the post–World War II period. The Japanese workforce was only 30 percent as productive as the American in 1960. But today, Japan has almost pulled even on average, and is far ahead of U.S. levels in key areas of tradeable goods such as automobiles and consumer electronics. Japan is expected to surpass the United States in overall productivity sometime between 1995 and 2001.

America's weak propensity toward capital investment and slow productivity growth are problems that no single corporation, not even the most successful, can tackle alone. These problems are closely connected to much broader structural issues in American life, which require government attention, leadership, and involvement, such as how people are educated in our high schools before they enter the workforce, or how low-cost capital can be made available for productive investment by the private sector.

One of the most telling summary statements of the situation is offered by Andrew Grove, CEO of Intel, a company that is actually outspending its Japanese rivals on R&D and has fought back tenaciously to regain market share in the ultracompetitive semiconductor industry. Says Grove somberly, "We are in an inexorable drift toward becoming a techno-colony by the end of the decade."[29]

The sad reality is that even though "competitiveness" has been a Washington buzzword for more than a decade—and even though the studies, commissions, and specific proposals for reform are legion—it is hard to identify a single major U.S. government initiative of the 1980s that actually resulted in positive change on any of the most central structural issues.

Even in its deeply troubled condition, the United States continues to generate an extraordinary degree of invention and innovation. Its economy still benefits from the self-correcting powers of markets, even if those corrections can no longer quite catch up to the excesses and abuses. And for at least some Americans—the top third or so—America continues to offer the highest living standards and the greatest opportunities anywhere in the world. Since virtually all political, business, and intellectual leadership springs from this top tier of American society, it is not surprising that we continue to suffer incredible disjunctions between what we know about what is happening in America, and what we are willing to do about it.

Tokyo enters the middle years of this decade consciously trying to reinvent the Japanese system to the benefit of Japan's powerful private sector corporations and the overall, long-term health of the economy. Washington, meanwhile, stared for a long time at the choices involved in reinventing America, yet remained unable to start the process and continually hoped not to have to. Perhaps the Clinton administration will at last succeed in breaking through the gridlock. But we will not know for another year or two.

Over the last generation, as Japan's economic success has attracted steadily more outside attention, American experts have often sought to discern Japan's "secret." At one point early on, the secret appeared to be its cheap labor. But since the mid-1980s, Japanese workers have enjoyed rough parity in wages with American workers. Later, the argument was made that Japan's secret resided in its cheap currency. But the currency argument hardly seems reasonable with the yen as strong as it has been these last few years. Then it was the regulated and protected state of Japan's domestic economy. But while Japan remains far more regulated and protectionist than other major economies, it has opened up so much—including to $50 billion per year worth of American imports—that it is no longer persuasive to make a case that rests on this factor.

The most recent preferred "secret" of Japan's success has been its low cost of capital: If Japanese companies can borrow more cheaply than American companies, they will naturally feel freer to invest for the long term. But as a result of the liquidity-draining measures taken to burst the bubble, Japan's current cost of capital has come close to parity with America's.

The truth is that all these factors have been instrumental in Japan's success at different times. Many still give Japan an advantage—but only a marginal one. After-tax real costs of capital are still a few tenths of a percentage point lower in Japan than the United States, for example. When wages are compared per hour rather than per month, the Japanese worker is lower paid, since he puts in more hours than the typical American. Some economists believe the yen is still too weak and should be revalued upward. Certainly, there is a broad consensus that the Japanese economy is still the most protected of all major nations'. But alone or even together, none of these advantages can fully explain Japan's success anymore.

Peeling away the layers of economic measurements, we are getting closer to discovering what lies at the very center of the Japanese miracle. As it turns out, the "secret" is not really economic, but social and political. It is the process by which Japan adapts readily and radically to new economic circumstances. More than any other country, Japan is able to make future-oriented choices about national direction, and to do so in a way that pulls the entire population along cohesively. This is a process we Americans should understand well. It is essentially the one we practiced in this country for most of our history.

Just as Japan's secret is not any one economic element like cheap labor or a weak currency, America's erosion of competitive power is not due to any one flaw. Our greatest weakness is the inverse of Japan's greatest strength. It is our refusal to make the tough choices necessary to adapt our system to the new challenges before us, and the way our society is fissioning out of control as a result.

2

The Coming U.S.-Japan "Detente"

The Coming War Isn't Coming

My book *Yen!* was among the first public warnings of a violent American backlash brewing against Japan. At the time of its publication five years ago, I argued that if farsighted leaders in both countries didn't intervene, and if circumstances didn't change, the fear, anger, and bashing on both sides of U.S.-Japan disputes could escalate into serious economic retaliation, a trade war, a financial war, and on the very distant horizon, even some sort of renewed twenty-first-century military clash.

In the last half-decade, the notion that the United States and Japan are on a dangerous collision course has become a mainstream view openly espoused by politicians, business leaders, and foreign policy experts in both countries. "Relations have suffered their most serious downturn in decades," *The Washington Post* reported in March 1992. "To a greater degree than in earlier crises, the current disputes have spread beyond specific differences over economic and security policies to a broader collision of two dissimilar societies, their leaders and peoples."[1]

Extreme voices have grown more vituperative. In Japan, attitudes have arisen that some in the media have dubbed *kenbei* (dislike of America) and even what one journalist called *bubei* (contempt for America).[2] Shintaro Ishihara, most famous in the United States for urging Japan to flex its muscles by selling its advanced computer chips to the Russians, now declares that with the Cold War over, Japan should say no to the United States even more emphatically than before. Ishihara favors a Japan that gives up on an arrogant, blameful, and economically defeated United States until Americans change their ways.

On this side of the Pacific, Daniel Yankelovich, the most insightful of all opinion pollsters, tells us that Americans are searching to replace the Soviet Union with a new national enemy and that Japan could be made to fill the bill.

Meanwhile Chrysler chief Lee Iacocca declared openly, "I'm a protectionist. And what's more, I'm proud of it." He urged the U.S. government to force Japan "to play by the same rules I have to play by" and to "retaliate if they don't."[3]

After visiting Tokyo with President Bush, Iacocca announced that he was "fed up" with Japanese inaction on American trade demands. "I used to believe the Oriental long view was a great virtue and something we could learn from the Japanese," he said in a fascinating and self-revealing statement. "I was wrong. It's not a virtue at all, it's a weapon, and we have to disarm them. We need to use our own weapon: good old-fashioned American impatience. That means demanding a solution to the problem NOW!"[4]

Senator Ernest Hollings, irked by remarks by Japanese politicians about the supposed inferiority of American workers, suggested that American workers "draw a mushroom cloud and put underneath it: 'Made in America by lazy and illiterate Americans and tested in Japan.' "[5]

Hollings was not the only one to rekindle the inflamed rhetoric of the World War II era. As Japan's stock market crashed, a major Japanese magazine ran an article alleging that a conspiracy of "Jewish money" was trying to destroy Japan economically, and make Japanese companies ripe for takeover. Anti-Semitic, anti-foreigner hate mail began showing up in fax form at the offices of foreign brokerage houses. A fax received at Salomon Brothers said, "The falling market has brought the suicide of several hundred people. Do you need more? Leave the country! Commit no more bad deeds in Japan."[6]

Perhaps the most sensational expression of conflict within the U.S.-Japan relationship was the 1991 book *The Coming War with Japan*, in which two American writers argued that a new military conflagration in the Pacific between the United States and Japan was not only possible but inevitable—and soon.[7] The book was a runaway best-seller in its Japanese translation. Indeed, it encouraged a widespread belief in Japan that many Americans think trade tensions are likely to escalate into a shooting war.

It is easy to hear the drumbeats. But the surprising reality, as we shall see below, is that U.S.-Japan friction may already have peaked. Although the chance of an American protectionist backlash is still there, especially if Japan fails to maintain progress on market opening, the economic relationship will probably continue to withstand the politics of acrimony and mutual recrimination as it has already done for a decade now. *No new war is coming—not even a trade war*—at least not in the foreseeable future. Japan is *not* going to become the new Soviet Union in the American mind.

To the extent that Washington-Tokyo power struggles might bear some resemblance to the Washington-Moscow conflicts of the Cold War, the apt analogy for the next few years will not be to the brinksmanship of the Cuban missile crisis. Instead, it will be to the era of "detente" in the 1970s when American and Soviet leaders first began contemplating the possibility of a warm peace rather than war, either cold or hot.

Japan as Metaphor

Two Japans exist side by side in the American mind. One is the "real" Japan. This is the country with which the United States has many substantive, specific problems of fairness and balance. To mention just a few of those at the top of a long bill of particulars: a cumulative $450 billion U.S. trade deficit with Japan over the last twelve years that is still running at roughly $50 billion annually; a Japanese vehicle market in which foreign companies have been able to get only a 3 percent share, compared to the nearly 30 percent Japanese companies get of ours; a highly monopolized distribution system that keeps foreign products out of the industrial supplier networks and off the retail shelves.

But another Japan has overshadowed the real one. This is the metaphoric Japan. It is America's alter ego—the country that succeeds where America fails, the country that is rising while America declines, the country that may be in the process of dislodging the United States from its position as preeminent global leader just as the United States once dislodged Great Britain.

Awesome as the real Japan can appear on the economic battle-field, the metaphoric Japan is more potent still. Japan-as-metaphor compresses together a great many ideas and sentiments about what American decline feels like to those who are already experiencing its downward pull, or at least fear they will soon. To a large degree, the metaphoric Japan has allowed people to put a label on primal images whipping through the collective American psyche and on the churnings wrenching the collective American gut. These are deep-seated American fears and anxieties about the future—about the loss of jobs, markets, and industries, the polarization of haves and have-nots, downward mobility, the end of the American century, the weakening of American beliefs and values, and the fading of the American dream.

It is a reality that the United States is losing the nearly full control it had in the 1950s and 1960s over its own economic destiny. Decisions about interest rates, capital availability, the value of the dollar, the development of new technology, jobs, and wages are increasingly influenced by events in Tokyo, Frankfurt, and elsewhere. Part of this is due to declining American economic power, but another part owes to the process of economic globalization itself. Most other countries have long understood—and accepted—the notion that they cannot fully control their economic destiny. In the United States, however, we are only groping slowly toward this realization. Accepting the new reality is particularly painful because we enjoyed the perception of being masters of our destiny for so long.

In the inchoate thought process from which metaphor springs, the instinctive assumption of the American tribe is that there must be a causal connection between Japan's success and America's failure. Mixed with appropriate doses of jealousy and envy, tinged with undeniable elements of racism, it is this belief that provides the impetus for Japan-bashing and various related strains of xenophobia, isolationism, and America-firstism. The Japan metaphor sometimes incites irrationality—congressmen taking pickaxes to Toshiba boomboxes; angry Detroit autoworkers smashing Japanese cars. Even when it doesn't incite such violent acts, it fans suspicion, distrust, and fear.

Yet the American people are not as unintelligent as Japanese politicians sometimes think. Even if ordinary Americans have difficulty identifying Japan on an unmarked map of the world, they came to undertand the metaphoric Japan quite well over the last few years. They began to know Japan as a kind of mirror image of America, practicing opposite policies from the United States on many fundamental questions.

They came to believe the Japanese have their work ethic intact, while Americans have lost theirs—even if they are angered when Japanese politicians say so out loud. Not only in opinion polls, but in auto showrooms, in consumer electronics stores, and at other points of purchase where it counts, Americans regularly exhibit their belief in the superiority of Japanese quality. They know that Japan saves and invests while America continues to borrow and waste; that the Japanese are comfortable thinking long term while America becomes shorter- and shorter-sighted; that Japan is a culture of consensus while America fragments into a barely sustainable collection of special interests.

The more Americans have become familiar with the Japan metaphor, the more they have understood that the enemy is not really Japan. In a recent poll, three-quarters of respondents cited the principal reasons for the loss of U.S. economic prowess as either (1) "the U.S. hasn't done enough to adjust to the new challenges of economic competition," or (2) "the U.S. work ethic and commitment to quality have declined." By contrast, only 19 percent blamed Japan for the deterioration of the U.S. position.[8]

To be sure, America continues to have a "Japan problem" with the real Japan, not the metaphoric one. The Japanese market is still closed to many kinds of American goods. This is true even in spite of the surprising facts that the Japanese Chamber of Commerce is fond of pointing out: Japan is now second only to Canada as a market for U.S. goods; Japan buys more from the United States than Germany and France combined; and Japan actually imports more from us than we do from Japan when measured on a per capita basis.

Even if Japan is making fewer corporate acquisitions in the United States these days, most of the ones that *are* being made, plus most that took place in the boom years of the '80s, represent the kind of ownership and control in American-based businesses that U.S. companies have not generally been able to obtain in Japan, at least until now. In fact, foreign investment is a less significant factor in the economy of Japan than in *any* other industrial country. When foreign business investment is measured as a percentage of GDP, Japan is judged only about one-twentieth as open as the United States. Even the most protectionist among Western European countries are more open to cross-border direct investment than Japan.

The international competitive "playing field" remains studded with hills, mountains, and gullies that have yet to be leveled. The disproportionate share of global peacekeeping costs still borne by the American taxpayer is a major factor. So too is a myriad of unfairnesses bred by the differences in approaches of the two systems: how patents are obtained, how corporations gain access to the work of research centers, how safety standards for consumer products are set and regulated.

In one recent study, the "playing fields" in Japan for foreign companies trying to sell consumer goods, soda ash, auto parts, construction services, and flat glass were all judged to be egregiously unlevel. Even when U.S.–based companies perform at high levels of quality in these fields—and even when they are able to sell their goods and services at prices way below Japanese norms—they have trouble competing fairly. Japanese cartels in these sectors keep promising to open their markets and yet keep managing to avoid letting imports in.

Even when progress is made, it is rarely complete: A decade ago, American soda ash companies simply couldn't sell their cheap, abundant, high-quality product in Japan. Today, after years of tough negotiating, U.S. producers have 20 percent of the Japanese market. Yet that is about 30 percent less than they would have if Japanese buyers judged soda ash purely on marketplace factors such as price competitiveness.

Soda ash producers obviously have legitimate complaints. The problem is that even if they gained 50 percent of the market—and even if other American producers enjoyed similar gains in sectors now dominated by the most unfair practices—the net effect on the U.S. economy would be marginal.

Disentangle the emotions from the Japan issue for a moment. Set aside the frustration of a country that keeps its rice market hermetically sealed and whose diplomats have argued in the past that foreign beef can't be digested because Japanese stomachs are different, or foreign skis can't be sold because of the different nature of Japanese snow. Such unfairnesses are maddening and outrageous, to be sure. But a sober, analytic assessment also shows that these issues are far from being the central problems in the decline of American economic performance. MIT economist Paul Krugman frames the issue this way:

> Predatory behavior by Japan—even though it happens now and then—is not a major part of our problem. If an earthquake were to wipe out Japan tomorrow, we would still have stagnant productivity, soaring income inequality, a fifth of our children in poverty, and a future compromised by the worst basic education and the lowest savings rate in the industrial world.[9]

If productivity isn't everything, it is almost everything, according to Krugman. For national living standards to improve over the long term, output per worker must rise consistently. The optimism and upward mobility of World War II veterans had much to do with the fact that they came home to an economy that doubled its productivity over the next twenty-five years. Men and women of that generation found themselves quickly able to enjoy living standards their parents had never imagined. By contrast, Vietnam veterans came home to an economy that had raised its productivity less than 10 percent in fifteen years. They found themselves living no better than their parents—and in many cases, worse. Krugman concludes:

> The slowdown of American productivity growth since the early 1970s has been the most important single fact about our economy. Over the first 70 years of this century, American output per worker rose at an average annual rate of 2.3 percent. During the 1950s and 1960s that rate was 2.8 percent. Since 1970, however, our economy has delivered average annual productivity growth of only 1.2 percent. Had productivity over the last 20 years grown as fast as it did for the first 70 years of this century, our living standards would now be at least 25 percent higher than they are.[10]

Had the United States maintained the historic levels of productivity growth to which Krugman refers, we might now enjoy 25 percent more wealth and resources with which to fund investments in our future and solutions to our problems. In all probability, our government budget deficit would be minimal.

Furthermore, if we had stayed our historic productivity course, General Motors would still be the world's most efficient auto- mobile producer, Zenith, Ampex, and an American-owned RCA would dominate global consumer electronics, and many of our businesses and industries that now find themselves threatened with competitive extinction in the new global economy would instead be world leaders.

Raising productivity, of course, appears to be primarily a func- tion of private sector management practices. In the 1970s and '80s, middle management became bloated, excessive salaries and perks became the norm for upper management, and much of American business turned into a dog wagged by its Wall Street tail. Companies lacked worker-training policies and paid little attention to quality. Often, they were seduced into "service" businesses that turned out to have remarkably low efficiency. All of this must be considered in trying to understand the productivity depression.

But government policies and budgets have more to do with productivity than the enthusiasts of laissez-faire economics would like us to believe. Apart from being the nation's largest employer whose own productivity growth is negative, government sets the agenda for raising private sector productivity in five major ways:

- Through fiscal policies, tax incentives, and financial regu- lations that encourage strong capital formation and the use of capital for productive investment by the private sector.
- Through direct investment in productivity-enhancing infra- structure. In the past this meant funding the construction of highways and ports; today it means those traditional elements plus their modern equivalents, such as data highways and teleports.
- Through investment in "human capital"—educating and training young people to make them as skilled, flexible, and productive as possible when they enter the workforce.
- Through direct support of R&D in the form of government- sponsored research projects, as well as indirect support in the form of tax incentives and other policies that encourage pri- vate sector R&D.
- Through programs that seek to ameliorate the social problems

that nag at productivity and ultimately drag it down—drug addiction and AIDS being potent current examples.

Candidates Clinton and Gore spoke eloquently on these issues during the 1992 election campaign, and it appears almost certain that there will be some substantive change. But for the last twenty years, the U.S. government has underinvested in every one of these areas, failing to support America's present competitive needs, let alone the future.

Nor has government played its role in creating the proper environment. No business person will dispute the importance of R&D to our long-term competitive abilities and economic health. Yet the United States trails not only Japan and Germany, but *all* major economies in per capita expenditure on civilian R&D. While Japan is now reaping massive productivity gains from using the nearly half a million industrial robots it installed over the last decade, the United States, which has deployed only one-tenth as many, has no significant government-sponsored program to develop industrial robotics.

No credible argument can be made that Japan, or any other foreign competitor, has much to do with weak American productivity growth. Indeed, by bringing new technology and new management practices into the U.S. economy, recent Japanese investments in this country have helped *raise* productivity in key industries. The Japanese presence has stimulated exactly the sort of competitive pressure that is in fact healthy for capitalism. For all its use as a central metaphor for America's economic problems, the truth is that Japan is not the source of our problems.

As the now oft-invoked cartoon character Pogo once remarked, "We have met the enemy . . . and he is us."

Revising "Revisionism"

A more intellectualized version of the Japan metaphor exists as well: *Japan as a different model of capitalism.* In this instance, the metaphor showcases a system that appears better adapted than our own to the needs and challenges of the twenty-first century. If the future is going to be driven by factors such as productivity growth, quality manufacturing, new technology, workforce skills, and ability to capture global markets, then the Japanese model must command our attention.

Experts have tried many ways to synopsize the differences between the American and Japanese models of capitalism. One of the best current analyses stresses Japan's roots as a "producer" society versus America's post–World War II incarnation as a "consumer" society. Another way of making the same point is to note that the Japanese state plays a more active role in planning the economy, while the United States relies on the philosophy of laissez-faire, which separates business from government and deliberately leaves the economy unplanned. Others see the difference best described in America's commitment to free trade versus Japan's mercantilism. Still others see it derived from deep cultural forces, such as the Japanese emphasis on the group versus the American emphasis on the individual.

Some explanations are geographic (an island people with few resources versus a continental people with abundant resources); some are religious (Japan's Buddhist-Confucian heritage versus America's Judeo-Christian heritage); and some are geopolitical (America spent the last forty years fighting the Cold War while Japan could focus exclusively on economic competition).

The bottom line of all these explanations is the same: *Japan is different—profoundly so.* This observation would seem to be elementary. Yet it took the development of a major new school of thought among Japan experts in the 1980s to popularize this crucial starting point: revisionism.

What "revisionism" seeks to revise is the old American belief that capitalism functions in basically the same way everywhere. Rooted in the ideas of Adam Smith, who described the laws of capitalism at its eighteenth-century birth—and reaffirmed by the Reagan and Bush administrations—the old wisdom held that as the Japanese became more prosperous, their marketplace would tend to converge with ours. The playing field would then become more or less level, and the Japanese would end up sharing American economic values and acting more like us.

The revisionists torpedoed this solipsistic American theory by demonstrating how different the Japanese model really was on every issue that arose in the 1980s. The old belief system that encouraged the White House to drive up the value of the yen against the dollar at the Plaza agreement in 1985, for example, was shown to be a complete fiasco in obtaining its desired results—a reduction in the U.S.-Japan trade imbalance. Classic laissez-faire economics suggested that a sharp upward spike in the Japanese currency would make Japanese products less competitive. Revisionists understood that the Japanese would find ways to become more productive, reduce costs, and if necessary, accept losses in order to hold on to market share.

Clearly, the two systems were not converging. Instead, the Japanese system was retaining its distinction. What's more, it was winning. Clyde V. Prestowitz, Jr., a former Reagan administration trade negotiator and one of the architects of "revisionism," argued that even the talk of a "level playing field" missed the point: Japan is playing by the rules of football and the United States is playing by the rules of baseball. No wonder Americans are getting mauled!

Or, as Jim Martin, an executive with Rockwell International's Tokyo office, puts it, "I don't know which system is better—Japan's or ours. But I know which one is winning."[11]

Stressing just how different—and successful—Japan was, the revisionists charted a set of solutions to America's competitiveness problems that entailed fighting fire with fire. In this view, America needs to learn from Japan and create its own government-led industrial policy that would foster, protect, and advance the interests of major existing American industries as well as critical new technologies of the future. Linked to such a national industrial policy must be a panoply of other government-launched initiatives and public-private sector partnerships in fields as disparate as public education, advanced scientific research, and health care, all serving the goal of refocusing the nation's priorities to meet the new challenges of global economic competition.

The budget deficit must be solved, the American financial system restructured, and virtually every institution in American life, from business-labor relations to the armed forces, rethought and redesigned. Only this sort of massive American version of *perestroika* would allow the nation as a whole to compete better with the new standards set principally by Japan, but also by other Asian and European competitors.

In the meantime, as America goes through this wrenching process of change, the Japanese economic machine must be held at bay. Revisionists argue that since Japan is "different" and doesn't respond to normal free market forces, tough-minded tools like "managed trade" and "reciprocity" are needed to keep Japan from further dominating the U.S. economy.

"Managed trade" means using government's power to set and enforce progress on specific trade goals. "Reciprocity" means seeking exactly the same kind of access to the Japanese market for American firms that the Japanese have in the U.S. If the American side doesn't get reciprocity, then Washington retaliates by closing off Japanese market access to the United States.

Demands for strict reciprocity are still mainly in the realm of threat, but when it comes to managed trade, the revisionists have made—and at least partially won—their case. Given the gross disparities in U.S.-Japan trading patterns, there can really be no free trade unless certain aspects of the trading system are managed. As it turns out, free trade and managed trade are not as mutually exclusive as they seem. Most trade in the world today is managed to some degree. The question is how well it is managed, and whether the particular management policies facilitate competition over the long term or create new barriers.

Those in the trenches of trade negotiations have recognized these realities. Even in the laissez-faire Bush administration, a growing emphasis on targeted management of specific problem sectors arose, such as getting the Japanese to agree that their private sector companies will try to buy $19 billion worth of U.S. auto parts, or that Japanese semiconductor users will buy 20 percent of their chips from American companies.

But the overt management of American trade remains confined to a few compartmentalized sectors. Negotiating positions are driven more by the self-interest of bellicose industrial lobbies than by a unifying national strategy.

Another problem is that a well-managed trade policy, if it is to support the goal of competitiveness rather than merely coddling uncompetitive companies, presumes a link to industrial policy. If government is willing to fight for a certain industry in international trade, it ought to be willing to take special measures to ensure the true competitiveness of that industry at home. We don't just want to force the Japanese to buy a small allotment of our cars or chips, we want to make sure that our products are the best quality, lowest cost, and most advanced on the market. This is for the good of our own domestic consumers as well as for long-term leadership in global trade. Unfortunately, what initiative Washington has shown in managing trade a bit better has not yet been complemented with the requisite domestic industrial policies.

Although the revisionists have been labeled "Japan-bashers," most of them are actually admirers of Japan's success. In most cases, their foremost concern is with promoting the renewal of the U.S. economy, not with attacking Japan. Consciously or subconsciously, however, they have been willing to arouse already-inflamed public sentiment against Japan in hopes of finding an acceptable platform for encouraging the domestic American changes they believe necessary.

By using the Japan metaphor, the competitiveness camp has been able to transcend its native ivory towers and inside-the-beltway think tanks. From my own experience as a journalist and commentator on competitiveness issues, I know that a discussion of competing models of capitalism is not the right stuff for TV and radio talk shows. But framed in the context of whether Japan is taking over the world from America, it is.

More critical still, the key programmatic ideas supported by revisionists are taken most seriously when posed as American national responses to the Japanese threat. This is especially true of industrial policy. A decade ago, it was an obscure bee in the bonnet of Harvard intellectuals and the left wing of the Democratic Party. But in the 1990s, even *Business Week* proclaims that the United States cannot hope to compete in the future without at least something resembling an industrial policy:

> Industrial Policy. The very phrase rattles the teeth. . . . It suggests government will pick winners and losers. Done badly, it would certainly hurt America. But with the Cold War over and a global economy taking shape, America needs to shore up its competitiveness. How? Certainly, by investing in education and infrastructure. But that's not enough. We must recharge the "knowledge base"—the basic science and technology that are the foundation of an advanced industrial society. Perhaps we should call it a growth policy.[12]

The New York Times adds:

> Industrial policy, the notion that government should help the industries and technologies of the future, is moving out of the dog-

house and into the limelight. The idea—derided by some Reagan
and Bush administration officials as a violation of *laissez-faire*—has
picked up steam because many Americans yearn for Washington
to do more to strengthen the economy. It has also been fueled by
concerns that more and more American industries are falling behind
their Japanese counterparts.[13]

The public buzz that exists about Japan has helped make Americans a nation of experts on the competitiveness crisis. Over the
last five years, I tracked the work of more than thirty commissions,
committees, and think tanks that identified what might be called
a "competitiveness gap" between the United States and Japan.
All of them proposed reasonably intelligent (and reasonably similar) solutions for what the United States should do to put its own
house in order. My library shelves added well over one hundred
new books, all with different emphases and styles, but all making
the same fundamental points. About six hundred pounds of newspaper and magazine clippings filled my office—a small sampling
of the total universe, to be sure—describing key events in the
erosion of American competitiveness. Even best-selling thrillers
and popular movies now routinely take the U.S.-Japan competition as their milieu.

All well and good thus far. But the last few years have also
pointed up an American tragedy that is a sad dilemma for well-
intentioned revisionists.

On the one hand, the revisionist action program for dealing
with Japan's mercantile, protectionist, and predatory practices has
found some support. The managed-trade policies used thus far
on autos and semiconductors are a good indicator of this trend.

A raft of proposals is now current that would go even further.
These measures ask government to protect U.S. industry from
Japanese competition, to restrict Japanese access to the U.S. market, to curtail Japanese investment, and to enforce collection of
billions in U.S. taxes from Japanese companies. Lobbyists for the
auto industry are trying to limit sales of Japanese cars in the United
States, for example. They are hoping to get Congress to endorse
the type of approach used in the European Community, where
it is not only Japanese imports that are limited, but cars made at
local transplant facilities as well.

As a result of such friction, Japanese companies have also become gun-shy about investing in the United States. Even when their investment would have many obvious benefits to a local U.S. community, the Japanese are choosing to avoid raising political hackles by staying away.

But the tragedy is that while there is enthusiasm to hit out at Japan on pieces of the problem, little action is taking place on the most critical part of the revisionist agenda—the development of an American economic strategy, an industrial policy, and the restructuring of our institutions. While good ideas abound, implementation in Washington has been marginal.

A world-class, globally competitive economy begins at home. And while certain American corporations have made heroic strides in improving their competitiveness, the U.S. government during the last few years has ironically succeeded in bringing about more change in *Japanese* economic policies than in our own. Indeed, the United States has moved into the unenviable position of having the worst of both worlds—managed trade policies that irritate our trading partners and are directed largely by special interest lobbies, combined with an absence of industrial policy to serve the strategic general interests of the American economy and workforce.

During these last five years, I have spoken individually with more than two hundred members of both houses of Congress on both sides of the aisle. Almost to a person they agree that the United States needs to cut its budget deficit, raise its savings rate, and encourage productive investment.

Almost to a person they agree that America needs to radically improve its basic K-12 educational system to compete in tomorrow's world. (How could they think otherwise? This has been the conclusion of more than three hundred federal studies on education since 1960.)

Almost to a person they agree that government ought to have some role in nurturing new technologies and new industries of the future, even if they disagree about the extent of such an industrial or technology policy.

Almost to a person they agree that our bloated entitlements structure, escalating health care costs, and rapidly expanding underclass represent costs to our society that ultimately take their toll on our national ability to compete.

Almost to a person they fear that if the United States doesn't act soon on these and related agenda items, we will find our prosperity eclipsed by Japan and perhaps the New Europe as well, and our leadership and influence in the world diminished.

And yet, no such set of changes have come about, even under the potent influence of the Japan metaphor. Even now, with a Clinton administration highly supportive of these ideas arriving in Washington, the needed changes will prove extremely difficult to realize.

For one thing, the actual implementation of a true competitiveness agenda requires massive new funds to pay for it. A conservative estimate is that the U.S. government needs to be investing about $300 billion per year more than at present in fields ranging from education and training to support for high technology. At the same time, a balanced federal budget is needed to bring down the cost of long-term capital, to cease choking off the flow of savings into government consumption and to start steering it into private sector investment. The mathematics is obvious but painful: a new $300 billion needed for investment plus $400 billion in current deficits to be eliminated equals a total of $700 billion, minus some increased tax revenue that would be the natural product of a healthier, faster-growing economy. Such stupendous sums can only be obtained through acts of extreme political courage that are currently tantamount to political suicide— real entitlement cuts, real defense cuts, real gasoline taxes, real wealth taxes, real burden sharing with our allies, and so forth.

Measured against the $700-billion-a-year gap between national economic investment needs and available funds, the $50 billion in U.S. trade deficit with Japan looks much more like what it is: a worrisome symptom, not a root cause of American economic decline.

Even if the courage was there to raise and reallocate the needed $700 billion, current political institutions are incapable of providing the vision, the blueprint, and the follow-up to see that the proper bang for the buck is achieved. Many voices in the competitiveness camp point out, for example, that in every other major industrial economy, education is the responsibility of the national government. Only in the United States is it in the purview of states and localities. Yet turning America's educational system over to today's federal bureaucracy hardly seems like the answer to the crisis in American public education.

Similarly, while the ideologues of the Reagan-Bush era were

wrong to insist that government is incapable of picking winners among future technologies, they were right in one way: If given a blank check to select the critical new industries of the future, *today's* governmental institutions are unfortunately more likely to opt for the interests of pork barreling than national competitiveness. Government itself has to change in order for the government programs favored by the competitiveness camp to work.

Thus, America has been paralyzed, running on the stored wealth of enormously productive prior generations and the incomparable innovation and productivity of a few continuously excellent sectors of the economy. Five years ago, it could be argued that the country needed to be "awakened" to what was happening in the world. Today, that is no longer the case. We are wide awake, and in 1992 voted overwhelmingly for change. Now we will see how much change the younger, more aware, more in touch political leadership of the mid '90s will be able to bring about as they battle the albatross of debt left in the wake of the '80s.

The revisionist critique of American policy toward Japan in the Reagan-Bush years was consistently on target. And revisionism's description of the fundamental differences between U.S. and Japanese societies remains generally correct—although the collapse of the bubble economy has opened the door to more real change in Japan than might previously have been assumed. It is even possible there will be greater convergence of the American and Japanese practice of capitalism, though no one should expect the major distinguishing features of the two systems to disappear soon.

It is revisionism's hostility to Japanese participation in the U.S. economy, however, that now needs to be rethought. This is so for two reasons.

First, because the "Japanese challenge" will simply not be as strong and visceral over the next few years as it has been in the past. Those who wish to continue to try to get Americans to take up the difficult choices involved in renewing the country's economic structure need to find new ways to communicate that program.

Second, and most important, Japanese participation in the U.S. economy (as well as that of other foreign investors) is ironically turning out to be a more positive force and a more productive approach to reindustrializing America and enhancing U.S. competitiveness than all the talk in Washington. While the politicians have dithered on industrial policy, Japanese companies have created hundreds of thousands of skilled manufacturing jobs in the United States. The Japanese are bringing manufacturing processes and techniques to the United States that would otherwise be absent. They are contributing to the rebuilding of domestic U.S. industries and the stimulation of new ones. They are creating R&D centers where American scientists and technologists can do advanced work in areas the U.S. government has chosen not to support.

The Japanese are of course acting in their own interests. They want to benefit from American research and advanced technology; they want to take advantage of the comparatively low cost of American labor in basic industry; they want to generate enough jobs in local markets to short-circuit protectionist political impulses.

But Japan's contributions to the American economy have become substantial enough that they can no longer be seen as some sort of conspiratorial chicanery to throw a few crumbs in our direction and divert our attention from the fact that they are outcompeting us. The Japanese have invested deeply in America, and their investments are paying off for the U.S. economy, as well as for Japanese corporate interests. Perhaps most critical, as the Clinton team attempts to develop a new policy toward Japan and as Washington now gropes toward incremental elements of industrial and technology policies, America can get Japan to contribute even more to our economic health by adopting a posture of long-term cooperation rather than erecting barriers. One plank (among many) of a pro-competitiveness program for the American future, therefore, is to encourage Japan, as well as European and other foreign investors, to solve bilateral problems not by exiting our domestic economy, but by contributing more to it—in addition, of course, to creating more opportunities and easier access for American companies in foreign markets.

Revisionists must come to grips with a fundamental reality about the American political and social landscape: The best solutions for restoring American competitiveness are not likely to come to pass. With the budget deficit as large as it is and the resistance to new taxes as politically strong as it is, the visionary kind of public investment needed to retool the American eco-

nomic structure is not likely to be made in the near term, even
if a political consensus is slowly forming that such action is ad-
visable—and even if the first few steps in the right direction are
at last being taken.

America has lost valuable time. Had government adopted a
meaningful competitiveness program a decade ago, a very different story would be told today. Instead, the United States squandered immense resources on the follies of the '80s—whopping
defense budgets that turned out to be against the grain of history
and a deeply flawed experiment in *de-industrial* policy that included huge tax breaks for the wealthy and the amazingly costly
deregulation of the financial system. For all the talk about how
government should not be in the business of picking winners and
losers, the Reagan-Bush policies *did* favor certain businesses. Unfortunately, they picked losers—defense industries and S&Ls.

Given that valuable time and resources have been lost, given
that even the most sincere and credible attempts to rebuild the
American economy will take a decade and perhaps a generation,
shouldn't America seek all the help it can get?

Machiavelli once observed that in a world where leaders are
forced to play by the laws of the jungle, the wise prince should
learn from both the fox and the lion. The lion is defenseless
against traps, the fox defenseless against wolves. "Therefore one
must be a fox in order to recognize the traps, and a lion to frighten
off wolves. Those who simply act like lions are stupid."[14]

In the new world of international economics, America must also
be sometimes lion and sometimes fox. At this particular historical
moment when Japan could use a more symbiotic relationship with
the United States to break free of its own structural problems,
and the United States could use all the new investment and
manufacturing technology it can get from Japan, the wise American policy is to encourage the symbiosis.

"Getting competitive" means "getting smart" as well as "getting tough." It sounds very "tough," for example, to favor limits
on Japanese car sales in the United States. But in reality, it would
be both "tougher" *and* more pragmatic to encourage Japanese
manufacturers to buy the factories being shuttered by America's
Big Three and rehire the tens of thousands of autoworkers who
have been laid off.

Under Clinton and Gore a limited version of a national "technology policy" has a fighting chance of coming into being. But to serve American interests in terms of jobs, skills, and the technological infrastructure of the United States, it must be global-minded.

"I believe the world has changed and globalism is the future," remarked W. J. Sanders III, chief executive of Advanced Micro Devices, in 1992 as he announced his company's alliance with Japan's Fujitsu.[15] Sanders has long been one of the most intelligent and outspoken figures in the U.S. electronics business—and one of those most vociferous on maintaining American competitiveness and getting tough with Japan on semiconductors. But now he is at the forefront of a critical shift in thinking about competitiveness.

As *The Wall Street Journal* puts it: "The new emerging philosphy is that U.S. and Japanese companies have complementary strengths and weaknesses in semiconductors, with the Americans strong on design and innovation and the Japanese contributing their superiority in manufacturing techniques."[16] The R&D costs are simply becoming too great, the necessary manufacturing volumes too large, and the markets themselves too globalized for companies to go it alone with nationalist strategies.

Certainly there have been failed cross-border alliances before, and the new wave of global partnerships will not be immune to cultural as well as competitive pressures. But Americans are no longer arrogant and naive as they were in the 1960s and '70s when they gave their technological secrets away to the Japanese too cheaply, never imagining they were nurturing their future competitors. And the Japanese are no longer out to conquer the world as they were in the 1980s. They have been reined in by a new political understanding of the objective limits on the game of global market share, and by reassertion of the laws of economic gravity in Japan. Now they have more in common with their American partners. They too must become more profitable and find new ways to bear the escalating costs of innovation in technological fields that are commoditized as fast as they are developed.

In this new atmosphere, the two best-known American showcase initiatives on technology policy—MCC, the electronics industry R&D group, and Sematech, the semiconductor consortium partially funded by the Defense Department—are both leaning toward more cooperation with foreign companies.

MCC's chief is Craig Fields, one of the most forceful voices favoring a U.S. technology policy. In fact, Fields's support for national industrial and technology policy initiatives led the Bush administration to purge him from his former post with the Defense Department. But after a year at the helm of MCC he declared his organization needed redefinition and a new vision of its purpose. While he still favors national efforts by business and government to collaborate, he now believes "it has become essential to work with foreign companies which supply parts and buy products in order to raise the international competitiveness of our participating firms."[17]

Sematech CEO William J. Spencer adds a similar perspective: "We're entering an era when nationalistic issues will continue to decline. Sematech gradually will become an international organization."[18]

Automobiles and electronics are the two biggest industries in the United States. If the former is virtually synonymous with twentieth-century industrialism, the latter is the proxy for the postindustrialism of the twenty-first century. Yet in both cases, there is hardly any such thing anymore as an all-American car or an all-American computer or an all-American semiconductor. To dream that there will be again someday is akin to tilting at windmills. Maintaining or restoring American competitiveness in key industries requires an intelligent U.S. strategy supported by the requisite resources from government and industry. But invariably, it will also involve cooperating with foreign partners.

In the early days of the Industrial Revolution, angry, exploited workers known as Luddites roved about England smashing the textile looms and other new machines of capitalism. Their anger was understandable, but the attempt to hold back the machine age was folly—and not at all in the workers' own interests. Nearly two centuries later, as the Postindustrial Revolution gathers momentum, something similar is happening. With Japan representing so much of the future in so many areas of economic activity, it is understandable that some Americans may want to smash its machines—mainly figuratively, and occasionally literally as well.

Opposition to foreign participation in the U.S. economy is being revealed as a kind of latter-day Luddite folly. It cannot hold back the new global age, nor return America to its former glory.

The time has come to stop seeing Japan as the source of our problems, and instead, to try to make it responsible for at least a part of our solutions.

3

The Portents of Peace

Fifty Years After Pearl Harbor

ON A VISIT TO JAPAN in 1989, almost every lunch or dinner with a prominent figure from business or government eventually threaded its way to the same question: "Tell me, Mr. Burstein," my interlocutor would begin, usually after the table had been cleared, "what do you think will happen in the United States on the fiftieth anniversary of Pearl Harbor?"

It was not necessarily my reputation as a futurist that caused my Japanese friends to ask me about this event still two years off. As I later discovered, they were asking almost every American they knew the same question. In typical Japanese fashion, they were compiling a huge, informal database to help them decide how to handle the problems posed by this milestone. They were most concerned that xenophobic politicians and media sensationalists would use the anniversary as a focal point for mobilizing American anger and frustration over economic issues into an organized Japan-bashing force of some kind.

By the time December 7, 1991, rolled around, the conditions were certainly ripe for something like this to happen. The United States was in the grip of a serious recession, with unprecedented mass layoffs taking place at major corporations from GM to IBM. The well-publicized trade deficit with Japan remained stubbornly high. A newly published study equated every $1 billion of the trade deficit with the loss of twenty thousand American jobs. The

1992 election campaign had begun, and Democratic hopefuls like Bob Kerrey, Tom Harkin, and Paul Tsongas were on the New Hampshire trail hitting out at the Bush administration's weakness on economic issues.

Leaders of Japan's Liberal Democratic Party (LDP) thought they might try to preempt a groundswell of Japan-bashing by issuing a formal apology for the attack on Pearl Harbor fifty years earlier. But this plan backfired when nationalists within the LDP refused to go along with a vote unless the United States apologized for dropping atomic bombs on Hiroshima and Nagasaki. The result was the worst of both worlds: The American news media alternately depicted Japan as *demanding* an apology from Washington and as *refusing* to apologize for Pearl Harbor.

Based on these conditions, the Pearl Harbor anniversary could well have proven incendiary. But it didn't.

The anniversary passed in a rather low-key way. Most of the public discussion focused on historical events, not contemporary U.S.-Japan issues. Even when discussing history, the American media proved generally balanced in perspective. Never before have American journalists and historians tried so hard to explain the "Japanese side" of the Pearl Harbor story, nor to describe the cynical machinations on the American side during the late 1930s and early 1940s. Several books were published purporting to prove that Roosevelt had advance warning of the attack, but chose to let it happen in order to precipitate the kind of crisis that would force America into war.

Concerned in part about offending Japanese advertisers, TV networks and newsmagazines went light on articles and programs dealing with present-day conflicts. Those that did appear tended to be balanced. If unfair Japanese trading practices were criticized, America's own failings were given equal time.

The 1991 Pearl Harbor anniversary did *not* turn out to be a barometer showing the rising pressure to bash Japan. Instead, it may have been the watershed when the tide of bashing actually began to recede. Perhaps America was becoming aware of the complexities of the issues, the futility of scapegoating, and the absence of easy answers. The new trend of U.S.-Japan "detente" was beginning to take hold.

The same week as the Pearl Harbor anniversary observations, Susan Hammer, the mayor of San Jose, California, officiated at a groundbreaking for a Sony corporate research center in Silicon Valley. "They used to say what's good for General Motors is good for America," she said. "Now, what's good for Sony is good for San Jose . . . and America."[1]

The New "Japan Question"

A certain greening is taking place within the once tumultuous U.S.-Japan relationship. The big, emotional battles have already been fought. Both sides are maturing. Slowly, Japan is becoming accepted as a force in American life and in the U.S. economy.

Relaxation of U.S.-Japan hostilities is now likely to be the major trend of the next few years, although certainly not without periodic flare-ups. Many factors support this trend and some have already been cited. But the following list adds much of the story.

1. You Won't Have Japan to Kick Around Anymore

The collapse of Japan's bubble economy means Americans will be experiencing considerably less expansion of Japan's business presence in our own backyard for the next few years. With reduced flows of Japanese capital, fewer corporate acquisitions of U.S. firms, less visible Japanese extravagance in the streets and shops of New York and Los Angeles, and more media attention given to Japan's problems rather than its triumphs, the public perception of Japanese ascendancy is going on hiatus.

In Danbury, Connecticut, Fujitsu shut down a sales office, laying off one hundred people. In Anaheim, California, Hitachi closed a small VCR plant. Toshiba put a planned new semiconductor plant in Oregon on hold. These and other such moves are indicators of a much-chastened Japanese business sector no longer expanding without regard to profitability and market conditions.

As Japanese money dries up from local real estate markets (as well as the U.S. Treasury bond market), it is very possible that the biggest criticism of Japan's presence in the U.S. economy will be that Japan isn't investing *enough*. "It seems like only yesterday that many Americans were worried about what they viewed as an invasion of Japanese capital," says Sam Nakagama, one of the New York financial community's leading pundits. "Now they must worry about the danger that some of that capital is going home."[2] Even more dramatically, veteran Wall Street economist Ed Yardeni declares that while Americans previously "were gnashing our teeth that the Japanese were taking over the U.S., now we're sweating bullets wondering whether the collapse in Japan will end Western civilization."[3]

The average American, whose real wages are still falling and whose job is still less than secure even in a so-called recovery, is not necessarily going to buy the good news song of the Hallelujah Chorus. But the intensity of his fear of "Japan taking over" *is* going to dissipate.

2. The Empire Matures

Even as the Japanese empire returns to full strength and reasserts itself in world markets, it is likely to be somewhat less rapacious. In its post-bubble sobriety, Japan is maturing as a global power. Just as the United States dabbled first at building a traditional colonial empire (by occupying Puerto Rico and the Philippines) before discovering more benevolent twentieth-century means of exercising global leadership, Japan too may have started down a false path in the '80s only to find a road more suited to its unique skills in the '90s.

Tokyo's elite decision-makers have come to understand (at least partially) the fear induced in the West by the relentless expansion of their business outposts. They know that their continued mercantilist behavior risks triggering protectionism and trade wars. Even without dreaded scenarios coming to pass, the perception of Japan as a pariah nation obsessed with its own interests breeds constant distrust and keeps Japan isolated.

With its empire now so global, Japan no longer wishes to be excluded from the structure of global decision making. Curbing the constant encroachments into foreign markets by Japanese companies—or at least slowing their pace—is one key step toward changing the way Japan is viewed by the club of developed countries that now controls most levers of world leadership.

The new Japanese understanding on this point dovetails with post-bubble insights into the problems of the domestic economy. Prime Minister Miyazawa himself has pointed out that the cult of market share has unduly stunted Japan's development as a consumer society. Everyone knows Japan's personal living standards don't match the wealth of its corporations. And some are beginning to question the thin profit margins businesses have been forced to accept, the low dividend payouts to investors, and the excessive working hours put in by employees—all in the name of maintaining an ultracompetitive edge. As a result, Japanese companies are beginning to impose some self-restraint on their once unremitting drive to capture global markets.

Japan's automakers, for example, possess the manufacturing resources, technology, and capital to put most of the U.S. auto industry out of business. But they no longer believe it a good idea to try to do so. Their new focus is on determining how far the U.S. political environment will allow them to go in taking market share away from the Big Three (29 percent of the U.S. market? 30 percent? 32 percent?). Once they determine the appropriate level, they will focus on making their percentage of the market as profitable as possible. That is why Toyota and other Japanese companies hiked prices on U.S. models in 1992, even in the middle of a desperately slow sales climate. In another era, they would have cut prices to gain market share during a recession.

In taking the pressure off U.S. companies and giving them some breathing room, the Japanese side will not only boost profits, they will also do themselves another favor by calming some American fears. The Ford Taurus will surpass the Honda Accord as America's best-selling car, and Americans will breathe a sigh of relief. That the Japanese side can revive the domestic American auto industry at will is the most telling fact about the power relationships over the long term. But never mind. The immediate appearance will once again be that of a somewhat diminished Japan and a resurgent U.S. auto industry. This pattern will be repeated in other business sectors as well.

3. Who Is Us?

More than half a million Americans now work for companies owned by Japanese interests. That stunning fact is but one indicator of the deepening roots of Japanese business in American life. States like Tennessee, Kentucky, and Ohio, which have been particularly hospitable to Japanese investment, now have scores of new Japanese-owned factories lining their highways. I-75, which runs through some of America's heartland, looks like a strip highway of Japanese industry, and is even known locally by some as the "Tokyo expressway." Matsushita operates its most automated plant here, making color TVs. AAP, an aluminum-wheel-making subsidiary of Hitachi Metals, reports that it lifted productivity 50 percent among its two-hundred-strong American workforce by introducing a variety of new manufacturing and management methods. And the sales manager of an industrial supply company in Troy, Ohio, says, "Without the Japanese, we'd be a Rust Belt."[4]

In Michigan, long considered hostile territory because of the dominance of the major U.S. automakers, Japan has recently been transformed from a "threat" into a "prime business opportunity," according to an officer of the local Chamber of Commerce. "It has taken us a long time, but Detroit has finally recognized the benefits of financial interaction with the Japanese."[5] Even in a huge economy like California, the nearly three hundred Japanese-owned factories located there provide a statistically significant percentage of employment and growth. Meanwhile, Japanese corporate philanthropy has now become nearly a billion-dollar annual business in the United States. The Japanese government is furthering this trend with an unprecedented domestic tax credit to companies that contribute to good corporate citizenship activities abroad.

Slowly, steadily, Japanese businesses are growing into fully integrated American enterprises. Most of the cars Honda sells in the United States are now produced at its Marysville, Ohio, plant—and a small portion of the Ohio production is actually exported back to Japan. Although there have been high-profile arguments over the "local content" of components within the Honda cars, and some of the high-value-added parts continue to come from Japan, Honda's local U.S. content is higher than that of Chrysler's Stealth model, which despite its American name-plate is actually made in Japan.

Sony produces nearly all its television sets for U.S. consumption in its American factories, carries on some of its most advanced research at U.S. centers, and is responsible for half a billion dollars a year worth of U.S. *exports*. In fact, subsidiaries and affiliates of all Japanese firms operating in the United States now account for nearly 10 percent of *all* U.S. exports.

At a research center in Princeton, New Jersey, sponsored by the Japanese electronics giant NEC, fifty American computer scientists and physicists are engaged in basic research ranging from fuzzy logic to neural networks. The lab's freewheeling approach is likened by one of its scientists to the good old days at Bell Labs, before restructuring forced that once premiere corporate research institution to orient itself more toward AT&T's bottom line.

Altogether, more than fifteen hundred Japanese-owned plants are now in operation in forty-seven states. The state tax breaks that attracted them to their particular locales represent the absence of an American national strategy, but their role in reviving U.S. manufacturing is undeniable. In addition, some three thousand formal tie-ups of various kinds have been made between American and Japanese companies in the last three years, including cross-border investment, technology transfer, joint manufacturing, and joint marketing agreements.

The six major Japanese investments in the U.S. steel industry made during the 1980s were surveyed by Gary Saxonhouse, a University of Michigan economist. He concluded that they were responsible for bringing the best of Japanese plant automation, computerization, and production control systems to the United States:

> With the adoption of Japanese processing and surface-coating technology made possible by these joint-ventures, American producers have been able to compete at home and in overseas markets once again on the basis of quality as well as price. . . . It has been well over a century since the U.S. economy has been on the receiving end of so much manufacturing technology transfer.[6]

Certainly, some Americans continue to feel victimized by Japanese business practices inside the United States. The number of lawsuits in which American executives say they faced discrimination when they worked at Japanese-owned companies is on the rise. So too are legal actions taken by American-owned companies that believe they were passed over in favor of Japanese companies in competing for supplier contracts. In fact, some Americans feel they have as hard a time cracking the mini-*keiretsu* of suppliers that have grown up around major Japanese manufacturers *inside* the United States as they have in cracking the Japanese market itself. Yet overall, respect for the genuine economic and social contributions of Japanese corporations in the United States is beginning to become the *main* trend in public discussion, rather than the criticisms.

Toyota, for example, has been criticized for importing too many of the high-value-added components it uses in its U.S.-assembled cars, for locating its manufacturing facilities in nonunion and predominantly white regions of America, and for continuing to oppose meaningful opening of Japan's domestic car market. Yet consider this *New York Times* account by a reporter who visited Toyota's plant in Georgetown, Kentucky, and examined the implications of what else was happening there besides the assembly of the popular Camry model:

> As more and more Camrys were built, accolades for the car poured in. Experts from the Massachusetts Institute of Technology came and concluded that Toyota's methods could help a factory make everything more efficiently, from cars to copiers, jet engines to dishwashers.

> In the four years Toyota has been making engines and cars here, tens of thousands of manufacturing executives and production engineers have journeyed here . . . convinced that what is happening here can change the American way of mass production. . . . Virtually every U.S. maufacturer is trying some elements of the Toyota system. . . .

> Toyota's assembly and engine plant has been an economic godsend to a region hurt by falling farm employment, particularly in tobacco, and cutbacks in areas like coal mining. Toyota jobs, with average pay about $17 an hour, are highly prized. Workers from 111 of Kentucky's 120 counties commute by car, a few almost three hours each way.[7]

In a similar vein, one of he most eloquent arguments in support of Japanese investment is proffered by Dr. Sheldon Weinig, whose semiconductor equipment company, Materials Research Corporation, was acquired by Sony in 1989. Faced with financing problems during a downturn in the market, Weinig had carried out an assiduous and ultimately unsuccessful effort to find an American or European buyer for his company before talking to Sony. Summarizing his experience afterward, he said:

What if we had not been sold? Would our brilliant team of scientists and engineers still be together working on the next generation of processing materials? Would the employment base that we have jealously guarded over 30 years be as gainfully employed as it is today? Would the Rockland County and New York state economies still be benefiting from our operations? Or the American economy? Would we have been able to continue making significant contributions to world technology? The likely answer to all these questions was no. But with our purchase by Sony, the answer to all of them seems to be a definitive yes.[8]

Analyzing the contributions foreign corporations are making to the American economy, Harvard University professor Robert B. Reich has gone so far as to suggest that the distinction between "American" and "foreign" corporations may not only be blurring, but even reversing itself in some cases. If Sony brings advanced high-tech manufacturing jobs to the United States, while Zenith, in an effort to cut costs, moves its TV production to Mexico or Taiwan, which is the true "American" corporation? Reich called attention to this question in a *Harvard Business Review* article with the provocative title, "Who Is Us?"

American ownership of the corporation is profoundly less relevant to America's economic future than the skills, training, and knowledge commanded by American workers—workers who are increasingly employed within the United States by foreign-owned corporations. . . .

If we hope to revitalize the competitive performance of the United States economy . . . we must open our borders to investors from around the world rather than favoring companies that may simply fly the U.S. flag. . . .

In the process of supplanting the American company, the foreign-owned operation can transfer . . . superior know-how to its American work force—giving American workers the tools they need to be more productive, more skilled, and more competitive.[9]

Reich is not an obscure academic. He served as the key economic advisor to Bill Clinton during the 1992 presidential campaign, and his ideas have been picked up widely within the Democratic Party. Previously, only overt "free traders" congregated within the Republican Party's right wing went out of their way to welcome Japanese investment in the United States from an ideological viewpoint, although state governors and local politicians always welcomed it from the practical viewpoint. Reich has now elaborated a line of reasoning that is ideologically attractive to Democrats and intellectuals on the left side of the political spectrum.

Reich's notion about the degree to which nationality in ownership is losing its meaning is overstated. Political power—and the future American standard of living—is not as easily reduced to issues of "workforce skills" as Reich suggests. Yet even so, he gives voice to another equally important reality—Japanese and other foreign-owned companies are making valuable contributions to renovating American competitiveness in ways that neither the American business community nor Washington has matched.

The fear of Japanese investment that existed when it was a new trend is now being replaced by a grudging recognition of reality: While "American" companies close down plants and lay off people, Japanese companies have opened plants and created jobs.

4. Buy American?

Those who are frustrated and fearful in front of the Japanese economic onslaught often wonder what practical steps they can take personally to strengthen the U.S. economy. One of the standard practical recommendations has been to "Buy American." In early 1992, the "Buy American" movement looked like it might become a popular groundswell, fueled by the nasty remarks about Americans made by Japanese politicians and the intransigence of Japanese automakers on issues relating to opening their market. One survey showed two-thirds of the American people saying they were "making a conscious effort to avoid Japanese products."[10] From the White House to the NAACP, the drive was on to choose American over foreign products.

American companies, both large and small, announced incentives to encourage employees to "Buy American." Monsanto, a major supplier of plastics, rubber, chemicals, resins, and fibers to the North American auto industry, offered employees one thousand dollars toward buying or leasing a vehicle assembled in the United States, Canada, or Mexico. In framing the program this way, company president Robert G. Potter had to grapple with Robert Reich's question about who, exactly, is us. He needed to be able to decide what an "American" car was.

The "American" names on cars can be deceiving: The Pontiac Le Mans is made in Korea, the Chevrolet Lumina in Canada, the Mercury Capri in Australia, and the Mercury Tracer in Mexico. Meanwhile, some cars with Japanese names like Honda, Nissan, Mazda, and Toyota are built by American workers in U.S. plants. What's more, the components under the hood of a car can come from just about anywhere.

Monsanto developed its own definition of an "American" car. It decided that any vehicle assembled in the United States was worth supporting, specifically including those made in Japanese transplant factories. Given the close integration of the U.S. auto industry with Canada and Mexico—and sales of Monsanto products to those countries—the company concluded that cars assembled there should also be supported.[11]

The rush to "Buy American" that season led to several follies. A town in New York had to buy earth-movers and was rumored to be ready to pick Komatsu equipment over models from John Deere. A local political hubbub ensued—how could the town buy equipment from a Japanese company at a time like this? But it turned out that the good old "American" company, John Deere, used Japanese engines in some of its equipment. Most of the Komatsu equipment, meanwhile, was actually made in the United States, despite the company's Japanese name.

In Los Angeles, "Buy American" fever broke out just days after county transportation officials approved the bid of the American subsidiary of Japanese giant Sumitomo to build $122 million worth of modern new rail cars for the city's fledgling experiment with modern commuter trains. In the wake of the Bush visit to Tokyo, the county was suddenly accused of having sold out the interests of American workers in accepting the Sumitomo bid over the lower bid of Idaho-based Morrison-Knudsen. Yes, the officials replied, the Morrison-Knudsen bid was lower, and yes, the company was U.S.-based. But they rejected it because the Japanese were experts at building the needed rail cars and had a proven track record of quality and on-time delivery. Morrison-Knudsen, on the other hand, had never built anything of the kind. "We weren't trying to export jobs," said the L.A. officials. "We were trying to get L.A. taxpayers the best deal for their money."

Amid demonstrations and allegations of economic treason, Los Angeles reopened the bidding process, dividing it into two orders. But when the first order was bid up for bid, no one replied. Sumitomo was gun-shy and did not bid again. Morrison-Knudsen, after all the furor, took another long look at the numbers and decided they couldn't make the rail cars profitably enough to warrant bidding! The "Buy American" movement had resulted in nothing to buy. When last seen, the L.A. officials were trying to horn in on a rail car order placed by the city of St. Louis for rail cars made by the German giant Siemens.

The point here is not that it is impossible to distinguish American from Japanese products, or that the world has become so globalized there's no point in trying. Nor is it that trying to find ways to support our own national economy is not a worthy goal. Far from it. Real issues are involved in these debates about nationality of ownership and local content. But Americans are beginning to appreciate that the "us versus them" mentality is not fully appropriate to global economic issues.

Japanese prime minister Kiichi Miyazawa slipped in and out of Washington for a meeting with President Bush in July 1992, with hardly a bit of public attention focused on the very same issues that had enjoyed such a high profile half a year before. This was in spite of the fact that the U.S.-Japan trade balance had taken a marked turn for the worse.

Some of the steam had clearly gone out of the zealous "Buy American" movement. This was attributable to many factors, but at least one of them was good news: After the collective jerk of the American knee, the collective American brain had begun to understand some of the new complexities of the issues.

5. *When Picking Up a Rock, Be Careful of Your Feet*

Americans who wish to "get tough" with Japan are discovering the meaning of an interdependent economic world: It is increasingly hard to design ways to punish Japanese companies for unfair trading practices without damaging American economic interests as well.

A good case study was the U.S. Commerce Department's stiff 63 percent tariff slapped on flat panel computer screens, which Japanese electronics companies were found to be "dumping" in the American market in 1991. The point of the tariff was to try to level the playing field so that the few remaining American manufacturers of flat panel screens could stay in business. It was perhaps a good idea in the abstract, but not in the tangled world of global business competition.

Toshiba and other leading Japanese screen-makers responded to the tariffs by closing down pilot programs to manufacture in the United States. The American economy was thus deprived of some of its best laptop computer manufacturing jobs.

American trade law is an irrational patchwork in general, but this case created a particularly absurd and counterproductive anomaly: A fully assembled laptop computer could be imported into the United States without duty, even if it *included* a Japanese-made flat panel screen. The tariff was placed only on those screens imported as stand-alone components. Thus, even American companies such as IBM, Compaq, Apple, and Tandy were encouraged to move their production of laptops to sites outside the United States where they could continue to acquire the Japanese screens (the most expensive component in a laptop) without paying duty. Once the computers were fully assembled, they could be imported back into the American market duty-free.

A spokesman for IBM called the decision "an eviction notice from the U.S. government to the fastest-growing part of the U.S. computer industry."[12] Practically everyone who has examined the facts now admits that the net loser in this case was the U.S. economy.

It is not just computer screens. Many kinds of protection that those concerned with U.S. trade policy fought for and eventually won have also backfired. Managed trade agreements that have imposed quotas or "voluntary restraints" on Japan have often ended up simply guaranteeing the Japanese a certain share of the American market, without enhancing domestic competitiveness. By enabling Japanese companies to know in advance what their share will be, they have also enabled these companies to maximize profits. In the case of machine tools, restraints froze the Japanese share of the market at its peak levels—and then worked to keep out lower-cost imported machine tool components from Taiwan and South Korea.

"The people who want to maintain the restraints are trying to fight a war that is already over," observes Brian McLaughlin, president of Hurco, an Indianapolis-based machine tool maker.[13] Hurco's own strenuous efforts to become more competitive on cost—and to develop East Asian markets—were hurt by U.S. domestic protectionism.

Less significant from the point of view of business strategy (but perhaps most telling of all from the cultural viewpoint) was the flap over the proposed acquisition of the Seattle Mariners baseball team by a group whose lead investor was Horoshi Yamauchi, president of Nintendo, the Japan-based video game company.

The movement against Japanese ownership of U.S. assets reached such a fever pitch in early 1992 that even baseball became a front of conflict. Nintendo was at first rebuffed in its bid to make a friendly investment in the Mariners, even though the offer was solicited by local businessmen as the best way to keep the team in Seattle, where Nintendo's U.S. operations have dug deep roots. The deal included local American investors and was supported by leading political figures throughout the Northwest. However, baseball commissioner Fay Vincent at first declared that non–North Americans could not, under any circumstances, own a piece of the national pastime.

Emotional arguments ensued about Japanese sports practices, which have kept American-born sumo wrestlers from holding top honors in Japan, or which prevent foreign ownership of Japanese teams. But eventually, Vincent and team owners relented and allowed Japanese participation in the acquisition of the Mariners, as long as the foreign investors didn't gain operating control. Baseball not only liked the smell of the Nintendo-led group's $125 million; the game also liked the big money possibilities suggested by globalization: international television rights, lucrative foreign markets for U.S. baseball merchandise, and perhaps one day, a real "world" series.

Sports fans and Seattle boosters were generally thrilled with the outcome of the baseball decision. The manager at a local sports bar near Seattle's Kingdome, where the Mariners play, summed up the inevitable quality of America's new globalism: "You have to remember that the Kingdome is a stone's throw from the Port of Seattle, where every day container ships load and unload. Seattleites have always known that they depend on the Asian Pacific Rim for their bread and butter."[14]

6. A Hot Political Issue Keeps Turning into a Nonstarter

In spite of the heated controversy that has surrounded U.S. policy toward Japan, the issue has never successfully made it into the heart of American politics—the electoral process. It is instructive to see what has happened to those who have tried.

In 1988, Missouri congressman Richard A. Gephardt launched his run for the Democratic presidential nomination amid a series of television commercials that called for getting tough with nations that didn't play fair. A thoughtful proponent of American competitiveness in the new global economy, Gephardt believed he could tap the deep vein of American fear and anxiety about Japan, give it a leadership voice, and build a political movement around it. Yet his candidacy was short-lived. In the postmortem carried out by most political pros, his hawkish stance on trade proved more a liability than an asset. It was a legacy that lasted throughout the rest of the campaign. Even as the U.S.-Japan trade imbalance surged to astounding new heights, Massachusetts governor Michael Dukakis, the 1988 Democratic Party nominee, kept Japan policy at the periphery of his campaign speeches.

Four years later, Virginia governor Doug Wilder, one of the first Democratic candidates to declare his intention to run for president, issued an appeal to other candidates to avoid "Japan-bashing" in the campaign. With over five thousand Virginians working for Japanese-owned companies making "everything from safety glass to soy sauce," and selling $1.3 billion worth of tobacco to Japan each year, Wilder said he wouldn't pander to people's fears about the Japanese "buying up America." Japanese investment in his state was a positive economic force, he said, and he wanted more of it.[15]

A new crop of candidates in 1992 did try to make issues relating to Japan part of their campaign—but only a very small part. When *Business Week* devoted three pages to a survey of the economic platforms of the original six Democratic hopefuls, the word "Japan"never appeared once.

The Democrats who *did* go on to focus on trade were forced out of the race early: Senators Bob Kerrey and Tom Harkin. In a déjà vu of the Gephardt experience, Kerrey created a television ad designed to make his tough stance on trade explicit. Aimed at voters in the wintry climes of New Hampshire, it depicted him as a goalie on the hockey ice trying to protect the American team's goal from foreign attack. As with Gephardt before him, the experts later concluded the ad hurt Kerrey more than it helped. Almost immediately after the ad aired, Kerrey slipped in the polls from 16 percent of the vote to 8 percent.

Even with election fever picking up in the summer of 1992 and candidates scurrying to curry favor with voters, a majority could not be mustered in the Democratic-controlled Congress for a key provision in a new trade bill that would have capped sales of Japanese autos and light trucks at current levels.

Bill Clinton succeeded so deftly in keeping Japan and trade policy out of the campaign that by the fall of 1992, the Japanese companies most likely to be affected by a turn toward protectionism in Washington began to see Clinton as the candidate of choice over George Bush.

Trying to make an issue out of Japan didn't work on the Republican side in 1992, either. Maverick Pat Buchanan got a momentary lift at the very beginning of his challenge to George Bush by openly proclaiming his commitment to "America first." He zapped the president's record with one-line zingers like "In 1988 Bush promised you he'd create 30 million jobs—but he forgot to tell you that they were all going to be in Yokohama." Yet almost as quickly as he emerged as a force, Buchanan faded, never winning a single primary from Bush.

The most interesting candidate of all, businessman H. Ross Perot, ignited a national movement in support of his run for the White House by using battle cries like "action, action, action" and promising to "make tough decisions." He offered a number of good generic ideas for restoring American competitiveness. He also made some pointed critical remarks on unfair Japanese trade practices and the revolving door of American officials who leave government to work for Japanese companies and trade associations. He attracted the support of several leading American "revisionists." If anyone was going to be successful in making Japan a campaign focal point, Perot had everything going for him.

Yet even in Perot's on-again, off-again presidential bid, Japan never surfaced as more than an occasional buzzword in Perot-speak. As on other major issues, Perot was never very specific about how he would reshape U.S. relations with Japan. Even had he been elected, Perot's own successful business dealings with the Japanese might have proven to be the model for his Japan policy, rather than his inflammatory political utterances on the campaign trail.

Thus, for all America's supposed xenophobia and willingness to bash Japan, voters don't seem to find candidates who espouse tough positions on trade particularly attractive. Politicians appear to be grasping this lesson.

7. Money Talks—And Silences

American politicians are not just coming to enlightenment about Japan out of their own inner development process. Japanese economic influence exerts a powerful cumulative effect on their thinking. One does not have to agree with conspiracy theories about Japanese motivations to recognize that with about *one hundred* U.S. congressional districts now heavily affected by Japanese investment, many congressmen are increasingly reluctant to adopt positions that could be construed as "anti-Japanese." The same is true of state governors who are in a race with each other to attract greenfield Japanese plants.

From American universities (which are the beneficiaries of Japanese corporate endowments) to the "movers and shakers" inside Washington's beltway (who are increasingly likely to be involved with the $400 million per year spent on Japanese political lobbying and image making), one sees the same tendency: Americans are beginning to be more circumspect in what they say and propose about issues having to do with Japan. Even CEOs of some American companies who used to be considered "trade hawks" have grown more careful. They now worry about the impact of their statements on their company's efforts to do business in the booming Japan market. And some fear that if they speak their minds on "unfair" Japanese competition, they won't be able to attract Japanese investors to their companies.

Much of this process has a dark, cynical side in which the Japanese exploit the openness of our society, and how far a few almighty dollars go in a culture obsessed with short-term profit and personal gain. American trade negotiators leaving their jobs to work for Japanese industry associations are clearly a part of this trend. No symmetry is possible here—it will be generations (plural), if ever, before American companies can hire influential Japanese to represent their interests in Tokyo, in the way that Japanese companies readily hire influential Americans in America today.

But there is a more positive side to the new American circumspection. Some Americans are actually coming to understand that in a global economy, the real interests of Americans and Japanese are increasingly intertwined. As their own companies and industries benefit more from partnership ties to Japan, they are not just being bought off, but developing a genuinely new interest-based perspective, as well as new knowledge about how Japan really works. As a result, they are less interested in taking confrontational positions, less willing to blame Japan for American problems, and more willing to consider dialogue and mutual problem solving.

With Chrysler CEO Lee Iacocca riding off into the sunset, American industry is losing its most visible hardliner on Japan. The dearth of business leaders rising up to assume his mantle suggests that others do not believe his confrontational style gets to the heart of the issues or encourages progress.

8. The Attraction of a $50 Billion Growth Market

That the Japanese domestic market has become progressively more open during the last ten years is being publicly recognized for the first time by the very Americans who do the most business in Japan. American companies now export about $50 billion worth of goods annually to Japan, and many see Japan as a huge growth market.

In a landmark 1991 study sponsored by the American Chamber of Commerce in Tokyo, most American businessmen said they face far fewer Japanese government trade restrictions now than in the past. Most also agreed that the rewards of doing business in Japan were high: Three-quarters said they expected their Japan-based subsidiary to earn *higher* profit margins than their U.S.-based parent.[16]

"While many managers based in the U.S. believe it is impossible to succeed in Japan, a growing number of American companies in the Japanese market are prospering," concludes the American Chamber of Commerce's chief, Edmund J. Reilly, who is also president of the Digital Equipment Corporation's successful Japan subsidiary.[17] It will take time for today's experiences of U.S. companies doing profitable business in Japan to counteract the legacy of information from the days when Japan was much more resistant to imports. But the trend is now moving in a positive direction.

One of the best recent books on doing business in Japan is *Cracking the Japanese Market* by James C. Morgan, the CEO of the U.S. company Applied Materials, and his son, J. Jeffrey Morgan.[18] The message of the Morgans' book is that competing successfully inside the Japanese domestic market is crucial for any world-class business these days. If you aren't in Japan, say the Morgans, you are not only missing 10 percent of the global marketplace, you are missing your chance to "gain new strengths in management, technological development, in quality control and production, in product design, and in new ways to satisfy customer needs." The American companies tested in the crucible of the Japanese domestic market will "become better organizations, better marketeers and better able to meet the requirements of the new global markets."

Such views are dramatic changes from the past climate of executives telling "horror stories" about the difficulties of doing business in Japan.

9. The Children Are the Future

Demographics are also beginning to work in favor of a more harmonious U.S.-Japan relationship. One hidden reason why the Pearl Harbor anniversary did not provoke more intense feelings is the simple fact that only about one in five living Americans is old enough to have meaningful memories of December 7, 1941.

Young Americans are the least likely group in the population to have negative feelings about Japan. They have grown up surrounded by appealing, exciting Japanese consumer products. While many older Americans say they would never buy a Japanese car, their children are only too happy to do so. Well-educated young consumers tend to believe that Japanese quality is far superior to American quality. The less-educated often do not even know that Anglophonic-sounding brands such as "Panasonic" or "Bridgestone" represent Japanese-owned companies.

The *most* sophisticated of today's American youth are not just devoted buyers of Japanese goods, but tend also to be interested in Japanese culture. Some have taken a Japanese language class—now offered in America's best high schools. Some are studying in business schools where discussion of Japanese management philosophy is part of almost every curriculum. And some just like to eat in sushi bars.

Whatever their level of exposure to Japanese culture, they are likely to have more positive attitudes toward Japan than any previous generation of Americans. Students graduating from college today were born in the 1970s—the time when Japanese cars and electronics products began to flood the American market. The influence of this generation's greater acceptance of and positive feelings toward things Japanese will grow throughout the 1990s. By the early part of the next century, it will be this new generation that will be most influential in defining American consumer tastes and shaping business and political trends.

10. The Complex Macro Environment

Finally, it must be noted that in today's global economy, Americans are increasingly aware that the challenge comes from many directions at once, not just from Japan. The rise of a German-led European Community, even if it is currently still groping toward unity, has underscored the multidimensional nature of competition in the new order.

Some American energy for tackling Japan-related problems has shifted to dealing with Europe, where pasta wars and oil-seed disputes can be nearly as rancorous as issues on the U.S.-Japan agenda. The inability to reach a successful conclusion of the GATT's Uruguay Round owes primarily to irreconcilable differences between Washington and Brussels, not Tokyo. Even America's generally happy relationship with its usually accommodating neighbor to the north, Canada, is now studded with angry debates over matters that range from lumber to beer to cross-border shopping.

That there are many challenges from many different directions diffuses the focus on U.S.-Japan frictions and puts them in a new context: America is experiencing less a "Japan problem" than the traumas of adapting to a new and complex international regime.

U.S.-Japan Relations in the 1990s

Detente, as may be remembered from the 1970s, does not imply absence of conflict. To forecast a de-escalation of tension in the U.S.-Japan relationship in the coming years is not to say that angry rhetoric, threats, retaliation, scapegoating, and bashing will disappear. Indeed, the political-economic landscape will continue to witness all kinds of transpacific hostilities. But unlike the last few years, when friction has constantly threatened to tear the U.S.-Japan relationship apart, tomorrow's hostilities will be contained within an increasingly institutionalized U.S.-Japan relationship that is moving toward a new definition of its parameters.

At a minimum, a relationship that is modestly more amicable than what we have seen up until now will prevail throughout the rest of the '90s. But what isn't yet known is whether this period of U.S.-Japan detente will be passive or active.

In the "passive detente" scenario, the two sides would setle quietly into a recognition of each other's new powers and constraints. They would do a lot of business with each other, but perhaps not significantly more than today's levels. The importance of the overall relationship would be de-emphasized. Each side would be inclined to focus more attention on *other* relationships. For Japan, that would mean its Asian neighbors, perhaps Europe, and perhaps the former Soviet Union. The United States meanwhile would be chiefly concerned with building a North American Free Trade Area with Canada and Mexico, and expanding its ties to Latin America and Europe.

In the "active detente" scenario, the new atmosphere of relative calm would allow the United States and Japan to consider the welter of ideas now in circulation that are aimed at maximizing the potential complementarity of the two societies, along with specific ways to achieve better balance and synergy between the two economies. That course is in the best interests of Americans as well as Japanese. Whether leaders on both sides will have the vision and courage to follow such a road remains to be seen.

Part II

PROBLEMS AND CHALLENGES

4

Continuous Improvement:
The Dawn of a New Business Order

The Lexus Factor

In the Japanese industrial heartland outside Nagoya, at the edge of the urban sprawl of Toyota City, lies the Toyota assembly plant known as Tahara. Spare to the point of being spartan, the orderly rows of low-slung buildings look like standard industrial issue— just a bare grade up from Quonset huts. Unlike American show- case facilities, Tahara has no elaborate visitor's center, no state- of-the-art executive offices, no futuristic design flourishes. Not a yen has been spent to make Tahara look like anything special. Yet beneath this appearance of prefab anonymity beats the heart of the once and future Japanese economic miracle.

Rolling off Tahara's assembly lines, among a mix of other ve- hicles, is the car with the highest rating ever given by *Consumer Reports*,[1] the car that J. D. Power & Associates has ranked for two years running as the best car on the road in the United States,[2] the car known in Japan as the Celsior, and better known in the U.S. market as the Lexus LS400. The plant also makes a variety of other Lexus and high-end Toyota models.

Despite the success of the Lexus, the visitor to Tahara has to look carefully to understand what is so special about the way it is made. As in other manufacturing plants in the industries for which Japan has become famous, the genius of the system is in the details—and the details themselves are often amazingly simple.

The factory floor areas, for example, are immaculate and the assembly line is relatively quiet. These characteristics would appear normal. Indeed, they *are* normal by Japanese standards. But to appreciate their significance, you have to have been inside a selection of American auto plants, where grime, dirt, and piles of junk can be the norm, and where the production noise is usually deafening.

Asked about the apparent quiet at Tahara, a Toyota executive, wearing a workman's standard blue company jacket, simply smiles and says, "We are trying to reduce the noise level further to make this a better working environment."

A stack of metal cutouts in the stamping area looks ordinary enough—until a blue-jacketed engineer points out the changes in the stamping configuration that have resulted from the employee suggestions that are part of the process the Japanese call *kaizen*—continuous improvement. In the beginning, ten components and fifteen dies were required. Two years later, just two components and eight dies are needed. The engineer, of course, is not satisfied: "We can probably reduce the number of dies still further."

Robotic arms dance in a ballet of simple motions that belie the complexity of the task they are performing. First they mount and tighten bolts. Then, the robotized laser detection equipment moves in to check every single bolt to see if the torque is sufficient. Elsewhere, the process is repeated: Robots do body welds or mount car door assemblies. Other robots follow using cameras and computers to check the precision of the work.

Toyota, however, doesn't think of the process as being especially automated. "Our goal," says an engineer, "is to find a harmonious relationship between humans and robots." And indeed, the most impressive thing about the Toyota plant is not the machines but the people. Their controlled, disciplined movements throughout the production system appear to mimic the robots, while their attention to detail combines robotlike precision with the intensity of human craftsmanship. There are no "attitudes" on display here; no "personalities," no outside-the-workplace issues brought to bear. Every person is doing his job as if his life depended on it—as if he or she really believed the slogans emblazoned on the walls: "Catch the Heart of the Customer," "Keep Customer Satisfaction Foremost in Your Mind," and "Strive for the Relentless Pursuit of Perfection."

Not only is each car tested as it moves through various stages of the production process, but every single finished LS400 is also subjected to ten different quality tests before shipment. This approach of "100 percent testing," increasingly common in quality-conscious Japan, stands in sharp contrast to the occasional sampling method that is the norm in many U.S. industries.

New recruits work with "buddies" as they learn multiple skills. A chart posted on the wall indicates each newcomer's name and which processes he has mastered to date. As is typical in the Japanese system, workers do many jobs at once and will float fluidly through the factory over the course of their careers. Managers have no reason to fear their huge investment in on-the-job training. Even today, with "lifetime employment" breaking down and "job hopping" more acceptable, the average Japanese will change jobs only two or three times in his life, compared to the American average of 12.5. And among those who join leading companies like Toyota, the majority will stay for a lifetime.

Perhaps the single most telling feature of the plant is the white thread that runs alongside the assembly line. By pulling it, any worker can stop the line at any time if he sees a problem. In most American auto plants—as with U.S. factories in general—management dares not entrust the workforce with such personal power for fear it will be abused. In Japan, the inverse syndrome operates: Because they have the power to stop the line at will, workers try hard *not* to use it.

Toyota City is itself a metaphor for the Japanese economic miracle. It was here, about halfway through the history of the automobile, that Keichiro Toyoda, the son of a nineteenth-century loom inventor, first set about turning the family textile equipment company into a car company. Impressed with what he had seen in travels to England, he dreamed of developing a Japanese-made car. In 1936, he realized his goal as the Toyota model AA rolled off the first primitive assembly line.

Today, Toyota City has become the Motown of the modern world. A giant company town, it is home to over half a million people, most of whom make their living in twelve nearby Toyota manufacturing plants and hundreds of related enterprises. The city is not particularly attractive and the quality of life outside the workplace leaves much to be desired from the viewpoint of Americans accustomed to a culture of consumption and leisure pursuits. But nobody takes the making of cars more seriously or in a more visionary way. "Problems" don't exist in the lexicon of Toyota engineers—only "challenges."

In the lobby of the corporate headquarters an exhibition from an "Imaginary Car Olympics" captures the Buck Rogers–like enthusiasm for engineering that permeates Japanese industry. One of these visionary vehicles solves the "challenge" of parking space shortages in small Japanese homes: It disassembles itself on arrival. The body of the car becomes a gate, the seats become door pillars, and the mirrors and meters take up double duty as door lamps.

Although nearly one in ten cars sold worldwide is a Toyota, the company is not the world's number-one vehicle manufacturer. That distinction still belongs to money-losing General Motors. But if it isn't biggest, Toyota is the richest, the most innovative, the most competitive. Put simply, it is "the best carmaker in the world," according to *Fortune*. "The company simply is tops in quality, productivity, and efficiency. . . . And it keeps getting better."[3]

As recently as 1989, on the eve of Toyota's introduction of the Lexus (and a similarly timed introduction by Nissan of its Infiniti model), the automotive world scoffed at Japanese plans to create a new class of cars to compete directly with top-of-the-line German cars like Mercedes and BMW. "Sure, the Japanese make mass market cars well," said a BMW executive. "But when it comes to the style, design, engineering, and craftsmanship expected by the world's most affluent customers, the Japanese will never match the German standards." The American business press, as well as some of the automotive trade press, echoed that sentiment. Some experts even predicted that the very idea of a Japanese luxury car was such an oxymoron that Toyota and Nissan were doomed to failure. When brake light and cruise control problems forced a recall of the Lexus just two months after its introduction, American automotive publications mused that Toyota might be in over its head in trying to make the Mercedes of the '90s.

Why there were so many skeptics is a bit hard to understand. Lexus and Infiniti, after all, were not introduced in the 1950s, when the Big Three had first scoffed at the thought of the Japanese trying to export cars (and when Secretary of State John Foster Dulles told Japanese leaders that their country was destined to suffer a permanent trade *deficit* with the United States). Nor were the new Japanese "super cars" introduced in the pre–oil crisis days of the early 1970s, when experts scoffed at the Japanese notion of focusing on small, fuel-efficient cars for consumers concerned about rising gasoline prices. Nor were they arriving in the 1980s when Americans had yet to understand the importance of the Japanese approach to quality control and other revolutionary aspects of what has been dubbed "lean production."

No, the new Japanese cars entered the U.S. market in the 1990s, when the U.S. automotive trade deficit already was nearly as much as the total U.S. trade deficit with Japan. Americans were already intimately familiar with Japanese abilities in the realm of automotive engineering. Indeed, the Japanese car had already become the chief symbol of Japan's industrial dynamism and America's corresponding erosion.

The economic stakes were also well known. The luxury car segment was growing faster than the automobile market as a whole, so it was a good business niche. The higher margins commanded by luxury cars could produce profits to offset extreme competitive pressures that the Japanese manufacturers themselves had introduced to the rest of the market through their relentless expansion of capacity. What's more, the margins on luxury cars could also be used to subsidize breakthrough engineering developments, which could later be incorporated into the rest of the fleet.

The politics of trade were prominent in Japanese thinking as well. Japan had promised to limit the number of its auto exports to the United States, but not the dollar value of them. Therefore, it made sense to transfer manufacturing of middle market cars to U.S. facilities, and concentrate on exporting higher-priced vehicles, which could earn greater profits on fewer units.

It should have been a no-brainer that the Japanese super cars would be successful. That so many experts doubted Japanese companies could become major players in the luxury car market tells us much about the sorry state of what passes for expertise on the Japanese economy.

Today, of course, no one doubts what Toyota and Nissan—and now Honda, Mazda, and Mitsubishi as well—can achieve with their higher-priced models. Within a year of its introduction, Lexus sales zoomed past both Mercedes and BMW in the U.S.

auto market. Lexus and Infiniti both shot to the top of J. D. Power's customer satisfaction charts as soon as they had been on the market long enough to be judged.

More incredible still, top-of-the-line Lexus and Infiniti models sell for ten thousand to thirty thousand dollars *less* than comparable Mercedes and BMW models against which they compete. Senior executives of the German car companies, like BMW's CEO, Eberhard von Kuenheim, have been known to complain that Toyota is underpricing the Lexus to buy market share. *Nein*, Herr von Kuenheim. It is actually Toyota's most profitable car, according to company president Shoichiro Toyoda. And there isn't much mystery about the key reasons. The ratio of workers to assembled cars at Mercedes and BMW, for example, is about twice what it is at Toyota. And while much of the "quality" at the German companies is derived from "rework" to make sure everything is just right, Toyota generates its quality principally through development of systems that make rework less necessary.

Thus, we encounter the lessons of what might be called the "Lexus Factor" as it operates within the Japanese economy. First, don't underestimate Japan's ability—over time—to enter any and all of the fields where others now exercise positions of global leadership. That is not to say that Japanese companies can or will succeed at everything they try, or that there haven't already been some real failures and less-than-successful Japanese efforts to chart new paths. The much-publicized "fifth-generation" computer project of the 1980s, for example, never succeeded in creating a new generation of computer technology.

But in manufacturing-related businesses, it is perilous to underestimate what the Japanese can do. Even now that U.S. companies are showing signs of reviving manufacturing skills, the Japanese have something more powerful working in their favor. In Japan, manufacturing is not something that just happens. It is a *system*. Even though some of the system's premises sound downright simplistic to American ears, the fact is that the system works. It cannot beat the best American companies in every field. But over time, it will outperform *most* American companies in *most* manufacturing fields.

As we shall see next, Japanese advantages may be small and subtle. But they are built into the competition from the beginning and become powerful determinants of the outcome as a result.

The Ten Core Competencies of Japanese Capitalism

Some of the components of Japanese competitiveness are rooted in the overall conditions of Japanese society. The homogeneity of the Japanese population, its neo-Confucian reverence for hard work, education, savings, order, and virtuous authority, and its island-nation zeal to develop comparative advantage in trade are cultural forces that shape Japanese thinking long before employees walk in the door of the workplace or managers weigh decisions.

But on top of this cultural infrastructure, Japan's business system has erected an elaborate network of approaches and practices that, taken together, tend to give it a *systemic* edge over others. As the revisionists have correctly pointed out, Japan practices a *different* model of capitalism from what America has traditionally known. It has different values, different beliefs, different goals, and different operating mechanisms.

Japanese capitalism is not just different. On a number of key issues facing the global economy, it is *superior* to anything else currently at work. Just as the United States embodied the most concentrated expression of capitalism's genius for most of the twentieth century, Japan is poised to play that role in the twenty-first century.

Capitalism Japanese-style represents the dawn of a new global business order. That is the fundamental reason why Japan has attracted so much attention, not just among Americans, but among business people everywhere. No intelligent business person can look at the Japanese system today and not, at the very least, feel challenged by it.

The core competencies of the Japanese economy described below are not meant to summarize the totality of the Japanese economic model. They are merely illustrations of some of its particularly potent features. As Japanese companies have honed these competencies in recent years, they have been able to reduce costs, improve quality, and add functionality and features to products faster than their global competitors. They have made what amounts to a revolution in manufacturing concepts, which has translated into astounding gains in productivity. All this helps explain the transition of Japanese companies from the tough competitors they were in the 1970s and early '80s to the *supercompet-*

itors dominating key markets and industries that they became in the late '80s and early '90s.

Of all the U.S.-Japan negotiations in recent years, the most intellectually interesting is the Structural Impediments Initiative (SII). In this series of bilateral discussions, Tokyo's negotiators tell Americans what they think is wrong with the U.S. system while Washington's team returns the favor. It is not very fruitful in terms of opening up markets, but it does highlight the real differences in the way the two systems operate.

The SII process has shed considerable light on the fundamental difference between Japan as a producer-oriented economy, and the United States as a consumer-oriented economy. In thousands of ways—some substantive and some small and subtle—the Japanese system favors producers (businesses, especially industrial and manufacturing businesses), while American society puts the interests of consumers first. It should come as no surprise that over the last decade, Japanese producers have revolutionized the business world, while American consumers have set the pace when it comes to purchasing power and lifestyles.

Both the United States and Japan are capitalist marketplaces. Both societies obviously incorporate producers as well as consumers in highly complex and dynamic relationships. The difference is in the balance and the structure of those relationships.

For two hundred years, the Anglo-American approach to capitalism, practiced first in Britain and later perfected in the United States, was clearly the most successful wealth-generating machine the modern world had ever seen. It yielded huge opportunity, enormous innovation and expansion of human knowledge, and massive increases in productivity that fueled rapidly rising living standards—all the while enlarging democracy and expanding personal freedom. Anglo-American capitalism's astonishing record of success seemed to prove the theoretical premises behind it, which originated with Adam Smith and were re-emphasized in the age of Ronald Reagan and Margaret Thatcher: free markets, free trade, maximum freedom for individuals, consumers, entrepreneurs, investors, and profit-making corporations.

For most of the last three-quarters of a century, the only meaningful large-scale challenge to the American model of capitalism came from the advocates of planned economies and public ownership, who put their scheme into practice in the Soviet Union and other socialist countries. The colossal economic, political, and human failures of this approach, now demonstrated incontrovertibly by the bankruptcy and disintegration of the Soviet Union itself, made it abundantly clear that the Marxist idea of a planned economy was anything but a viable challenge to American capitalism.

Japanese capitalism, however, has succeeded where socialists and Marxists failed. In creating a successful blended economy that enjoys a thriving competitive marketplace yet maintains intelligent mechanisms for public planning, management, and control, the Japanese have achieved what the Anglo-American theory of capitalism held to be impossible.

In Anglo-American theory, only competition, with all its ruthlessness and "creative destruction," can continue to cleanse the system sufficiently to continue its optimum functioning. Thus, when American corporate power become too concentrated and abusive (first in the days of the Robber Barons, then in the aftermath of the Roaring '20s), the system responded by busting up companies and curbing their influence. Japan, however, has found a way to develop behemoth yet enlightened corporations. In the Anglo-American system, corporations are driven by the pressure to maximize *profits for shareholders*. In Japan, their motive is not so much maximizing profit as maximizing employment, long-term corporate growth, and *benefits to stakeholders*—which include workers, supplies, and the nation itself.

For much of this century, the American model was the trailblazer not only in terms of the raw wealth created, but in its equitable distribution. Now, as the American model breaks apart, it is continuing to work at world-leading levels of excellence in some areas while failing miserably in others. As a result, U.S. society is becoming less "middle class" and more polarized between the "haves" and "have-nots" of wealth, education, and skills. Japan, meanwhile, has taken over the American mantle as the world's most middle-class society. The decline of so-called family values in the United States is only a mirror image of the decline of the upwardly mobile, American Dreaming mass of middle-class families. Although much Japanese wealth remains in the hands of producers and corporations, that portion which is distributed to individuals and consumers is more evenly distributed than anywhere else in the world. And nowhere else are living standards rising with such uniformity.

The Japanese model has proven so successful that it has influenced most of the other economies of East Asia to follow similar paths. It has even had an impact on Europe. The shock of Japanese global competitiveness was one of the factors encouraging support for EC unification and for the development of policies incorporating many of the virtues of the Japanese system. The European style of capitalism that is evolving today is squarely positioned between the extremes of the American and Japanese systems, but is perhaps leaning slightly toward the East.

The balance of economic forces is now in flux in both the United States and Japan. Prime Minister Miyazawa and other Japanese politicians have begun to say their country needs to become a "lifestyle superpower" as well as an economic superpower. The latest annual "white paper" on international trade from MITI argues that quality of life should replace economic expansion as the chief aim of Japanese government policies. Meanwhile, Americans are being forced by the harsh marketplace realities of the last few years to consume a bit less and produce a bit more.

But while considerable change lies ahead in the superstructure of the two societies, it is unlikely that there will be fundamental change at the base—at least not anytime soon. Japan will continue to be the world's leading producer society. It is from that elemental reality that it draws both its global competitiveness and its value as an intellectual model and an international partner.

Japan is manifestly not without its serious systemic weaknesses and faults. The list is long, and criticisms of the Japanese system by the Japanese people themselves are legion. The very factors that make Japan so homogenous also make it somewhat less brilliant and less creative than the most talented sectors within American and European societies. But while the strengths of American and European societies appear to be staying only just ahead of the centrifugal forces threatening to tear them apart, Japan appears to maintain a somewhat wider margin of effective planning and control over its future.

Winston Churchill once observed, "No one pretends that democracy is perfect or all-wise. Indeed, democracy is the worst form of government except all those other forms that have been tried from time to time."[4] In a similar way, the Japanese model of capitalism is far from ideal. However, it just happens to enjoy a margin of improved performance over the models practiced in

America and Europe. That difference—small as it may be when all the strengths and weaknesses are toted up—is the source of most Japanese gains in productivity, economic efficiency, wealth, and international competitiveness.

Let us now take a closer look at some of the core competencies that make individual Japanese companies so excellent, and the Japanese model of capitalism as a whole so powerful.

1. Continuous Improvement

The Japanese approach to business known as *kaizen*—"continuous improvement" in English—is so deceptively simple that many American executives refuse to entertain its relevance to the complex challenges they face. Despite Japan's reputation as a rigid, inflexible, and hierarchical society, the fact is that inside leading Japanese companies, certain kinds of change—particularly the ones that matter most in the international competitiveness race— are constant. Manufacturing methods and processes are questioned, challenged, and adapted with a lightning speed that belies the image of slow-moving, blue-suited consensus.

Simpler, cheaper ways to make and do things are constantly sought. Of course, this happens in various ways in American business as well. The difference is that in the United States, changes tend to be instigated only periodically, and usually as "big ideas" from the upper ranks of management. In Japan, the emphasis is on small, incremental changes that flow out of the daily experience of the production process. Virtually every major Japanese enterprise has explicit goals, broken down department by department and function by function, for cost reductions, design speedups, production time decreases, and improvements in quality.

The process of continuous improvement lies at the base of what experts at MIT's International Vehicle Program have termed "lean production"—the revolutionary manufacturing system of the future that combines the scale of traditional mass production with the specialized skills and customization capabilities of historic craft production. In the words of Professor James P. Womack and his team, which studied the global auto industry for five years, lean production is "lean" because "it uses less of everything compared to mass production—half the human effort in the factory, half the manufacturing space, half the investment in tools,

102

half the engineering hours to develop a new product in half the time."[5]

Marrying the low costs of mass production with the quality, flexibility, and innovation of craft production, the "lean" approach was born at Toyota and quickly diffused to the rest of the Japanese auto industry. Now, it is spreading to other industries in Japan and around the world. The MIT experts believe lean production "will change everything in almost every industry—choices for consumers, the nature of work, the fortune of companies, and, ultimately, the fate of nations."[6]

Contrasting mass production as perfected in the U.S. industrial system with the emerging lean production of Japan, the MIT study observes:

> Perhaps the most striking difference between mass production and lean production lies in their ultimate objectives. Mass producers set a limited goal for themselves—"good enough"—which translates into an acceptable number of defects, a maximum acceptable level of inventories, a narrow range of standardized products. . . .
>
> Lean producers, on the other hand, set their sights explicitly on perfection: continually declining costs, zero defects, zero inventories, and endless product variety.[7]

Two forces inside Japanese companies make the improvement process literally continuous. One is the importance accorded to engineers. With half the U.S. population, Japan has twice as many engineers working in civilian industry. This vast cadre of technical talent is constantly refining the production system and business systems more generally. In fact, many CEOs of Japanese industrial companies worked their way up through the engineering ranks— unlike American chief executives whose background is usually in finance or marketing.

A second force is equally important: the ordinary employees. Foreigners tend to think of Japanese workers as docile automatons—"ants," in the infamous words of former French prime minister Edith Cresson. Yet management regularly seeks—and gets—the suggestions of employees on all issues, great and small. The carefully maintained suggestion statistics are mind-boggling. Major corporations measure worker ideas in the millions per year. At one electronics company, a "suggestion drive" was organized recently when workers failed to match the prior year's pace of twenty-three suggestions per worker per week. Obviously, there is much psychological and social benefit in organizing workers to interact with the company in this way. But these suggestion programs are not a management tool for keeping workers happy. They are critical to improving products and the production process. MIT's Womack concludes that the Japanese approach changes not only the way employees work, but more important, the way they think.

American R&D departments may be more innovative in their abstract thinking skills than their Japanese counterparts, more worldly or more sophisticated. What makes the Japanese system different is the degree to which R&D is not a separated function, but is integrated into the daily life of the company. As Japanese professor of management Ikujiro Nonaka says:

> The centerpiece of the Japanese approach is the recognition that creating new knowledge is not simply a matter of "processing" objective information. Rather, it depends on tapping the tacit and often highly subjective insights, intuitions, and hunches of individual employees and making those insights available for testing and use by the company as a whole.

> To create new knowledge means quite literally to re-create the company and everyone in it in a nonstop process of personal and organizational self-renewal. In a knowledge-creating company, inventing new knowledge is not a specialized activity—the province of the R&D department or marketing or strategic planning. It is a way of behaving, indeed a way of being, in which everyone is a knowledge worker.[8]

2. Total Quality and Zero Defects

Closely related to continuous improvement is the Japanese approach to quality. The search for quality in Japanese enterprises is seen as a constantly evolving discipline requiring daily fine tuning. By now, everyone literate on U.S.-Japan issues knows that the basic work in developing the corporate practice of quality control was actually done in the United States by people like W. Edwards Deming, who went on to become more influential in Japan than in his own country. And almost anyone who works for a major U.S. corporation has, by now, attended at least a few corporate seminars in recent years on how to improve quality.

The new American focus on quality has paid off in many ways. According to a J. D. Power survey, the average car made at a Big Three auto plant in 1991 had only 20 percent as many defects as the average car a decade earlier. *Some* American Ford plants actually obtained lower defect ratios than *many* Japanese plants. But on average, the Japanese cars still have defect ratios significantly lower than American cars—1.1 defects per car versus 1.5.

While American academics have contributed a great deal to the study and discussion of quality, Japanese enterprises are the leaders in implementation of almost all of the new techniques. These include new efforts to achieve "zero defects" (organized plans to reduce failure rates in the manufacturing process to statistical insignificance), to integrate "competitive benchmarking" (competing internally against the standards set by the leading corporations in a certain field), to create "pokayokes" (designing parts in ways that prevent workers from installing them incorrectly), to deploy just-in-time inventory delivery (systems that require consistent quality and coordination throughout the chain of suppliers), to build in customer definitions of quality through QFD techniques (Quality Function Deployment), and to use "robust designs" (where certain kinds of problems in the field are foreseen as inevitable and designed around).

In one recent sudy of five hundred automotive, banking, computer, and health care companies, the Japanese outperformed their American rivals in each of five quality considerations: the importance placed internally on customer satisfaction, the weight given to competitive benchmarking as a practice, the diffusion of time-based competition techniques, the degree to which process simplification was used, and the frequency of performance evaluation as related to quality.[9]

Japanese quality gurus are now leading the charge to move the science of quality upstream from the factory floor to the design process and even the research phase. Meanwhile, there are disturbing signs that enthusiasm for U.S. drives centered on "total quality" goals may be withering. In spite of high-profile success stories, such as Motorola's use of a quality program to cut $700 million in manufacturing costs over a five-year period, only one-third of U.S. companies surveyed in a recent Arthur D. Little study reported success with their quality programs. According to one McKinsey expert, two years after their introduction, the majority of programs "grind to a halt because of their failure to produce the hoped-for results."[10] The Conference Board, the American Quality Foundation, and a number of consulting companies reported waning corporate interest in quality issues during 1992.

Having mouthed the mantra of quality for a few years, short-term-minded American businesses are complaining that the results aren't showing up on the bottom line. While some companies have institutionalized new thinking about quality, most have not been successful. And many of those that perceive their programs as "failures" are throwing them overboard.

3. R&D: Tomorrow's Competitive Battles Today

A first look at trends in R&D spending within different economies would suggest that the United States leads the world in this category. Yet when *military* R&D spending is discounted, America actually trails almost every industrial economy in the percentage of GDP devoted to *commercial* R&D. Japan, which devotes nearly 3 percent of its GDP to commercially oriented R&D today—and is aiming for 3.5 percent by 1996—becomes the world leader when R&D is measured this way. The United States allocates less than 2 percent.

Even those figures may underestimate the growing commercial research gulf between the two countries. New Mexico senator Jeff Bingaman, who chairs a congressional subcommittee on technology, argues that Washington's methods of compiling such statistics are out of date and off base. Although the Japanese population is only half of America's and its economy is only two-thirds the size, Bingaman believes that "it is close to certain" that the Japanese are outspending Americans in absolute dollar terms on civilian R&D. According to news accounts of the debate over the numbers, the new way of valuing Japanese R&D allocations should "send shock waves through the U.S. industrial community."[11]

However one counts the numbers, the bottom line is the same: Across a broad range of businesses, Japanese companies, which were the R&D followers of the last generation, are now the R&D leaders.

While Japanese companies have recently curtailed some of the outsized investments they had been making in plant and equipment, the end of the bubble economy has generally not derailed the growth in R&D spending. Honda, for example, announced a fiscal 1992 cutback of 11 percent on capital spending to $640 million—yet *augmented* its R&D budget to a whopping $1.5 billion. Fujitsu boldly declares in full-page ads in the U.S. business press: "This year we'll spend more on R&D than most of the Fortune 500 will make in sales."[12] From food products to plastics, from fabricated metals to machine tools, annual R&D budget increases have typically been in double digits every year since the mid-1980s.

It is also important to note that the huge investment made by the American economy in *military* R&D—over 60 percent of all R&D dollars spent annually by the U.S. federal government—no longer has the same synergistic effect on the civilian economy for which it was known in the past. As weapons systems have become increasingly exotic and specialized, the flow of benefits to the rest of the economy has slowed. Some experts argue that the historic relationship between consumer and defense technologies has actually been reversed. The greater flow of benefits may now be *from* the R&D done to develop new consumer products and processes *to* the defense sector.

"Today's leading-edge technologies in microelectronics, computers and telecommunications are found, not in Defense Department laboratories but in private industry," says a recent report by the Council on Competitiveness. "Moreover, consumer products, not industrial products, are frequently driving state-of-the-art technology, as the video camcorder so clearly demonstrates. Instead of industry adapting defense technology breakthroughs to commercial markets, the Defense Department is increasingly adapting commercial technology to its needs."[13] Many of those new commercial technologies, such as the video camcorder, are now pioneered and perfected in Japan.

Management expert Peter Drucker describes new and even more powerful trends in the Japanese approach to R&D:

Everybody now knows that the Japanese can bring out a new product in half the time it takes their American competitors and one-third the time it takes the Europeans. And everybody also knows that major U.S. companies are reorganizing their research and development work on the Japanese model, along cross-cultural lines. But the Japanese are already moving to the next stage.

They are organizing R&D so that it simultaneously produces *three* new products with the effort traditionally needed to produce one. And they do this by starting out with a deadline for abandoning today's new product on the very day it is first sold. . . .

By deciding in advance that they will abandon a new product within a given period of time, the Japanese force themselves to go to work immediately on replacing it, and do so on three tracks.

One is the *kaizen* continuous improvement process of achieving specific manufacturing goals, such as a 10 percent reduction in cost within fifteen months along with a 15 percent increase in performance characteristics—"enough in any event to result in a truly different product." Another track is "leaping"—developing a new product out of the old. The third track is breakthrough innovation.

Increasingly, the leading Japanese companies organize themselves so that all three tracks are pursued simultaneously and under the direction of the same cross-functional team.

A leading Japanese industrialist says that since the mid-1980s, American firms have been rushing to install Total Quality Management (TQM) programs.

That'll take 10 years before it really works—at least that's what it took here. This means it will work in America around 1995. By then, we'll have Zero Defects Management and will again be 15 years ahead.[14]

The most recently compiled statistics show that U.S. industrial R&D spending (on an inflation-adjusted basis) peaked in 1989 and has been dipping steadily since—often under the pressure of trimming expenditures to meet the burdens of corporate debt. Not only have Japanese companies followed the opposite course and continued to increase R&D spending even in difficult economic times, but their American affiliates have also bucked the U.S. domestic trends. Foreign companies (largely Japanese) now

account for over 12 percent of all domestic U.S. industrial R&D—
a 200 percent increase from a decade earlier.

Japanese companies, it would seem, are more concerned with
investing in the future competitiveness of their U.S. operations
than their native-born American colleagues.

4. Process Innovation

Related to the drive for quality, drawn from the emphasis on
continuous improvement, and closely connected to the commercial focus of Japanese R&D is the strong bias in Japanese companies toward *process* innovation, as distinct from American
emphasis on *product* innovation. Being "results-oriented," American R&D programs tend to concentrate their resources on the
search for new products. Japanese companies, while no less eager
for hit products, put the lion's share of human resources and
research budgets into improving their processes instead.

Americans tend to think up great new products—and then find
manufacturing them a major challenge. The Japanese approach
improves manufacturing processes to the point where new products emerge from the new capabilities of the processes. For example, while American researchers may be busy designing a
breakthrough computer chip that will pack even more information
onto the head of a pin, Japanese companies are figuring out how
to eliminate tiny particles of dust from the "clean rooms" needed
to manufacture such sensitive devices.

A super "clean room" developed by Tadahiro Ohmi at Japan's
Tohoku University is rated at 10^{-6}, which means less than one
particle of dust per 350,000 cubic feet of air—significantly more
dust-free than today's best commercial clean rooms. Ohmi believes Japan has been able to develop such temples of high-tech
manufacturing because its best engineers work in production. "In
America, the best minds remain stuck in design," he warns. And
unless that changes, "I'm afraid Americans will fall behind in
every case."[15]

The story is repeated across the gamut of many new industries.
No one questions America's indigenous design capabilities in
many advanced fields. But as the pioneering days of new-age
industries such as semiconductors come to an end, power is shifting to the manufacturing side of the equation.

"Innovation is sexy, manufacturing is not," says economist Marie-Louise Caravatti. "American business does not recognize that manufacturing processes are the biggest factor in determining product quality and price." Caravatti studied the research budgets of more than 1,119 large U.S. manufacturing companies. She discovered that 81 percent of the corporate research budgets went into product innovation versus a scant 19 percent to process innovation. In Japan, the allocations tend to be nearly opposite. Her conclusion? "A dollar of R&D in Japan is at least three times more effective in terms of international trade than an R&D dollar spent in the United States."[16]

The Japanese emphasis on process is also reflected in the way their businesses develop costing formulas and procedures. In American companies, new products are typically developed quite apart from cost. A product is researched, its characteristics are envisioned, it is then designed and engineered, and the appropriate components or supplies are purchased from outside. The cost of all of this, plus overhead, marketing, and profit, is then aggregated and divided into a presumably profitable unit selling price.

This contrasts with a Japanese preference for developing a target cost early and then designing and refining processes that will allow the company to meet that cost. According to Harvard professor Robin Cooper, American business tends "to build up a model of a product, determine what it's going to cost, and then ask whether we can sell it for that. The Japanese turn it around: They say, 'It's got to sell for X. Let's work backwards to make sure we can achieve it.' "[17]

A recent study by A. T. Kearney put some useful comparative numbers on new product development.[18] It turns out that Japanese companies suffer about 40 percent fewer development setbacks than U.S. companies in bringing new products to market and spend only one-third as much time debugging finished products. The Japanese approach doesn't necessarily lead to more good ideas for products. Instead, it leads to more successful new products that are more competitive from the beginning, and more easily subject to continuous cost reduction as they move through their life cycle.

"In recent years, Sony, Matsushita, Nissan, and Toshiba have all had a large number of hits," say corporate strategy experts

Gary Hamel and C. K. Prahalad in a *Harvard Business Review* article analyzing who's winning the race for corporate imagination. "Is this because they have more reliable market research . . . ? No, they've simply been at bat more often." By getting more new products to market than Western competitors, they have "a higher rate of market experimentation" and a faster learning curve.[19]

Hamel and Prahalad argue that the 1980s were the decade when global competitive battles were won "by companies that could achieve cost and quality advantages in existing, well-defined markets." But in the decade ahead, the winners will be those that can "build and dominate fundamentally new markets" such as "speech-activated appliances, artificial bones, micro-robots, cars that park themselves," and other products that "make the inconceivable conceivable" and create new "competitive space."[20]

Even if Western companies learn the skills necessary to close the gap on cost, quality, and cycle time, they may not prove as adept as the Japanese at developing the new products that will spawn the big new global markets of the future.

5. The Robot Explosion and Flexible Manufacturing

The use of robots in industry was an exciting new idea in American business a decade ago. But robots turned out to be more twenty-first-century sizzle than steak. Aside from a few specific applications (such as welding and painting in auto plants or moving factory supplies from place to place), engineers had trouble getting the robots to be flexible and dexterous enough to warrant the cost of developing and deploying them. Declining real labor costs in U.S. manufacturing also became a factor in designing out the once-imagined brave new world of factory automation. Given the short-term time horizons of most U.S. businesses, the investment in robots, even if they could be made to work properly, looked increasingly less attractive as labor became cheaper.

Most U.S. manufacturing operations have either stopped trying to robotize their operations, or have reduced their future visions of automation significantly. By the time Cincinnati Milacron sold its robotic tools division in 1991, every last American company that had attempted to mass-produce the robots themselves had left the business. In 1992, General Motors exited its successful robot-manufacturing joint venture with Japan's Fanuc—for the ultimate short-term goal of selling its ownership interest to its Japanese partner for cash.

In Japan, the road to robotization has also been paved with disappointments. However, with their longer-term time horizons for the payback on business investment, the Japanese stayed the course long enough to see the beginnings of success. For Japan, there are important social questions at stake. Fearing both the rising cost of labor and its scarcity in a graying population, Japanese manufacturers have found the robotization solution more appealing than other options such as importing foreign workers or moving more jobs offshore. Furthermore, as Japan has blazed new manufacturing trails in electronic miniaturization, a growing number of assembly operations have become virtually impossible for even the most skilled human hands. At the Sony plant in Kohda, for example, camcorder production requires printed circuit boards made up of two thousand separate tiny components. Robots do about 98 percent of the assembly work. They are a requirement not of the future but the present.

Japan now has a "robot population" that will soon reach half a million. This is about seven times as many robots as are found in the United States, and about ten times U.S. levels when measured on a per unit of GDP basis. Definitions of what is and isn't a robot vary in the two countries. Yet it is evident that a yawning, widening "robot gap" exists, and that the decisive move to robotization in Japanese industry is beginning to pay off handsomely in augmenting productivity and quality in industries like automobiles and semiconductors. The more experience Japanese companies develop with robotics, the more precise, dexterous, and flexible the system will become—and the wider the applications.

Linked to robotics is the emerging field of "flexible manufacturing." These are factory systems that have been designed to be easily adaptable from one product to the next generation of the same product, or a different product altogether. In general, Japanese software development lags behind American levels. But specialized software to redirect robots and other parts of the assembly process is quite advanced.

Toyota has succeeded in filling out a widening model line of Lexus automobiles—four-door sedans, two-door sedans, sports coupes, and so forth—while using the same basic platform and production line. This ability to combine economies of scale with customized features has eluded other luxury car manufacturers.

Retooling costs are moving down dramatically in Japan, as the same factory floor equipment is used for an ever-wider variety of products. In the last five years, consumer goods companies have developed so many different products loaded with so many different configurations of features that Japanese mass production is beginning to appear more like customized production. A new weapon in the international economy is the ability to completely surround the products of competitors with product offerings targeted at every segment of the market.

Nissan executives speak of achieving a goal called the "five anys"—being able to manufacture any product in any volume at any time in any part of the world by anyone. Manufacturing experts, both American and Japanese, predict that the "flexibility war" of the late 1990s will be just as significant to global business competition as the "quality war" was in the 1980s. Soon we will be hearing the stories of the Japanese factory that can make virtually any product, of theoretical break-even points cut in half, and of whole new ways to run businesses based on the kind of flexibility that allows for constant product evolution.

Fumio Kodama, a visiting professor at Harvard's Kennedy School, notes that flexible manufacturing has made production so fluid in Japan that Americans may have difficulty even trying to learn from the Japanese example. According to Kodama, the example changes before it can be emulated. "Due to the rapid change going on in Japanese industry, by the time Americans identify and prepare to import some concept, Japan has already moved on to the next stage."[21]

Kodama contends that the current reductions in Japanese capital spending reflect not so much the burst bubble as the triumph of flexible manufacturing systems: Companies have to make major investments in fixed equipment less frequently. Once a major new system is installed, corporate budgets shift emphasis from capital investment to process-oriented R&D as new uses for the same equipment are designed.

Flexible manufacturing systems also cut design and product changeover times because the same basic production equipment is being maintained and used by the same engineers. This fuels what Deutsche Bank economist Kenneth S. Courtis calls "Just-

In-Time-Development-And-Design." Not only can Japanese car makers develop, design, and begin to produce an entirely new model in about half the time it takes other world manufacturers, but they are also gaining the ability to customize each car to unprecedented degrees within a mass manufacturing system. These skills and resources, Courtis believes, are already in place but are not yet fully used owing to Japan's economic slowdown. As they are deployed in the years ahead, they will have an "explosive effect on world competition."

Japan, Courtis says, "will at last be understood not as a nation of imitators, but as playing a role comparable to that of the United States in the 1950s and '60s—the world's chief laboratory for new product innovation."

6. Critical Technologies

Opponents of "industrial policy" often say that government should not be in the business of "picking winners and losers." From the logic of this argument, it is easy to conclude that no one knows what the great technological breakthroughs of the future will be. Obviously, there is some truth to this. The whens and hows of certain breakthroughs are unknown, as are their real-life implications and applications.

Yet it is patently *not* true that tomorrow's key job-creating, economic-growth-stimulating technologies are unknowable. Obviously, unforeseen advances will trigger the development of whole new industries. But the basic list of critical twenty-first-century technologies is widely known and agreed upon by scientists, technologists, and experts in technology policy. Indeed, the list doesn't vary much from North America to Europe to Asia. It is roughly similar whether it is drawn up by the U.S. Commerce Department, Japan's MITI, or private think tanks.

In one of the best available studies, the private-industry-sponsored U.S. Council on Competitiveness looked into five broad aeas of technology likely to have a heavy impact on the future: materials and associated processing technologies, engineering and production technologies, electronic components, information technologies, and powertrain and propulsion technologies. Under these headings, ninety-four specific technologies were identified, such as superconductors, robotics, genetic engineering, applications software, neural networks, artificial intelligence, fiber optics, structural ceramics, microprocessors, optical information storage, natural language recognition, alternative fuel engines, and rocket propulsion.

The study, published in 1991, concluded that the U.S. economy, which two decades earlier would have dominated virtually every item on such a list, now maintains a clear lead in only about a third of the ninety-four areas. It is weak or has fallen seriously behind in another third, and is struggling to keep pace with Japan and other global competitors in the remaining third.[22]

A study undertaken in Japan by the Committee for the Year 2010, a body that advises the prime minister, reached similar conclusions in evaluating how 101 different technological segments would evolve over the next decades.

Japan's ascendancy in critical technologies is not an accident but the result of a core competency in its overall economic structure that leads it in this direction. Elements of this competency include the overwhelming emphasis on training engineers and scientists, pooling research in leading-edge fields through government-business partnerships and consortia that exist in almost every emerging niche of technology, and the deep pockets and high levels of vertical integration within corporations, which allow them to plow resources into research investments over a long period before having to show a profit from them.

The influence of government on Japanese industry has declined somewhat in recent years—a point that American opponents of government-led "technology policy" are quick to stress. Yet even though Japanese corporations no longer need the helping hand of government, MITI still helps seed new technologies and organizes their early development. A new MITI project, for example, calls for half a billion dollars to be spent over the next decade on "real world computing." It is an effort to develop a variety of initiatives in neural networks, massively parallel computing, and related technologies in order to discover which approaches to computer systems are most capable of emulating the human brain. In another instance, MITI has organized twenty companies to participate together in research funded at nearly $200 million to investigate "micromachines"—robots small enough to operate within human arteries or hair-thin fiber-optic lines.

The extent of Japanese technological leadership is not always fully appreciated. In August 1990, for example, a blue-ribbon panel of American scientists and business leaders went before Congress to plead their case for funding a program aimed at getting the United States back into the race with Japan to commercialize the benefits of recent scientific discoveries about superconductors. The key point of this five-year effort would be developing a powerful electromagnet driven by superconductivity. But just five *months* later, while Congress was still considering funding this *five-year* effort, Japan's Sumitomo group announced it had *already* built a prototype of the very same electromagnet.

Even taken as an isolated case, the story is significant. Superconductivity could well be to the twenty-first-century economy what the automobile industry was to this century. But it is *not* an isolated case. Japanese business has undertaken the world's most targeted and systematic approach to developing and exploiting the *commercial* potential of many critical scientific developments.

A stark indicator of what is happening in corporate control of new technology is the way Japanese companies have come to dominate the annual list of patents awarded by the U.S. Patent Office.

Top Five Companies Ranked by the Number of U.S. Patents Issued, 1978 vs. 1990

Company	1978 Patents Awarded	Company	1990 Patents
General Electric	820	Hitachi	908
Westinghouse	488	Toshiba	891
IBM	449	Canon	868
Bayer	434	Mitsubishi Denki	862
RCA	423	General Electric	785

It should be emphasized that this list does not derive from Japan's patent office—where Japanese companies, as a result of the many peculiarities and protectionist features of the Japanese system, dominate patent awards. The above list is of *American* patents awarded by the U.S. Patent Office. As the chart shows, the first four of the top five companies patenting the most new innovations in the United States in 1990 were *all Japanese*. (It is also worth noting that seven of the top ten companies on the list are either Japanese or European. Only three are American—

General Electric, fifth, Eastman Kodak, seventh, and IBM, ninth.)

John Akers, the embattled CEO of IBM, has seen the future. In 1991, he wrote a widely circulated memo blasting the internal workings of his own company—America's most successful corporate performer of the last forty years. He pointed out that while IBM dithers, Japanese computer companies, once considered unimaginative also-rans, have steadily gained ground. His confidence in his own company's U.S. operations was so badly shaken that Akers decided to move development of IBM's smallest, most technology-packed computers out of the United States to Japan.

The point is not that America is about to cease to be a technological leader. In many areas—applications software, telecommunications, biotechnology, aviation and aerospace—American businesses not only lead the world, but are likely to continue to do so well into the next century. What is important, however, is that Americans not be blinded by our successes in these areas to the broad, long-term challenge posed by the Japanese approach to developing new technology.

John Young, president and CEO of one of America's best high-technology companies, Hewlett Packard, gets to the heart of the problem by analyzing popular "myths" about American technological leadership:

> The first, which I call the "sunrise industries" myth, goes like this: "Sure, our traditional manufacturing industries are under siege, but we still lead in the new, high-growth, high-tech segments." The high-tech trade balance may have looked good in the early 1980s, but that ended in 1986 when the U.S. witnessed its first-ever trade deficit in high-technology segments. With technological innovation, the financial rewards are cumulative. If you lose one round, it's very hard to get back in the fight.

> The second myth is about "the leading edge." It says even if the U.S. has trade problems in technology, they're only at the low end in consumer electronics. We're ahead in leading-edge technology. Again, facts refute the myth. In terms of dollars it's true our biggest trade problem in electronics involves TVs, audio equipment and VCRs. However, America is also falling behind in several critical generic technologies including integrated circuit fabrication, optical information storage, and robotics. And consumer electronics is not all "low-tech." Many HP engineers feel the degree of sophistication

in the design and packaging of today's home video camcorders is the most advanced of any product family they've seen.

Myth three—the copy-cat—says that though other countries have caught the U.S., they've done so by aping us. The Japanese, especially, are incapable of innovating on their own. This was true in the early years following World War II but today, U.S. patents tell a different story.

The "Nobel Prize" myth says that the U.S. leads the world in Nobel laureates, our research universities are the best, so we have the strongest technology infrastructure. This is misleading in two ways. First, we must ask whether the breakthroughs that win Nobel Prizes actually help win the fight. We focus on the pursuit of basic knowledge but give little thought to its application. Second, our technology infrastructure is showing signs of strain. We've been living off the fat of the land, doing little to ensure future generations of technology and trained people. In real terms, federal funding for university research facilities declined 95% over the past 20 years.[23]

7. Relationship Capitalism: The Keiretsu System of Business Alliances

One of the new issues unfurled by American negotiators at the structural impediments talks in 1991 and 1992 was the problem of *keiretsu*. These are the interlocked groupings of Japanese companies that dominate the economy. Just the leading six of these groups account for roughly one-quarter of Japanese GDP. *Keiretsu* companies and their affiliates make up less than 1 percent of all businesses in Japan, but they account for more than half the market capitalization of the Tokyo Stock Exchange.

In its purest sense, the term *keiretsu* refers to a handful of immensely powerful families of diverse operating companies, usually centered on one of the major city banks and connected to one of the major *sogo-shosha* (global trading houses). The traditional *keiretsu* include some of the best-known names in Japanese business, such as Mitsubishi, Mitsui, and Sumitomo. These groups have business histories that go back hundreds of years. Indeed, the biggest *keiretsu* are modern reincarnations of the infamous *zaibatsu*—the corporate groupings broken up after World World II by MacArthur and the U.S. occupation forces on the

grounds that they had promoted Japanese militarism and imperialism. These *keiretsu* tend to be "horizontal" in nature, sprawling
across businesses from financial services and real estate to chemicals, electronics, glass, and oil.

Mitsubishi counts nearly two hundred companies in its group,
which stretches from Meiji Mutual life insurance to Kirin beer,
Nikon cameras, and Mitsubishi automobiles. The group as a
whole does well over $300 billion worth of business annually. One
shouldn't expect to go to a dinner of Mitsubishi group managers
and find brands of beer being served other than those from group
member Kirin.

Describing the group of companies around Dai-Ichi Kangyo
Bank, one observer remarks, "When the *Sankin-kai,* or president's
council of the DKB group, gets together for its monthly lunch,
the presidents of the world's largest bank (Dai-Ichi Kangyo), the
world's largest textile company (Asahi Chemical), and the world's
second largest computer company (Fujitsu) are at the table, along
with the heads of Kawasaki Steel, Isuzu Motors, cosmetics maker
Shisheido, and a couple of dozen other companies."[24]

While there are differing levels of integration—the Mitsubishi
keiretsu is relatively tightly organized; the newer DKB group much
looser—all *keiretsu* function as what Shoichi Saba, former chairman
of Toshiba (a company loosely affiliated with the Mitsui group),
calls a "society of long-term relationships."[25] Typically, members
own some of each other's stock and give preferential treatment
to one another as customers and vendors. Prohibited by law from
establishing holding companies to buy and sell their own stock,
Japanese companies have a strong incentive to keep shares in the
hands of friendly partners.

The *keiretsu* system is diametrically opposed to American capitalism's fears of corporate girth and the resulting U.S. approach
to antitrust policy. Unlike the American system, Japanese *keiretsu*
organizations find it second nature to target and promote new
industries, technologies, and market opportunities via the shared
resources of the group. The *keiretsu* prevents anything remotely
resembling shareholder rebellion or hostile takeover. If a serious
financial problem arises at an affiliated company, the group will
find a member company to absorb it or bail it out.

One of the most interesting features of the system has been
the ability of *keiretsu* companies to share the pain of economic

downturns. The stability and resilience that arises from such woe sharing has helped Japanese companies continue to invest and expand market share globally during recessions, often at the expense of foreign companies that are compelled to cut back.

Hot on the trail of yet another potential "key" to understanding the Japanese economic system, foreign economists have probably done more exhaustive analysis of the *keiretsu* system than their Japanese colleagues. In addition to the typical horizontal *keiretsu* established around the major banks, Western experts also speak about other types of *keiretsu* crucial to the organization of the Japanese economy. These are the "production" (or "vertical") *keiretsu* and the "distribution" *keiretsu*.

The "production" *keiretsu* involve the relationships between major industrial companies, such as Toyota or Matsushita, and the dozens, or even hundreds, of smaller supplier companies that provide the parts, components, and services crucial to making the "just-in-time" production system function like clockwork. Even when no ownership or cross-shareholding exists, the members of this kind of *keiretsu* live and breathe to serve the interests of the industrial company at the hub of the network. One of the reasons large Japanese companies appear so dexterous at developing new products or ramping prices down rapidly has to do with their influence over supplier companies. The bigger companies use the power of their relationships to force their partners to speed up delivery times or accept lower profits when necessary.

"Distribution" *keiretsu* control the complex maze of relationships between the factory, or the docks, and the consumers and end users of both Japanese and imported goods.

In addition to these kinds of *keiretsu*, some American academics have broadened the notion of *keiretsu* to include all kinds of partnerships and special relationships within the Japanese business world, such as small business cooperatives and big business strategic alliances, consortia, and joint ventures.

The reason U.S. negotiators have taken aim at this system is that the web of relations among *keiretsu* members creates a built-in bias against going outside the "family" to procure equipment or supplies or to obtain products for distribution. Congressman Richard A. Gephardt has said that the *keiretsu* system "lies at the heart of the incompatibility" between American and Japanese capitalism. Many American companies with high-quality goods to sell in Japan simply can't get them onto store shelves, because of the way the distribution *keiretsu* control the channels to retailers. Similarly, American makers of auto parts and electronic components claim, with plenty of evidence, that Japanese manufacturers are willing to pay more to buy from fellow production *keiretsu* members than to buy supplies from American sources.

In response to a combination of American pressure and a changing domestic policy, the *keiretsu* system is currently undergoing some change. A high-level consensus has already been reached on the need to overhaul the distribution system in order to make channels more competitive and improve the lot of the Japanese consumer. As a result, the power of distribution *keiretsu* will ebb over the next few years, with better opportunities for American businesses created as a by-product.

The stable cross-shareholdings that once cemented business relations between banks and their related trading houses and industrial companies are also weakening. But the basic proclivity of Japanese companies toward building highly integrated networks of business relationships—especially the vertical integration of the production *keiretsu*—is *not* likely to change too radically. And for good reason: The system works remarkably well. In a recent survey of Japanese executives, nearly 80 percent favored reforming distribution *keiretsu* to gain efficiency and bring benefits of competition to the customer. But only about 20 percent favored significant changes in the production *keiretsu* system.

The truth is that Japanese *keiretsu* are not so dissimilar to American companies like General Motors, U.S. Steel, or AT&T in their glory days—or even IBM today. In fact, Japanese corporations are organized in ways that might resemble American corporate structure had not antitrust laws come along, and had not investors and executives of recent years favored breaking up large corporations for the short-term benefit of the stock price.

The basic belief at the heart of the *keiretsu* system—that long-term business needs are best met by controlling production and distribution either in-house or through close alliances and stable long-term partnerships—is hardly unique to Japan. But back when General Motors was run like a *keiretsu* in the 1930s, '40s, and '50s (controlling virtually every part of its production process, buying up auto parts companies, and even buying up competing automobile companies), there were few foreigners trying to crack the American market, so the issue never emerged as a source of international trade tension.

In a de facto way, American business is coming to recognize the wisdom of the Japanese approach to integration. Looking in the Japanese mirror, American companies see some of the features that made themselves great in the past. The recent trends in mergers and corporate alliance building as well as the establishment of several consortia in the computer industry and other fields all reflect an understanding that companies that once found no difficulty going it alone now need long-term partners. Even automakers are giving up their once jealously guarded trade secrets in order to pool research in areas like pollution control technology to meet new clean air standards, although they still have to fight an anachronistic, uphill battle with the U.S. Justice Department's antitrust watchdogs any time they try to collaborate.

It seemed for a time in the 1980s that the model for future success in business was highly decentralized, specialized, and niche-specific. American business literature of the last decade focused on these themes. But the reality is that today's products, as well as the global competition that surrounds them, are so complex that it pays to control or coordinate as many of the variables as possible.

Even while American trade negotiators decry *keiretsu* arrangements, those who have studied the issue closely cannot avoid recognizing their virtues. Says Princeton economics professor Alan S. Blinder, "The sturdy, but not indestructible, relationships that constitute the production *keiretsu* seem to artfully combine the contrasting virtues of hierarchical control and market competition."[26] Production *keiretsu*, he concludes, might be "a better coordinating mechanism" than open markets for some U.S. industries.

Baruch College professor Yoshio Tsurumi claims that in today's global economy, where companies become so dependent on their suppliers, they are at considerable risk if they cannot count totally on those relationships for quality, delivery times, and upgrading as technology evolves. The *keiretsu* provides an organized framework for these relationships. It is not an archaic industrial structure, but an advanced, modern one, he says. Rather than urging the Japanese government to break up the *keiretsu*, Tsurumi believes Washington should "encourage American companies to join them."[27]

Some of the very American business leaders who most want in to the Japanese market are now posing the internationalization of the *keiretsu* system as an alternative to what might be fruitless foreign efforts to try to get the Japanese to dismantle it. One of those is Joseph T. Gorman, CEO of auto parts maker TRW. His company is a leader in both the European and American markets. Yet the *keiretsu* system has prevented TRW from getting anything more than a small fraction of the Japanese market, even though many TRW products are considered fully competitive on quality with available offerings in Japan. Says Gorman, "I believe there is much to admire about the *keiretsu* system, which has been very effective for the Japanese. My only complaint is that the *keiretsu* tend to exclude outsiders. . . . My advice to Japan is to either get rid of the *keiretsu* or open them up to foreigners."[28]

8. Capital Formation

In the midst of Japan's adjustment to its hair-raising $3 trillion meltdown in stock values, it seems counterintuitive to argue that the Japanese economy is particularly outstanding at capital formation. But aside from the disasters suffered by stock and real estate speculators in the last few years, the Japanese financial system has continued to be extraordinarily effective at the task financial systems are ideally supposed to perform: delivering capital resources where they are most needed to promote economic growth.

In this regard, it is important to look at what did *not* change before, during, and after the bubble. Household savings rates, for example, have remained stable at around 13 to 16 percent on a net disposable income basis over the last decade. The average American household, by contrast, is only able to save about a third as much. What's more, despite a host of liberalization measures, including the deregulation of capital controls in the mid-1980s, most Japanese household savings flow into low-yielding domestic instruments such as the postal savings system and government bond funds.

Japan thus continues to enjoy not only a vast pool of savings, but one that costs banking institutions relatively little to attract and maintain. This provides a basic building block for the financial system's ability to lend money to businesses at rates that are low by world standards, even when they are cyclically high by Japanese standards. The fact that the Japanese government runs a budget surplus helps enormously as well. Unlike the United States, where government borrowing consumes the lion's share of national savings, *most* of Japanese savings are available to be tapped for the investment needs of business.

Corporations also enjoy a number of strategic financial advantages over American competitors. The very largest companies are able to call upon relationships with their main banks (which are also often their largest shareholders) to borrow money at rates significantly below true market interest. Japanese companies are also under virtually no stockholder pressure to pay large dividends. American companies pay about 54 percent of after-tax profits to shareholders; Japanese companies only half as much. Typically, the difference between those two ratios becomes money allocated to either or both of the twin engines of Japanese business growth—capital investment and R&D. Although proposals are current to increase dividend payout ratios, few experts foresee Japanese companies adopting the rich payouts demanded of U.S. companies by short-term-minded U.S. investors.

Much has been made of the recent curtailment in capital spending by Japanese companies. Yet even after most major companies sliced significant chunks from their capital spending budgets in 1992, the total percentage of Japanese GDP allocated to capital spending for the fiscal year fell only to the levels typical of the mid-1980s. It is likely that the Japanese "capital investment bust" of the next few years will restore the "normal" situation, where the Japanese economy "only" outspends the U.S. economy by a per capita factor of 125 percent to 150 percent on new plant, equipment, and capital stock, instead of the abnormal 200 percent plus of 1988–91.

And then there is that huge Japanese trade surplus, now running at more than $100 billion per year. For the last dozen years, Japan's trade surplus has been recycled into foreign investments almost on a dollar-for-dollar basis. In essence, large Japanese companies have been able to fund their asset-buying sprees abroad and their deep penetration of economies from the United States to Europe, Latin America, and Southeast Asia entirely out of trade-surplus-generated funds. In this sense, expansion of Japanese business interests abroad does not compete for funding with domestic projects, although there may be some short-term readjustment to counteract the downside effects of the bubble bursting. Japan thus enjoys a situation in which the world economy—and the United States economy in particular—bears the cost of internationalization of Japanese companies.

Although some American and other foreign experts have raised questions recently about just how real Japan's cost-of-capital advantage may be, the Japanese themselves know its powerful impact. "Japan has created a system that makes it possible to lower the cost of capital, enabling corporations to build up their competitiveness," says Masasuke Ide, research director at the Nomura Research Institute. "Japan selected strategic industries and lowered the cost of their capital, establishing a system which assures victory in the global market," he adds bluntly. "The fact that Japan was too successful in this has caused a problem in international society."[29]

The Japanese financial system is not entirely virtuous, as the scandals of the last few years have shown. The stock market operates as a fixed casino when it is going up, and is almost out of control when it is going down. The routine corruption in Japanese political circles makes the most pork-barreling American politicians look saintly by comparison. And real estate values, even now that they have plummeted from their peaks, are nothing short of irrational. Yet with all its problems, the Japanese financial system remains consistently more adept at creating the conditions under which business can make sound long-term investments than any other national financial system in the world.

9. The Ultimate Capital—Human Capital

Every commentator on global issues recognizes that the future coming toward us is one in which brain power will count far more than brawn power. The link between education and training on the one hand, and corporate success on the other, is inexorable. In an era when the process of creating wealth relies increasingly on rapid introduction of new technology, information, innovation, and creativity, "human capital" becomes the ultimate capital. The societies possessing the most efficient means of diffusing knowledge and skills will emerge as the leading economic powers.

Knowledge has always been power, but never more so than today when military might, ideology, natural resources, and other kinds of global power tools are less important than they have been, even in the recent past. The question is: What kind of knowledge—and who must have it? In this regard, Japan and the United States are positioned for the future in two nearly diametrically opposed ways.

America is home to the world's most excellent university system and much of the world's most innovative, breakthrough work in science, technology, and creative pursuits of all kinds. But it is also home to a crisis-ridden basic K-12 educational system, a government that sees no role for itself in implementing national policy on public education and skills training, an expanding and structurally unemployable underclass, and a slowly closing window of educational opportunity for the children of the middle class.

In Japan, the picture is quite different. Although growing resources are being allocated to basic science, and creative pursuits are increasingly encouraged, the structure of the system remains much less conducive to breakthrough innovation than the American model. Yet underlying the system as a whole is an evenly distributed diffusion of basic knowledge and skills to the vast majority of people through a functional public education system and corporate training programs.

For a country where the future is taken so seriously, the Japanese approach to educating and training young people does not, at first, seem suitable for the demands of the twenty-first century. It relies heavily on rote memory and conformity to standardized curricula. Universities may play a critical role as networking centers for future business and social relationships, but they are not particularly good at research or advanced work and do not provide most of their graduates with the rigor and breadth of knowledge typical of the American university experience.

On balance, however, the Japanese system works better than the American system to achieve the desired results. The Japanese K-12 public school system is not only far less costly than the American system, but provides 33 percent more days of education per year—240 in Japan versus 180 in America. By the time they graduate, Japanese high school students have had the equivalent of four extra years of education over Americans. And that's not counting the intensity of homework in Japanese schools, the additional hours spent in *juku* (after-school cram courses), or the fact that normal school days in Japan are focused on the fundamentals of education, not the social and moral agenda that Americans insist their school systems take up. Those are some of the reasons why Japanese functional literacy rates run at 99 percent (versus 82 percent in the United States), high school completion rates are 90 percent (versus 73 percent in the United States), and average twelfth-grade achievement scores are nearly twice as high as American scores in subjects like geometry and algebra.

Given those world-leading elements of the Japanese educational system, it is not surprising that private sector companies are able to mold and train workers with relative ease, move them from one area to another as business needs evolve, and maintain a high degree of labor discipline and social harmony. Japan's "human capital" may not emerge from its high schools and colleges with the grand ambitions of American graduates. Japanese students may lack some of the all-round intellectual sophistication of America's best and brightest. Nevertheless, on *average* they make up a more readily trainable workforce.

"Japan's real 'secret,' " says Princeton's Blinder, is that the Japanese have "broken down the 'us versus them' barriers that so often impair labor relations in American and European companies. They do so by creating a feeling that employees and managers share a common fate. To paraphrase Lincoln, a well-run Japanese company is of, by, and for its people."[30] Blinder suggests that the Japanese model of capitalism has found the way to avoid the vaunted tradeoff between equality and efficiency. In Japan, he believes, management does not have to choose one or the other. Instead, greater equality works to promote greater efficiency:

American executives will tell you that it is risky and expensive to make large investments in employees who may soon resign or be laid off or to guarantee job security in a changing business world. They are right. But there are also benefits: A highly trained work force is more productive; a multiskilled work force is more flexible; employees with job security welcome rather than fear innovation. . . . To a significant degree, Japanese workers cooperate with management because their welfare is tied up with that of the company. . . . It is in managing people . . . that America can learn the most from Japan.[31]

The American system, with its emphasis on individuality, its encouragement of creativity and diversity, its great universities, and perhaps most important of all, its free market that offers immense financial rewards to talented people, continues to be the best vehicle for producing certain kinds of knowledge, specialized skills, and innovations. The United States continues to lead the world in advanced technologies and advanced services, which might broadly be classed as the "software" component of the new world economy—everything from Hollywood scriptwriting to computer program writing, from innovative financial services to innovative fast food services, from the design of telecommunications systems to the design of computer chips, rocket engines, and bioengineered pharmaceuticals.

The Japanese system, meanwhile, continues to produce the broadest base of skilled, talented, readily employable workers ready to sally forth and make many of the world's best and most advanced manufactured products. The Japanese economy maximizes the output of global "hardware," epitomized by automobiles, computer memory chips, and consumer electronics of all kinds.

The experts most bullish on America's future argue that "software" skills are inherently more advanced and more economically important than "hardware" skills. In this view, the increasing erosion of America's leadership in manufacturing is not just an irrelevance, it is a sign America is moving upstream to where the new value will be added in the future global economy. Japan, meanwhile, remains excellent only at the old, traditional industrial-age skills of mass manufacturing.

T. J. Rodgers, the combative CEO of Cypress Semiconductor, a Silicon Valley company that makes specialized computer chips, is one who holds this view. He describes the semiconductor industry as experiencing two battles simultaneously: "One battle is over manufacturing, which the Japanese have been winning. The other battle is over innovation, which the U.S. has been winning."[32] Although Rodgers acknowledges that the old-line

American electronics companies have been losing the manufacturing race, he believes that the "smaller, nimble companies"—such as his own—are winning the more important race.

Comforting as this view may be, it misreads the future and the road to getting there. For the present—the 1990s and the first decade of the twenty-first century—the manufacturing of "hardware"-type products is still likely to dominate global trade and shape the competitiveness of leading economies. The U.S. trade deficit with Japan in manufactured goods, for example, exceeds the U.S. surplus with Japan in services by a factor of nearly ten. Even if being good at services is the way of the future, the U.S. economy cannot afford to lose the quality of being good at manufacturing.

The experience of Rodgers's own outstanding company demonstrates the implications of this trend. Once Rodgers said he could compete with anybody on cost and quality in manufacturing the custom-designed chips for which Cypress is famous. But in 1992, the company was finally forced to close down its California manufacturing facilities. It moved assembly offshore, laying off two hundred of its nineteen hundred employees in the process. Rodgers himself acknowledged, "We are the last company in Silicon Valley to do assembly here; all our competitors already assemble offshore. We can no longer afford to keep our assembly operation."[33]

Cypress is still a world leader in the design part of its field, but the flow of benefits to the local economy it once generated has been significantly curtailed. Indeed, even though electronics now employs more people than any other U.S. industry, total domestic employment in this field of the future was down from a 1989 high of 2.6 million to only 2.3 million in 1992. The president of the American Electronics Association, J. Richard Iverson, calls the trend toward disemployment in U.S. electronics "disastrous." Even with the world market for electronic products and services rapidly expanding, he notes that the U.S. share of the overall pie has been "shrinking dramatically."[34]

America's "human capital" of talented people in software-driven and future-oriented sectors of the economy is obviously a precious resource. The argument in this book is that it is a resource that *may* save the American future—*if* it can be protected and used more strategically. But those are big ifs. As the Cypress case illustrates, a dwindling percentage of the population consists of upwardly mobile Americans with software skills. They are trying to support an economy in which a growing percentage of the population has less than globally competitive hardware skills and fewer opportunities to work at hardware jobs.

The gap is widening between America's ability to design products and to manufacture them. AT&T made headlines in 1992 when it announced a new videophone concept that could bring this long-awaited product into the price range of ordinary consumers. As market researcher Albert Lill notes, AT&T may have pioneered the technology and may hope to lead its manufacture, but "in the long run, it's difficult to see anybody competing against the Japanese" in this field.[35]

Simultaneously, a broadening brush of social crisis is sweeping across the American landscape—the problems of the underclass, poverty, racial tension, and failing public education, to name but a few. These forces are beginning to impinge on the lives of even the most skilled and affluent sectors of the U.S. population, with the result that American society is polarizing more sharply. This process threatens to cannibalize even the areas of present American strength.

In Japan, meanwhile, the pool of "human capital" is much more evenly suited to the economic tasks at hand. As skilled Japanese workers produce world-leading tradeable goods for their companies, they are also producing the profits and trade surpluses that allow Japan to buy on the open market abroad the skills and technologies it has been slow to develop internally. Japanese companies have acquired interests in nearly four hundred important U.S. high-technology companies in the last seven years, as well as hundreds of companies with specialties in other kinds of global "software" skills from investment banking to entertainment and retailing.

Because of the abundance of breakthrough scientific and technological work accomplished in the late twentieth century (the lion's share of it by Americans), the next generation of global economic development is likely to be fueled more by successful commercialization of what is already known than by the discovery of new knowledge. This is especially true in light of the hundreds of millions of new consumers currently gathered around at the peripheries of the developed world's Triad, and the new markets that are emerging in Eastern Europe and the former Soviet Union, China and other parts of Asia, and Latin America.

In commercializing what is known, the Japanese pool of human capital, and the Japanese system itself—with its emphasis on process innovation and continuous improvement from the factory floor upward—is nearly optimally organized.

As for developing what is not yet known, Japan may not be as poorly positioned as it looks. Lester Thurow, dean of MIT's Sloan School of Management, points out that it is not such a bad thing to be a "mere" imitator and improver on the breakthrough first made in other countries:

> In the nineteenth century, the United States was known as a nation of copiers. The great inventions that started the Industrial Revolution (the steam engine, the spinning jenny, the Bessemer steel furnace) were British inventions. Americans were famous for taking these inventions and making them work 10% better than the British—much as the Japanese are today famous for taking American inventions and making them work 10% better than the Americans. Historically, copying to catch up is the name of the game.[36]

Just as America eventually surpassed British and European levels of breakthrough innovation, Japan may ultimately surpass the United States. But it is not clear that it needs to do so in any across-the-board fashion to become the world's leading economy. The United States enjoyed the world's biggest GNP for nearly half a century before it surpassed European scientific achievements. At the rate Japanese government expenditures for basic research are rising and U.S. budgets are falling, however, the transition this time around may take much less than half a century.

10. Strategic Globalization

It is often said that the Japanese are not very "internationally minded." This is more than a little bit ironic. Somehow or other, without being very "international" in their outlook, the Japanese have managed to penetrate foreign cultures, understand consumer tastes, and develop not just the right products but the right marketing strategies to match. No other business culture is as deeply involved in exporting to *all* the major markets of the world *and* building productive capacity simultaneously inside those markets.

The core competency involved here is not globalization per se. Business leaders in every part of the world understand the importance of globalizing their operations. American businesses have long led the way in this effort. What is unique about the Japanese approach is the long-term, strategic, and systematic approach taken to globalization.

In the Japanese experience, globalization actually began at home in the 1950s, with the targeting of key international industries as fields in which Japan hoped to compete. MITI and other government agencies designed tax incentives, organized research consortia and production cartels, and issued "administrative guidance" measures of all kinds in order to stimulate the growth of new industries. First in products marginal to world economy (such as cameras and motorcycles) and later in industries at the center of global business (such as automobiles, steel, and electronics), government policymakers set the agenda and laid the groundwork for business to succeed.

Today's Japanese government bureaucrats will acknowledge that this process entailed heavy use of protectionism and managed trade tactics—although they will insist in the same breath that all that is now in the distant past. Between 1950 and 1980, the process of changing both image and reality of "Made in Japan" was highly directed by farsighted government ministries and agencies.

In the industries that Japan had "targeted," foreigners with more advanced products were often kept out of the domestic market until Japanese companies had engaged in their own internal Darwinian struggle to select the fittest and most competitive among them. From laws that forced foreigners to form joint ventures if they wished to enter certain businesses, to a patent system that compelled foreign companies to give away technological secrets, to careful allocation of overseas market share to exporters, Japanese officialdom intervened in a myriad of subtle ways, all with one goal: to create a globally competitive export machine that could earn for Japan the foreign exchange needed to buy oil and all the other raw materials the resource-poor Japanese islands lack.

It is true that government planners play a much less intrusive role in shaping industrial policy today than in the past. Japanese companies are big and strong enough to make their own industrial policies these days. The price of raw materials has fallen so far, while Japan has found so many ways to add value to its finished goods, that the country no longer needs a grand strategy in order to produce a trade surplus. But government's visible hand has certainly not disappeared altogether.

In some cases, government planners are still doing exactly as in the old days—for example, bringing together Japanese companies into a satellite-development consortium in order to enhance competitiveness in a field now dominated by Americans. Under criticism from Washington the incipient satellite consortium project was formally abandoned in 1992—but it is still, in fact, functioning in an informal way. So too are a host of projects designed to enhance Japan's competitive standing in new technologies and businesses where leadership is now firmly in U.S. hands. These fields include space science, jet aircraft manufacture, and superconductivity. Since the revaluation of the yen in 1985, government agencies have worked closely with business to create a new, more technologically intensive industrial base for Japan's future as an exporting nation.

MITI, JETRO (Japan External Trade Organization), the Ministry of Finance, the Economic Planning Agency, and numerous government and private sector organizations have developed a new management function: trying to harmonize Japan's industrial policy with business practices in the West. Thus, when the Japanese government announces that it will lower its voluntary restraints on auto exports to the United States to more acceptable levels, ministry officials work behind the scenes to cut deals reducing each company's allotment of the American market accordingly. MITI in particular is busy trying to encourage Japanese companies to *import* more from the United States and other countries and to create new megatechnology projects in which foreigners can participate. In other words, the same competency at market management once used to nurture Japanese exporting industries is being used to solve at least a few of the political problems that have arisen as a result of their great success.

The machinery of Japanese industrial policy is now so well oiled that it sometimes appears to run itself. With only minimal guidance from the government, Japan's private sector has moved collectively and strategically through several new stages of globalization in the last decade. In quantifiable waves, Japanese direct investment flowed first to the United States, next to Western Europe and East Asia, and now to Latin America, Eastern Europe, and perhaps someday soon to the former Soviet Union.

Not only was the geography of this investment well choreographed, but so too were the industries into which it moved, such as autos and auto parts, consumer electronics, computers, semiconductors, and financial services. British investors may own quantitatively more American assets than do the Japanese, but no foreign investor group can match the way Japan has focused its investments in key sectors and emerged with large ownership chunks of targeted industries. This trend is most noticeable in the United States, but it is also in ample evidence in Europe and in emerging markets such as Korea, Southeast Asia, and Mexico. One country becomes a center for Japanese production of semiconductors, another for appliances, and another for auto parts. As the degrees of investment rise, some Japanese companies have reassembled on foreign soil new networks of their own component suppliers and business partners that mirror *keiretsu* arrangements back home.

In 1990, the total value of Japanese corporate production outside the borders of Japan was estimated at $170 billion. By the early part of the next decade, some experts believe, that figure could rise to a trillion dollars, with Japanese companies employing several million workers in foreign countries. In most places, workers and politicians alike will be very grateful for those high-paying jobs in comparatively high-skilled industries.

Americans may be critical of Japan. Europeans may be downright paranoid. Chinese, Koreans, and other Asians may harbor both long-standing cultural antipathy and bitter memories of their experiences at Japan's hands in World War II. But in each major region of the developed world's "Triad," Japanese business has succeeded in making itself a powerful and growing force. Unlike the United States at its zenith of multinational corporate expansion, the Japanese business community does not ride on the backs of a global military presence, nor has it relied chiefly on dispensing government munificence. The Japanese may not be well liked abroad, but they have built relationships of economic interdependence that transcend sharp political and cultural differences.

Shying away from the baroque and now overly costly structures of American global power, Japanese relationships are targeted and efficient. They are focused on what most of the world now most wants: capital, technology, trade, jobs, know-how, advanced industrial equipment, and high-quality consumer goods. Like its production system, Japan's interactions with the global economy can be characterized as lean. The Japanese have invested less than Americans in becoming a global power, and are achieving better economic returns.

Productivity, Productivity, Productivity

Every major world economic power has unique strengths. In fact, Japan has had to hone its particular competencies to make up for what it lacks—blessings such as raw materials and open land, which Americans take for granted.

But in today's world, under today's conditions, Japan's particular core competencies combine to achieve consistently higher rates of average national productivity gains than anywhere else in the developed world. Japan today is 350 percent more productive than it was in 1960. The United States, meanwhile, is scarcely 50 percent more productive than it was in 1960. A look at the chart opposite shows how constant these trend lines have been for three decades.

In short, Japan's core competencies are a recipe for productivity growth, not to mention increased competitiveness on the world economic stage. And productivity growth, more than any other factor, is what makes a society richer, more abundant, more successful. Throughout much of modern history a correlation can also be established between societies with steadily improving productivity and the willingness of those same societies to embrace humane, progressive, and visionary values. What is more, productivity growth is a virtuous circle. The bigger the gains, the easier it is for business and government to invest resources in their country's future—and thus claim a future stream of productivity gains as well. It is when productivity is ebbing or stagnating—as it has been in the United States—that the vicious circle develops of claims on the future outpacing economic growth, making it ever harder to invest in tomorrow.

A review of the core competencies will show that most of them relate most directly to manufactured products. Japan remains

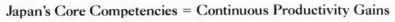

Japan's Core Competencies = Continuous Productivity Gains

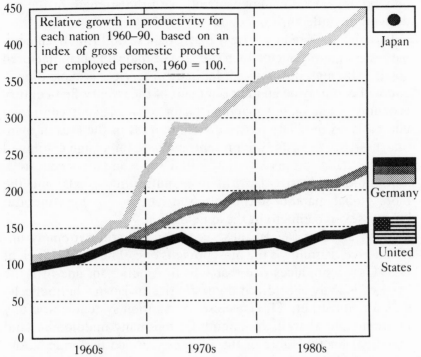

Relative growth in productivity for each nation 1960–90, based on an index of gross domestic product per employed person, 1960 = 100.

Source: *The New York Times*.

much more of a manufacturing-oriented economy than the United States. In making the broad (and maddeningly imprecise) distinction between manufacturing output and service output, Japan derives 44 percent of its GDP from manufacturing, while in the American economy, the comparable figure is about half that.

The rapid growth of the service economy in the United States of recent years has no doubt improved the quality of American life in many ways. But it has been a serious drag on productivity. Labor productivity in the tradeable goods sector of the U.S. economy rose at the extremely healthy annual average of 3.5 percent during the 1980s, yet the service economy, which employs far more people, brought down the national average dramatically as a result of its meager 0.7 percent annual gains.

Japan, on the other hand, is an underserviced economy, which will undergo a significant service sector expansion as the overall paradigm shifts. Yet the overseers of the Japanese economy show no sign of dropping their basic belief that the service sector should only be developed commensurately with the strength of the underlying manufacturing sector.

It is also important to stress that Japanese and American companies compete principally in the area of tradeable manufactured goods. Although the cross-border trade in services is expanding—and will certainly be an important part of the twenty-first-century economy—it is only a marginal factor today. Japan's continued emphasis on productivity-raising techniques in the area of manufactured goods is, for the present, a recipe for a large continued Japanese trade surplus with the United States and other countries. The more productive Japan is in manufactured goods, and the more global markets it controls, the harder it is for American businesses to compete in these fields.

Many areas of the Japanese economy are still extremely unproductive. Farming is the most obvious one. The highly efficient U.S. farmer produces rice that sells in America for one-fifth the price of heavily subsidized domestic rice in Japan's hermetically sealed rice market. The Japanese distribution system is woefully unproductive as well, containing far too many middlemen (and markups) for the value of the business service performed. And at the same time that many companies are experiencing a labor shortage, most also carry large numbers of unproductive or underused people on their payrolls. This is true even in Japan's large manufacturing industries, some of which are still considerably less productive than U.S. norms. However, the "paradigm shift" that is gathering steam currently (as we shall see in Chapter 5) is designed in large part to address exactly such remaining inefficiencies and anomalies in the Japanese economy.

Based on the expectation that Japan will continue to excel in its areas of core competency *and* make significant improvements in its unproductive areas, some international economists believe Japan can surpass the United States in absolute economic output by the beginning of the next decade. That is certainly where the trend lines point, although one always has to be cautious projecting even the sustained trends of the past onto the unknown future.

Nevertheless, consider the bald reality indicated by the following progression of statistics about national shares of total world output of all goods and services:

Year	Japanese Share (%)	U.S. Share	Combined Share
1960	3	36	39
1990	15	23	38
1999 (forecast)	19	18	37

Together, the two countries have consistently made up roughly the same total world output for more than thirty years. But the American part of the equation is being steadily reduced. In 1960, the U.S. share was twelve times greater than Japan's. By 1990, it was just one and a half times greater. And, according to some forecasts, by decade's end, Japan—which has only half America's population—may well have an economy that outproduces the United States.

That is a stunning proposition. A Japan capable of outproducing the United States by the year 2000 would mean one in which each Japanese worker was *twice as productive* as his American counterpart—and *twice as wealthy.*

A projection made by *Newsweek* magazine, based on data from the International Monetary Fund, goes even further, extrapolating recent trends not just to the year 2000, but over the next *fifty* years to 2041. Such a method is obviously flawed. Far too many variables can arise in fifty years' time—new oil shocks, the great Tokyo earthquake, wars, revolutions, and unimaginable technological and social changes. Certainly, Japan's recent economic woes would skew the numbers significantly if one assumed they might continue for any length of time.

Yet even so, the numbers are eye-opening enough to merit mention: Fifty years of Japan's progrowth economic trends would increase Japan's per capita GDP fivefold from $24,000 annually in 1991 to $123,000 in 2041. Meanwhile, fifty more years of current U.S. trends would result in meager increases for Americans—from a 1991 per capita figure of $22,000 to $36,000 by 2041.[37]

Having started off just slightly behind Japan's per capita GDP in 1991, Americans would end up producing *only a third* as much wealth as the Japanese by 2041. America's economy would then measure up to Japan's perhaps as poorly as Russia's compares to America's today.

In 1992, even the Bush administration recognized the problem,

at least in word. In the president's Annual Economic Report, it
was noted that "without adequate productivity growth, America's
standard of living will neither keep pace with the expectations
of our citizens, nor remain the highest in the world."[38]

Yet "adequate productivity growth" is not taking place in the
United States, and hasn't for a long time. *None* of the key recommendations offered by experts who have studied the problems
were implemented in the last dozen years. This was true not only
for the controversial, politically charged ideas like developing
strategic national industrial or technology policies; it was also true
for the constant stream of bipartisan consensus recommendations
to cut the budget deficit and raise the savings rate in order to
promote long-term productive investment. Bill Clinton, of course,
campaigned on a program of changing this record of ignorance
and national denial. Yet regardless of how much change he is able
to achieve, one can rest reasonably assured that Japan, using the
core competencies it has honed within its own economy, as well
as a host of other talents, will continue recording not just "adequate" results, but world-leading, superior productivity growth.
The bubble has burst, the stock market has melted down, but
the basic mechanisms of the Japanese economy remain intact,
well positioned for the future.

5

Paradigm Shift

Premonitions of the Bubble

The summer of 1987 was hot and rainy in Tokyo. In the government district of Kasumigaseki, some of Japan's most efficient bureaucrats sweated out the heat in the old wing of the Ministry of Finance (MoF), where air conditioners were few and far between. They also sweated over the future. For the first time in Japan's postwar miracle history, the nation's financial system was moving out of their control.

The yen was rocketing upward in value against the dollar in one of the most far-reaching role reversals of currencies and wealth imaginable. Two years earlier, under great pressure from Washington, Tokyo's central bankers had agreed to accept a major upward revaluation of the yen. The American theory was that as the yen rose, it would force the price of Japanese exports up along with it, making Japanese goods less competitive on world markets and reducing the politically sensitive U.S. trade deficit with Japan.

The premise had been accepted—a stronger yen—but not the conclusion of a weakened export sector. Soon after the 1985 Plaza Agreement launched the yen into the stratosphere, efforts began to turn the long-resisted appreciation of the yen into a virtue rather than a fetter on Japanese global competitiveness.

Some benefits were self-evident. With their yen garnering twice as many dollars in the foreign exchange market. Japanese companies could build new plants in the United States and elsewhere, expand their global operations, acquire new technology and new marketing channels, and diversify into new businesses—all at deep discounts in yen terms. Meanwhile, the inevitable American penetration of the Japanese market would be retarded by the high local costs U.S. companies had to bear as they tried to take advantage of market-opening measures Japan had finally made.

Most important, the era of *endaka* (strong yen) could be used to manufacture a crisis of a kind. Stodgy Japanese businesses would be prodded into changing their product mix and their production methods. A strong currency would compel them to move away from the price-sensitive exports of the past, such as steel, and encourage them to enter high-technology businesses where quality and features determined international market competitiveness. Bemoaned at first as the potential cause of unemployment and recession, *endaka* could instead serve as the catalyst Japan needed to adapt itself to the new era of advanced technology and globalized markets.

To help make the transition as painless as possible, business would require easy access to cheap capital. The Bank of Japan (BoJ) was prepared to comply aggressively. No sooner had the Plaza meeting ended than the BoJ began pumping liquidity feverishly into the financial system. The official discount rate was cut time and again in 1986–87, bringing benchmark borrowing rates down from 6 percent to a record low of 2.5 percent. BoJ policies inflated money supply by an average of over 10 percent per year in the late '80s, reaching a torrid, unprecedented annualized rate of nearly 13 percent in 1988.

By 1987, the restructuring plan was working well. Japan had shrugged off whatever loss of competitiveness a stronger yen might have implied in foreign exports. High-quality, ultracompetitive Japanese goods were flooding the world market like a scene from *The Sorcerer's Apprentice.* Contrary to American economic projections, the end was not nigh for the Japanese exporting machine. In fact, 1987 would be a record year for Japan's global trade surplus.

The wind was clearly at Japan's back. Even oil, Japan's biggest import expenditure, was tumbling in price, creating a huge additional windfall for an economy that had long assumed it would have to pay forty dollars a barrel forever.

Under normal conditions, the huge increase in money supply

might have had a highly inflationary effect on the "real economy."
But in Japan it didn't, at least not at first. The combination of a
superheated economy, a staggering global trade surplus, collapsing
raw material prices, a U.S. market that sucked in every import
it could find, a Japanese currency doubling in global value, and
the gusher of liquidity pouring out of every banking spigot in the
country created massive *asset inflation* (and stupendous paper
wealth) without interfering much in the daily operations of the
real economy.

For most Japanese, the summer of 1987 was a boom time. Tokyo
was drunk—literally, on enormously overpriced liquor flowing out
of Ginza bars where Japan's new global power was celebrated,
and figuratively, on financial liquidity that made ordinary Japanese
corporate managers look infallible.

With so much liquidity flowing into the financial system, *too
much* money had begun chasing too few investment vehicles. The
Japanese bid up the price of everything that could be construed
as an asset, starting with stocks and real estate, but moving
quickly on to golf club memberships and more dubious financial
instruments. The buckets of Japanese liquidity sloshed abroad
as well. Capital flows had only recently been deregulated, but
the Japanese didn't waste a moment pouring their excess funds
into buying up foreign companies, stocks and bonds, real estate,
artworks, and luxury consumer goods. No matter how many buckets of liquidity the Japanese spilled abroad, when next they looked
they seemed to have more than when they started.

Such a situation outwardly resembled economic nirvana. Big
Japanese companies issued warrant bonds with 1 percent yields
and used the proceeds to build new plants and buy up foreign
assets. Meanwhile, Mr. and Mrs. Watanabe borrowed enough
money on the massively inflated value of their tiny Yokohama
home to buy a collection of condos in Waikiki, the south of France,
and the Australian Gold Coast. But this was worldly temptation,
not nirvana. And the men of the Ministry of Finance were growing
worried.

Long trained as downside planners rather than upside dream-
ers, and well schooled in the Japanese "bicycle theory" (which
holds that if every Japanese doesn't keep pedaling, the economy
might fall over), the men of MoF didn't like the speculative excess
they saw bubbling up all around them. Toyoo Gyohten, the

thoughtful and articulate vice-minister, was one who was especially worried.

"The stock market has reached unsustainable levels of speculative excess," he told me in 1987, when the Nikkei average was still "only" around 26,000—more than 13,000 points shy of where it would be after two more years of speculative excess. "Many people think it would be better if stocks would stop rising and consolidate their value for a while." In a quiet, professorial voice, he confided a truth as simple as it was profound: "We Japanese are very good at making things, producing things, managing enterprises. This is the strength of our economy. Our best interests are not served by this rampant public speculation."

It would take two more years to form the consensus necessary to take action. The bubble was causing no visible damage to the economy, and most companies were thriving as never before. Those concerned about the situation argued that the atmosphere of *zaitek* (financial engineering) was eroding the base of the economy. But the evidence was mixed at best. Even the much-vaunted manufacturing sector was improving its capacity to manufacture as it used its newfound global financial power to buy foreign assets, move low-skill jobs offshore, and invest in the high-value-added manufacturing systems of the future. The argument that the runup of stock prices was inherently unsustainable looked less and less valid as the market continued to hit new record highs month after month, year after year.

In point of fact, the bubble *was* causing some real and potentially devastating long-term problems. Real estate prices, which had been too high to encourage rational use of land for two decades, were now soaring out of sight. "Classless" Japan was being polarized into archly divided camps of homeowners, who were enormously wealthy on paper, and those who would never be able to afford a home. Companies were finding new land too expensive to acquire for new production sites. Record public infrastructure budgets were consumed largely in land acquisition programs rather than actual construction of new bridges, roads, industrial parks, and towns.

With money to burn, some of it was being used unwisely. Banks were overlending on real estate, driving prices up still further. Companies were plowing huge sums into capital investment— some of it creating excess capacity, the very operation of which would only worsen Japan's labor shortage and drive corporate profit margins down further. Hungrily buying assets abroad, investors were gaining reputations as the "ugly Japanese." Political issues of Japanese "overpresence" were causing friction in many foreign markets. Much to the chagrin of the Japanese business establishment, asset inflation was allowing shadowy real estate tycoons, who had been marginal figures inside Japan's own economy, to emerge as some of the chief planters of the Japanese flag abroad.

The stock market's rise was creating unrealistic expectations of never-ending capital appreciation. Analysts at the big securities firms made the case for why stock prices would keep ascending forever. But not all regulators and planners sipped from this bottled bathwater. They had the benefit of a deep institutional memory of such things as the great Tokyo stock market crash of the early 1960s and the days of double-digit interest rates, dollar shocks, and oil shocks in the 1970s. They knew that the mob psychology driving stock prices up could, under certain changed conditions, drive them down again even faster, creating an unstable and unpredictable atmosphere in which anything might happen.

Japanese administrators crave order and stability not only because their nation thrives on it, but because of what has happened before in times of instability and disorder. Unspoken in the late 1980s were the deepest institutional memories—memories of a Japan characterized by violence, political terror, and assassinations in the 1920s and 1930s; the Japan that turned national power over to an elite class of militarists and imperialists who then led the nation to disaster.

More pragmatic worries were also voiced that summer in the MoF's smoke-filled corridors of power. The stock market runup was causing a structural change in the nature of Japanese wealth. This was beginning to lead, in turn, to changes in power and political relationships. The big four securities firms—Nomura, Daiwa, Nikko, and Yamaichi—were garnering influence far beyond their lowly status in the Japanese scheme of things.

Industrialists viewed stockbrokers as little more than glorified "pickle salesmen." Yet here was Nomura suddenly emerging as Japan's most profitable corporation—more profitable by far than Toyota or Sumitomo Bank or other proud blue-chip companies. Young people graduating from the best colleges were flocking to the recruitment drives of the brokerage houses, rather than the old-line banks and industrial companies. Avaricious "nonbank" banks were growing up outside the direct supervision of the regulatory authorities. Japan's underworld *yakuza* were greenmailing, money laundering, and organizing syndicates to trade insider information. In the process, these gangsters were institutionalizing powerful roles for themselves in the financial community.

Meanwhile, the "normal"manipulation of share prices on the casino-like floor of the Tokyo Stock Exchange—which the MoF men had always known about and winked at—was now reaching staggering proportions. The profits of inside information were no longer going simply to oil the LDP's traditional political machine. Now, they were being used by upstarts to gain quick influence in politics.

Japan's best-known modern scandal—the Recruit affair—was not yet public knowledge. But the facts about Recruit's influence buying were known, at least in broad outlines, to the men of the MoF in 1987. In this economy of excess liquidity and astronomical asset inflation, influence was shifting to those like the little-known newcomer Hiromasa Ezoe, chief of the Recruit corporate empire. His business spanned new kinds of ventures from computer services to placement of temporary office workers. His success attracted widespread jealousy. He compensated for this by spreading his wealth around in the right places. In just a few years, he had managed to insinuate himself into the campaign and personal finances of many major political figures in Japan. Eventually, some 160 notables would be exposed as having taken tainted funds.

Other insider-trading and influence-buying scandals were also becoming known to MoF. In this sea of corruption, MoF's own top officials as well as prime ministers and would-be LDP leaders were all implicated. Those who wanted to rein in the excesses of the bubble economy began to understand that in order to do so, they had to be willing to challenge entrenched political leaders.

But even as many Japanese leaders had become caught up in the cycle of corruption, a broadly shared philosophical bent existed inside government and business institutions against allowing the financial services sector to become too influential. America, after all, had allowed itself to become an economy of Wall Street "money games." The result was that its industrial structure had been hollowed out and it could no longer make many things competitively. If Japan wished to avoid a similar fate, its leaders would have to take action to burst the bubble and accept the consequences.

Despite the outward appearance of a permanent boom economy, Gyohten and his colleagues at MoF had reason to be worried, as did their counterparts at the Bank of Japan, at MITI, and throughout many, although certainly not all, leading institutions of Japanese political and economic power. Today, MoF men say they believed it was up to the Bank of Japan to puncture the bubble, and they claim to have lobbied hard for BoJ governor Satoshi Sumita to raise the easy money discount rate. Sumita was averse to spoiling the long-running party with the tough remedy needed. Even so, he reluctantly oversaw rate hikes in May and October of 1989. The fact that they did not have much effect allowed him to argue that a further tightening of monetary policy could not be counted on to address the brewing problems.

"As early as 1988, most all the financial authorities recognized the problem," recalls Takeshi Ohta, a former BoJ deputy governor. "But we were too preoccupied with scandals to focus on tightening money supply. Monetary policy is a consensus policy in Japan, and it took us until 1989 to get the support we needed from government, business, and the public."

The development of that consensus was given a strong nudge by inflation rates, which approached 4 percent in 1989—a mild figure by American standards, but catastrophic in inflation-phobic Japan. It became obvious that the bubble was doing economic damage not just on social and structural issues of the future, but in the here and now. For those who had previously opposed intervention, the prospect of roaring inflation gave them a face-saving way to change their stance.

Had the Bank of Japan moved to reduce the money supply in 1988, some experts contend, asset prices might have stabilized at their then-current levels. Others argue that much of the damage could have been prevented had BoJ acted decisively as late as the middle of 1989, before the last huge runup of the Nikkei averages. Better late than never, the reins of command at the Bank of Japan finally passed to Yasushi Mieno, a forty-year veteran of the bank's bureaucracy. Assuming control at the end of 1989, Mieno made clear that a new tough-minded order had arrived.

Making a Virtue of Necessity

Mieno appeared to many as a bull in the delicate china shop of finance. He declared an open war on asset inflation, and he meant what he said. Ominously, he compared the rising tide of inflation to a "loose thread of a kimono," which, if left unattended, could unravel the entire Japanese economy.[1]

Before he could begin getting the job done in earnest, Mieno first had to win a war of nerves with the new minister of finance, Ryutaro Hashimoto, a dapper politician once voted the handsomest public figure in Japan. Hashimoto was more an expert on politics than on monetary policy, and his eye was undeniably on the prime ministership. Not surprisingly, he was reluctant to be the one to encourage the necessary monetary tightening.

With Japan heading into a new election season, Hashimoto believed rising interest rates would have negative political implications for a government already reeling from scandal and a growing erosion of public confidence. Hashimoto urged Mieno to wait for the previous upticks in the discount rate to take effect. The press was rife with unprecedented leaks as charges and countercharges flew between MoF and BoJ. The two institutions had often disagreed in the past, but never so vehemently or so publicly. Mieno won the tug-of-war. Eight days into his tenure, he raised the discount rate again. Four days after that, the stock market peaked. Investors realized that the days of easy money were finally over.

Under Mieno's forceful hand, interest rates were raised continually until the discount rate hit the practically American level of 6 percent. Banks were virtually forbidden to lend on new real estate projects. The tidal wave of liquidity was dammed. Money supply growth was squeezed down from 13 percent to barely 2 percent.

The effects were dramatic. The stock market began its nearly three-year-long swoon. Property prices began retreating from the realm of the extragalactic back to the merely stratospheric. With the scent of blood in his nostrils, especially as new financial scandals from the bubble era left hardly a major Japanese political figure standing, Mieno ran his own show his own way. He drove interest rates too high and dried up the money supply too much, triggering more asset deflation and crisis in the financial system than was needed to normalize the situation. By the time he tried to ease credit again two years later, the stock market had lost so much confidence that interest rate cuts were greeted with yawns if not perverse new sell signals.

Tetsuo Tsukimura, the bellwether forecaster of Tokyo market trends at Smith Barney, was among the first to announce the death of the bubble economy in February 1990. But two years later, while others were hoping that credit loosening would keep the Nikkei's head above the 18,000 level, Tsukimura scoffed and intimated the market could fall as low as 6,000.[2] Others were equally despairing. "I'm planning for a seven-year recession," announced Kazuhiko Nishi, founder and president of Ascii, one of the most notable Japanese entrepreneurial high-tech companies.[3]

Yet Mieno may well have succeeded in bringing off the impossible. He was able to squeeze three trillion dollars of phony value out of the stock market, and even more out of the real estate market. He did it in such a sustained and measured way that no out-and-out panic arose, and none of the worst-case scenarios have been realized—at least up until now. Throughout 1990 and most of 1991, he was even able to attack the bubble while the real economy grew faster than any other in the world.

In retrospect it seems obvious that Japanese bureaucrats first acted too aggressively in creating the liquidity needed by business to combat the negative effects of the rising yen. Next, they acted too slowly to bring the bubble they had created back to earth. Finally, they acted too rashly and went too far once they moved into the damage-control mode.

The entire process reveals the inherent weaknesses of a system where government is anything but transparent, conflicts of interest between the regulators and the regulated are rampant, markets operate less than freely, informed public debate is skimpy, and the press is hardly independent. (Japan's leading financial daily, the *Nihon Keizai Shimbun*, which was itself implicated in a major national financial scandal, referred to the bubble economy a mere twenty-seven times during the years when it prevailed—1985–89. However, since 1990, when government policy shifted toward bursting the bubble, the same paper has printed more than five thousand articles about bubble economics.)[4]

If anyone thought the Japanese economy always acted as a well-ordered, well-planned, well-controlled, and homogeneous machine, the roller coaster of recent years shows otherwise. Even when it was obvious that the bubble was getting out of control, the most control-minded Japanese officials found themselves at an embarrassing and dangerous impasse, unable to get the genie of diverse market and political forces back into the bottle.

For all the mishandling of Japan's economy in the last eight years, Americans ought not be too quick to judge. Both the United States and Japan faced a mind-boggling array of new economic conditions in the 1980s. A short list would include deregulation, globalization, floating exchange rates, and new technologies that rewrote old rules of value, accounting, debt and equity markets, and business practices in general. The downside of adjusting to these changes included financial excesses, mindless speculation, and corruption aplenty in *both* countries.

But on a bottom-line basis, Japan fared better than the United States. It enjoyed far more real growth. It undertook vastly more productive investment inside the country and a more visionary course of investment outside the country. And it managed to raise the living standards of almost all of its people in the process, even if it still has a way to go to match American norms.

Japan, not America, experienced the real supply side revolution of the 1980s. Some of the excess "supply" of capital has now dissipated. Yet for all the talk of "collapse," it is important to remember that the combined evaporation of stock and property market value from 1990 through 1992 claimed less than 20 percent of the total value of Japanese assets. While American financial authorities wrestle with the enduring economic disabilities created by Reaganomics, their Japanese counterparts feel free to declare that "the decline in asset prices has had no substantial impact on the real economy."[5]

Some excess capital was squandered, the lion's share was not. In the boom years, Japanese businesses poured so much into capital investment and R&D that it will take some companies into the mid-'90s just to begin to use what they built. In fact, the capital investment boom has laid the groundwork for an almost brand-new Japanese economy of the future.

In the United States, meanwhile, R&D budgets are still falling and capital investment is up only marginally. Whereas the American economy burdened itself with three times as much new debt as new capital investment in the last decade, Japanese capital investment far outpaced increased debt levels. Many American companies are still paying for the immensely overleveraged capital structures they took on in the debt binge of the 1980s. But large Japanese companies are witnessing their best debt-to-equity ratios in the history of postwar Japan.

The banking systems in both countries are still burdened by unresolved debt problems on a grand scale. But Japan's excesses—as well as its achievements—have taken place without recourse to huge borrowings from foreigners or from the next generation of workers. Japan enters the global economic competition of the twenty-first century with a virtually brand-new industrial base. Perhaps even more important, it is ready to compete without the shackles of American-style debts placing potentially unbearable burdens on its national future. The world's most unsentimental financial observers—currency traders—seem to understand all this quite well. As Neal Cavuto, of the CNBC financial news network, observed at the height of Europe's currency crisis in September of 1992, "The dollar is no longer a safe-haven currency. That honor goes to the Japanese yen."

Almost all Japanese financial service companies face a long, uncertain climb back to their former solidity and global prestige. Overleveraged individuals and small companies are trying to cope with ferocious squeezes and the fallout from bankruptcies, especially in the real estate and construction sectors. Some twelve thousand companies went under in 1992. In Japan, that's a lot of bankruptcies, even if it pales by comparison to the nearly three-quarters of a million personal and corporate bankruptcies filed in the United States annually. The effects of these disasters are real—Japanese suicides are up and so even is unemployment, albeit modestly.

But the worst appears to be over for most sectors of the Japanese economy. Speculative froth has been blown out of the system. Inflation has been quelled. Corrupt financial practices have been reined in.

Some experts even deny a post-bubble recession ever took place. "If an economy doesn't experience large-scale unemployment, if companies remain profitable (even if less so than before), and if GDP increases remain in positive territory for the year, I don't think you can really call it a recession," says Hitotsubashi University economics professor Yukio Noguchi. He acknowledges that his own views are at odds with those of other experts who feel the country has been pinched plenty by the recession. Nevertheless, his point has a measure of validity. After all, while more than three million Americans lost their jobs in the U.S. recession of the early '90s, only about two hundred thousand Japanese workers joined the ranks of their country's unemployed.

The bursting of the Japanese bubble was a necessity. It *had* to be done. Its effects will probably be more complex and longer-lasting than the Bank of Japan initially thought. But the economy appears set on a course of making a virtue out of this rather painful necessity.

An American business magazine observed ruefully:

> It hardly seems like justice that Japan should have let its financial markets run so wild, and in the end, get off so easily. Or that its excesses should result in so little tangible pain, while the rest of the industrialized world struggles with long unemployment lines. But when citizens have savings that are three times the size of their liabilities, and when companies are world class exporters, economies can be quite resilient. Even when Japan is down, it seems to come out way ahead.[6]

A High-Stakes Debate About the Future

An irony of Japanese economic planning is that managers spend a great deal of time trying to figure out how to minimize risk, avoid failure, and avert disaster. And yet nothing works to spur the Japanese to new successes as well as the failures and disasters that befall them, along with the risks they are then forced to take to overcome adversity. Every major "shock" Japan has faced in the last quarter-century has ultimately been good for improving its system. The same may now hold true as Japan recharts its economic course after the bursting of the bubble.

In this regard, the American and Japanese economic experiences have begun to diverge in fundamental ways. Japan, although criticized within and without for being visionless, actually faces up to its domestic problems with a stream of new visions and practical action plans. The United States, whose leaders talk glibly about grand global visions (such as George Bush's "new world order"), and whose capacity to absorb adversity is demonstrably immense, nonetheless went out of the business of trying to steer an economic path toward any specified domestic goal or vision sometime in the mid-1980s.

In the mid-1970s and again in the early '80s, both nations faced energy crises. Japan launched a concerted drive to change its sources and uses of energy. It is still taking active measures to reduce its reliance on imported oil, even now that such imports are "cheap" by recent historical standards. The United States, on the other hand, toyed with energy-related planning only in the heat of the moment. As soon as the crisis subsided, efforts to develop a long-term energy policy were jettisoned. America today is *more reliant* on imported oil than ever. Amazingly, Japan has reorganized its use of energy so completely that even with its lack of indigenous resources, oil imports make up scarcely more of its GNP than they do in the United States, a country with vast domestic resources.

Similarly, when the great currency realignment of the 1980s took place, Japan reorganized its entire economy around the assumption of a strong yen. The United States not only pursued a disastrous policy course in driving down the value of its own dollar too far, but then proceeded to make no concerted national effort to recapture the advantages of a weak currency.

Now we are witnessing the responses of the two societies to the financial excesses and other experiences of the new global economic age. Once again, a concerted Japanese response is taking shape that is likely to retool the economy in new ways to meet future challenges. In the United States, meanwhile, visionless drift was the rule in the final days of George Bush.

Unlike the past, when national policies sought to solve particular problems, the initiatives gaining ground in Japan today cast a much wider net. They seek to re-engineer large parts of the entire social, business, and political structure. The point is not so much to prevent another bubble from arising, but to use the atmosphere of flux, confusion, and transition in the wake of the bubble's collapse to galvanize substantial long-term change in direction of the Japanese economy.

On a 1992 Japanese TV program, anchorman Sadatomo Matsudaira traced the history of previous Japanese "crises"—and the *kee-wahdos* (a Japanese phrase appropriated from English, which means "key words" or "buzzwords") to provide the solutions to the problems. "Energy efficiency and export drive" was the *kee-wahdo* of 1973–74, after the first oil shock. "Streamlining and shifting operations abroad," was the *kee-wahdo* of 1985–86 in response to the strong yen. But what should be the *kee-wahdo* in response to the collapsed bubble? The anchorman pointed only to a question mark.[7]

The recognition that there is no single focal point for change may itself be an indicator that Japan is getting ready for the deepest social restructuring it has experienced since World War II.

Sony chairman Akio Morita, always an innovator, identified perhaps the most sweeping *kee-wahdo* possible: "reinventing Japan." He argued that the Japanese business system itself needed a "new paradigm." In a controversial 1992 article in *Bungei Shunju,* one of Japan's leading magazines, Morita addressed the problem of why Japan instilled so much fear and resentment abroad. Showing how the Japanese business system had worked *too well* in making Japanese manufacturing companies internationally efficient and competitive, he proposed a strategic shift of priorities to bring Japan more into line with world business norms.[8]

In intentionally seeking to make Japanese business less relentlessly market-share-driven, Morita sought to marry Japan's two biggest challenges—improving the quality of life of its own people and integrating Japan more harmoniously into the world economic system. He proposed a set of interlinked solutions to the two problems.

Japanese workers, who log two hundred hours more per year than Americans and five hundred more than Germans, should work shorter hours and have more holidays, Morita suggested. Salaries might be increased so that more of Japan's corporate wealth would be shared with its employees, who could then enjoy a better quality of life. Japanese companies, which pay notoriously low dividends, should consider increasing payouts to shareholders. Industrial companies should develop more equitable partnerships with their suppliers and vendors, instead of pressuring them incessantly. Corporations should also get involved with community causes and devote more of their resources to philanthropy, corporate citizenship programs, and protection of the environment.

Morita argued that if such measures were actually taken up by Japanese business, the global playing field would be leveled in a meaningful way. Western companies would have a chance to gain back market share from Japanese companies, which would now bear costs and burdens more closely approximating those borne by Western companies. This deliberate forsaking of some aspects of Japanese corporations' global competitiveness and market share would be doubly in Japan's interests: On the one hand, it would reduce political friction and improve cooperation between Japan and the other leading economies of North America and Europe. It would also lay the groundwork for an even grander road to the borderless economy of the future envisioned by Morita—the harmonization of key areas of the global framework, such as antitrust, labor, and tax law. Such harmonization would allow cross-border corporate competition to focus fairly on the playing field of "creativity," which Morita defined as "technological innovation, product planning and marketing."[9]

At the same time as Japan reduced friction with other major economies, the measures outlined by Morita would solve the key problems of the Japanese domestic agenda by bringing a better life to Japanese workers and consumers, heretofore under-rewarded by the Japanese economic miracle.

Calling for a profound change in national thinking, Morita said it was imperative that Japan stop acting like a country still trying to rebuild from the ruins of war. It was time to take account of the fact that the period of rebuilding was finished, and that Japan was now an economic leader with global responsibilities.

Summarizing his views, Morita said in a speech:

> Japan needs a new paradigm for competitiveness. The efficiencies of Japanese corporations allow them to absorb razor thin profit margins which few Western companies can match. These practices do not violate the rules of international competition. The problem is that they fail to embrace the *spirit* of competition found in the United States and Europe. It comes as no surprise then that foreign competitors sometimes call the Japanese approach "unfair."

> With a new commitment to harmonize its management and competitive practices with those of the majority of nations, Japan will be well prepared to assume a more significant global role.[10]

Morita's views were immediately challenged in many quarters. They were explicitly rebuffed by Takeshi Nagano, chairman of Nikkeiren, the employers association. Nagano was piqued that Morita would propose wage increases just as Nikkeiren was negotiating annual wage settlements with the major unions. It didn't matter that Morita's ideas were focused on gradual change over a number of years. Nagano took them as aid and comfort to the unions at a moment when he was trying to hold the line on wages. "What Morita said is wrong," he declared summarily.[11]

Traditional business leaders worried that Morita's course would take them away from what they know and do so well—and into uncharted territory. Tadahiro Sekimoto, president of the giant electronics firm NEC, questioned Morita's appeal for Japanese companies to base themselves more on profitability and less on market share. Market share, Sekimoto said, "is a reflection of a company's strength. If share increases, profits increase."[12]

Neonationalists like Shintaro Ishihara criticized Morita for wanting Japan to harmonize its business practices with those of the declining West, instead of just "saying no" to America and Europe. Political reformers argued that Morita's points about changing business practices missed the key issue of shaking up and restructuring Japanese politics. And more than a few American skeptics questioned whether real action would follow the appealing words about change.

James C. Abegglen, one of the foremost American experts on Japanese management practices, skewered the Morita program as "contradictory in effect, impossible to implement at the company level, and largely pernicious in . . . impact on the economy." Yet in the very next breath, he emphasized that Morita's objectives were "entirely commendable" and that efforts such as Morita's to redefine Japan's role and position were extremely important.[13]

Whether one agreed or not with Morita's particular proposals and emphases, he was demonstrating that it was possible for a Japanese business leader to question the sacred cows of long-held beliefs and propose not just small incremental changes, but sweeping, systemic change as well.

For all the dust kicked up by Morita's comments, it is probable that his vision of the future course of Japan should take is not far off the mark of what will eventually happen. Many of the negative reactions can be attributed to fear and conservatism, rather than to real disagreement. Some in the Japanese business community, many in government, and a clear majority of public opinion at large responded favorably to what Morita had to say.

Other leading figures were saying similar things out loud as well. Masaya Miyoshi, director-general of the influential Keidanren, criticized "corporatism" in Japan. He argued that in the domestic context, the Japanese system produced a "herd mentality" and a compulsion on the part of employees to center their lives on work and company. In the international arena, the Japanese corporatist approach allowed companies to have "few qualms" about "disrupting the existing order in Western markets" without regard to the consequences.[14]

Toyota president Shoichiro Toyoda, a man of carefully measured words, put forward the view that "Japan has come this far on the strength of work, work and more work. But overwork and overachieving without regard for our fellow human beings does no good for anyone. The time has come to get in step with the rest of the world." Japan, he said, should promote a better quality of life at home and do more to contribute to the greater good of the global community. He warned that Japan must correct its history of being "too ignorant of and too apathetic about the feelings that our growing influence arouses in people and nations around the world."[15]

Other voices promulgated other far-reaching agendas. Even Prime Minister Miyazawa positioned himself at the forefront of calls for social change. Japan, he said, should become not just an economic superpower, but a quality-of-life superpower as well.

Opening the 1992 session of the Diet, Miyazawa said, "We must shift from a producer-oriented society to one with the priority on consumers and ordinary citizens."[16] According to the prime minister, elements of that transition would include better housing, shorter working hours, shorter commuting time, fuller employment and better opportunities for women, more balanced growth in the regions outside Tokyo, greater emphasis on creativity, and more attention to Japan's international responsibilities. "It is a private matter whether people find satisfaction or a feeling of affluence in their lives, but it is up to us to arrange the environmental infrastructure so that they are able to do so," he declared.[17]

The words sound promising, but many Japanese question

whether such extensive change can be achieved without political reform. So too do foreigners who have watched the Diet gridlock over other burning issues, especially those relating to Japan's international responsibilities. In trying to make amends for its inaction in response to the Gulf War crisis, for example, the Japanese parliament spent over a year debating a measure strongly backed by the government that would allow token peacekeeping troops to be dispatched to future international troublespots. Long after the world had already concluded that Japan was shirking its share of international obligations, the issue finally came to a vote. The opposition engaged in a unique Japanese filibustering technique known as the "ox-step." Walking as slowly as possible to the ballot box in a ritual designed to try even a Zen master's patience, the filibusterers forced a further watering down of an already heavily compromised initiative. In the end, the government was authorized to dispatch no more than a token force of two thousand peacekeepers in future crises. Under the new law, they can be dispatched only under UN command, only in situations where Japanese peacekeepers are welcome by all warring parties, and only to areas where a cease-fire is already in force. If the cease-fire breaks down, the Japanese peacekeepers are to leave.

It is often said of the Liberal Democratic Party that it is neither very liberal nor very democratic—and not much of a party either. The LDP is actually many parties within a single party, and the internecine warfare among organized factions is frequently quite sharp. But it still manages to present a relatively unified face to the public. Its forty-year lock on power has made Japan essentially a one-party state. Debate takes place, to be sure, but not in the public, participatory fashion Americans tend to associate with democracy.

In the wake of Recruit and other scandals, Japanese socialists temporarily made some gains. For a time during 1990–91, they threatened to re-emerge as real challengers to the LDP. Quickly, however, it became evident that they had no workable program for Japan's future. After a few months of fascination with socialist leader Takako Doi, the public lost interest, even though as a socialist, a Christian, a powerful public speaker, and a woman, she offered about as new a style for a Japanese politician as might be imagined.

Most of the LDP's top representatives are now tainted by scandal and the party itself is increasingly disliked by the public at large. "Younger-generation" leaders are few and far between and many of these in their forties and fifties are veterans of the same kind of backroom dealings as their elders in any event.

None of this has prevented the LDP from reasserting its primacy, however. Kiichi Miyazawa may have been forced to resign as finance minister in the wake of the Recruit scandal, but he was quickly back on the scene, assuming the top job as prime minister after only a brief political penance. Former prime minister Noboru Takeshita, also felled by Recruit, continues to press the flesh like a Japanese version of Richard Nixon. His faction still calls the shots, even after another political payoff scandal forced Shin Kanemaru, the Takeshita faction's operational strongman, to resign in 1992 as LDP vice-chairman. No matter how tarnished the Takeshita faction's reputation, it remains virtually impossible for anyone to ascend to the prime ministry without their blessing.

Increasingly cynical about such leaders, and increasingly embittered that theirs is a "first-world economy with a third-world political structure," the cautious Japanese public, long accustomed to suffering in silence, is edging closer to speaking up and demanding change.

New political parties are being proposed. A few tentative steps have been taken toward organization. Morihiro Hosokawa, a former LDP stalwart in the upper house of the Diet and a descendant of an ancient Japanese feudal clan, has launched the Japan New Party, which takes aim at what he calls a "moribund political system," which is "out of touch with the realities of the world."[18]

One of Hosokawa's supporters elected to the Diet in 1992 is Yoshio Terasawa, an internationally known Japanese business figure who ran the headquarters of Nomura Securities in the United States for many years. Terasawa says the Japan New Party will work to take politics out of the hands of politicians "who are in bed with the big corporations and interest groups" and put political power into "the hands of consumers and ordinary citizens." Japan's wealth is of little use if its own people can't enjoy it, argues Terasawa. Citing the case of his relatives who still live without central heating or flush toilets, he notes that living standards are better in the United States than in Japan.[19]

But perhaps even more so than in the United States, the grip of Japanese institutional political power is overwhelming. Trying to draw inspiration from American political mavericks, Hosokawa told journalists during the 1992 election campaign for the upper house of the Diet that he wanted to use TV call-in shows to reach the people directly. But Japan doesn't have call-in shows, and on-air political campaigning is strictly controlled.

Meanwhile, Rengo Sangiin, a group of upper house members backed by Japan's leading labor union, has begun to differentiate itself from the LDP across a range of issues. According to political science professor Takeshi Sasaki, this group has become the favored party of people under forty and of Tokyo residents, and now offers "the greatest potential as a counterbalance to LDP."[20] And Kenichi Ohmae, director of McKinsey & Co.'s Japan consulting practice, is trying to organize Seikatsusha—the Consumer's Party. Ohmae is one of Japan's most novel thinkers, and his analysis is instructive:

Japan's basic problem of excessive centralization has been created by the forty-year dominance of a single political party. A powerful, highly-centralized, "provider" government was appropriate when Japan was a developing country. Right after the Pacific War, Japanese per capita GNP was about $350 per year. We didn't have much-needed schools, roads, hospitals, railroads, or harbors, so the government built them. . . .

The role of government should have changed, probably around 1979–80, when per capita GNP reached $10,000. No change came, however, because the people in power quite naturally believed they had been very successful and were thus quite popular.

But this was a fallacy: They are *not* popular, and they remain in power only because people haven't had any other choices. . . . What I am proposing is the establishment of a new political party, the Consumer's Party, which will represent people who are on the receiving end of government services. I am also advocating a shift to regional autonomy and open markets, to giving people the choice of the best and cheapest from anywhere in the world. Such an antithesis to the current LDP-controlled central government is gaining in popularity. Six years ago, when I first made these proposals, I received many death threats. Today, my books are selling quite well, and those telephone calls have stopped.[21]

It is very possible that the LDP will break apart in the years ahead, that new political parties will arise, and that Japanese politics will be enlivened with new democracy and a new diversity of views. Even if such scenarios fail to materialize, the business community—which is Japan's most effective instrument of change in any case—appears prepared to take a number of initiatives that could greatly alter the fabric of Japanese society.

Real change will come, but it will come in the Japanese manner—slowly. "Economists can make all sorts of arguments about how Japanese companies will be forced to make changes," observes Koichi Hori, of the Boston Consulting Group's Tokyo office. But as for quick or drastic Western-style change, "It's just not the way things happen here."[22] Nissan's former chairman Takashi Ishihara believes fundamental change will come—but it will require "ten or twenty years."

That may be too pessimistic. Consider how much change Japan absorbed between 1985 and 1992: the successful shift from heavy industry to high-technology and from an export-led to a domestic-led economy, deregulation of major government monopolies, liberalization of the financial system, globalization of companies, restructuring of industries to digest the impact of the strong yen, and major new advances in R&D. In all of this one sees a portrait of a highly dynamic society at work. Japan in 1993 is incredibly different from the Japan of just a few years ago, even if it *seems* at times unchanging.

Japan is capable of *at least* as much economic, technological, and social change during the remaining years of this decade as it experienced from 1985 to 1992—perhaps much more—if the stranglehold of its political system is loosened, and fresh ideas are allowed in.

6

Heading Toward the Millennium: The Next Japan

The Crash as a Rite of Passage

In the Roaring '20s, the American economy appeared golden, its growth curve unending. Innovation, productivity, and optimism poured from the rich veins of the Jazz Age. Yet with the debacle of the 1929 New York stock market crash and the Great Depression of the 1930s that ensued, the powerful American economic machine ground to a halt. By 1932, the gilded promise of just a few years earlier seemed like a sad, nostalgic dream.

Out of those experiences, American society developed a new set of assumptions. An activist government with a grand vision and a liberal, Keynesian economic agenda was born. A coalition of social forces grew up around Franklin D. Roosevelt that would dominate U.S. political life for the next half-century. The economic pain of the 1930s was deep. But a decade later, the United States was back on its feet. It had become the most productive, dynamic, and vibrant society the modern age had yet experienced.

A similar rite of passage may be occurring in Japan today. The trajectory toward world power that emanated from Tokyo in the Roaring '80s was simply too torrid to be sustained. It skipped over too much developmental ground, leaving Japanese businesses and government institutions breathless as they tried to cope with new challenges. Now, as Japan picks up the pieces of past recklessness, it has the opportunity to develop a new set of assumptions. These *could* provide the basis for a Japan whose model of capitalism may well still emerge as the world-leading force in the next century.

Not one but five "New Japans" are being born—five dramatic sets of changes, which are converging in a 1990s Japanese version of the American "New Deal" of the 1930s. These changes bring with them new economic and social assumptions for the future. In each case, progressive impulses are moving Japan more toward traditional American values—traditional, that is, in the sense of America at its zenith of excellence in midcentury, not the extremes and excesses of our contemporary *fin-de-siècle* ways.

Japan's deepest-rooted core values will probably not change much. But enough of the society's operations are being questioned to imagine that even if Japan does not become more like what America *is* today, it may become a bit more like what America once *was*.

The vast majority of Japanese business, political, and intellectual leaders say they want their country to enjoy a richer, more diverse internal life as well as a more harmonious relationship with the external world. The changes detailed below are steps on the road toward those goals.

Today's geopolitics and geoeconomics have a curious, ironic symmetry. Just as America needs to move more in Japan's direction in saving, investing, and producing more while consuming less, Japan's best chances of making the changes it must make lie in a combination of new leadership and new ideas domestically *and* a closer relationship with the mirror-image society on the other side of the Pacific, the United States.

The Consumer Society

The shift toward becoming more of a consumer society is probably the biggest and most far-reaching change on the Japanese landscape. Obviously, Japan is very much a consumer society to begin with. Its streets are lined with fast food franchises, including ever-trendy American names like McDonald's, Kentucky Fried, Häagen-Dazs, and Mr. Donut. Even in a recession, the department stores of Tokyo's Shibuya district are jammed with young shoppers. Japanese homes, however small, are nonetheless crammed with the latest electronic goods. The average household contains 5.3 remote control devices for consumer electronics hardware. The penetration of some consumer goods, such as color TVs and washing machines, is actually higher in Japan than in the United States.

The transition from an export-led economy to domestic-led economy has already been made. In fact, most of the stunning economic growth achieved from 1986 to 1990 was fueled by domestic demand. The old American image of Japanese workers slaving away in low-paid jobs to make products for export is now part of an ancient history belonging to the 1960s and '70s. The United States and Japan are no longer even in different leagues in terms of economic dependence on exports. Japan derives a little less than 10 percent of its GNP from its exports; the United States a little more than 7 percent. The 3 percent differential *is* statistically significant and should not be glossed over. Nevertheless, the Japanese are consuming the overwhelming majority of goods and services they produce right at home.

But the Japanese *could* (and by all rights *should)* consume a good deal more. No other developed world economy has Japan's moderate level of individual and household consumption in comparison to business spending.

In order for consumers to consume more, some powerful existing barriers to consumption must come down. But if and when the barriers fall, the consumer could become the key to Japan's next phase of economic growth in much the way the American consumer was responsible for quantum leaps made by the U.S. economy in the 1950s and '60s. Increased consumption may also hold the key to reducing Japan's chronic and politically troublesome trade surpluses. This is true even though the imagined correlation between increased consumption and increased import absorption has proven to be something of an economic chimera in the past.

Reducing their astronomical savings rates by only a few percentage points, Japanese consumers could easily spend about $300 billion a year more than at present. Theoretically (a word that cannot be overemphasized here), $300 billion of new spending on consumer goods and services would be enough to wipe out Japan's trade surpluses with the United States and Europe entirely *and* add 5 percent annual growth to Japanese GDP—*all the while* avoiding the pitfalls of American-style overconsumption and retaining the highest household savings rate of any major economy.

Having been a producer society for so long, the Japanese economy has a supply-side rather than demand-side bias. Trained to fear the dangers of Westernization that lurk in the dark, shadowy world of consumption, Japan must actually *learn* how to consume intelligently.

One key focus of change will be on land and tax policy. Japanese farmers, trying to raise rice and other land-intensive crops in the rocky Japanese countryside, have ended up among the world's most *inefficient* and heavily subsidized producers. Not only are huge tracts of land in the countryside reserved for farming, but an incredible one-seventh of metropolitan Tokyo's land base remains zoned and taxed for agricultural use.[1] In spite of the obvious inefficiencies bred by Japan's farm policies, it has been extremely hard to get the farmers off the land. As in most industrial countries, political power in Japan remains skewed toward rural districts, which are over-represented in parliament.

Like Europeans and Americans, the Japanese retain a deep nostalgia for their nineteenth-century ways and the foods that keep their culture intact in spite of massive change in other fields. The cultivation of rice has been likened to a religious undertaking. Most consumers do not find it objectionable to pay five to seven times the world market price for a kilo of rice in order to ensure Japan's self-sufficiency in this staple.

The notion of self-sufficiency in rice has been taken to absurd extremes. In the 1992 "Sushi Boy" case, for example, a Japanese company of that name tried to import low-priced frozen sushi from its plant in California to serve in restaurants in Japan that target consumers who want fast food at budget prices. But sushi, after all, is mostly rice and only a little bit fish. Although they eventually relented, authorities at first blocked the imports, arguing that bringing frozen sushi in from California was impossible under the regulation forbidding the import of products in which rice makes up 80 percent or more of total weight.

Because of the extraordinary power held by the farm lobby, getting farmers off the land has proven to be a glacial process thus far. Adopting the related measures of freeing agricultural import markets to bring in much larger quantities of foodstuffs has been equally difficult, as has moving toward the ultimate goal: more rational overall land use.

Change is now in the wind, however. Momentum is gathering

for political redistricting that would give more influence to urban dwellers. The unusual shortages of rice for processed foods that occurred in 1992 as a result of bad weather and poor harvests also helped create a new business reason to consider imports. Above all, the outlook in the countryside is changing. Some 31 percent of farmers say they would be happy to get out of farming. The average age of rice farmers is rising—fifty-six years old currently. "The problem is being solved through attrition," as one Japanese economic journalist muses in a rather clinical fashion.

As land devoted to agriculture is reduced over the coming years, several simultaneously salutary effects could be felt: First and foremost, new land resources will be opened up for construction of new towns, housing developments, shopping malls, public works projects, resorts, and industrial areas. All of these uses will stimulate consumption. The expansion of available land for development in rural areas could also help bring down the ridiculously high price of real estate in major urban centers and foster the decentralization Tokyo and other cities need so desperately. The more rational and market-driven land-use policy becomes, the more pent-up consumer demand can be released—and the more realistic it will become to talk of improving the quality of life for the average Japanese. The government's Economic Planning Agency wants to see workers in big cities able to buy their own homes for five times their annual salary—a goal that can only be met by putting new land into use to reduce real estate prices.

Next, increased reliance on imported food will significantly reduce the cost of groceries to Japanese households, which now spend about 25 percent more than Americans on a daily total calorie intake that is one-third less. Assuming that the requisite liberalization measures are taken on tariff and nontariff barriers, and the distribution system is demonopolized, Japanese consumers could realize tens of billions of dollars in annual savings. This additional purchasing power could then be shifted into consumer industries more productive and more important to Japan's future than agriculture.

Finally, as Japan moves toward purchasing more of its food supply from abroad, its troublesome trade surpluses with food-exporting countries should see considerable improvement. To be sure, Americans frequently overestimate the potential of an open Japanese agricultural market. Japan is already the largest agricultural export market for American farmers. As the market reaches fuller liberalization, the Japanese will purchase only some of their increased food imports from the United States. More will come from China, Southeast Asia, Australia, and Europe, both Eastern and Western, as Tokyo seeks to defuse many different bilateral tensions with its many trading partners. Nevertheless, it is quite possible that a Japanese agricultural market freed of all tariffs and other major constraints could absorb at least twice as much imported food as it does today—in other words, another $40 billion or more annually. Such import expenditures will not be bad for Japan. Instead, they will have a positive, rationalizing effect: Putting $40 billion more a year in the hands of Japan's trading partners not only reduces political friction, but allows its partners to buy that much more higher-value-added Japanese export items.

Other changes are also necessary—and in the offing. Japanese businesses *are* serious about reducing working hours, even if official rhetoric on this point has run consistently ahead of the reality. In 1992, for example, average Japanese working hours fell by 2 percent—about a week's worth of work.

Even so, Japanese workers still put in the equivalent of eight working weeks per year more than Americans. Achieving the more-or-less official goal of an eighteen-hundred-working-hour year—which would mean rough parity with American working hours—is "not an impossible target," believes Japanese labor leader Naoto Omi.[2] The hand of organized labor in pushing for reduced hours is being strengthened by the labor shortage the country faces, he says, but management attitudes are also becoming more enlightened. Corporate committees are being formed "charged with devising schemes to reform work routines, raise hourly productivity, and realize the 1,800-hour goal." In fact, Japanese companies know full well that they can reduce working time without necessarily losing output. Especially in offices, Japanese workers often put in overtime as a way of demonstrating company loyalty, even when they aren't actually doing anything productive.

Using *kaizen* techniques to promote efficiency in general, augmenting automation of industrial production through robotics, and letting the ripcord go on the as-yet-to-unfold white-collar desktop computer revolution, Japanese workers of the late '90s will be clocking no more hours than Americans. As a result, they will free billions of man-hours for consumption-type activities: shopping, home improvement, entertainment, hobbies, sports, travel, and other leisure pursuits.

Plans for Nissan's "Visionary Factory" on Japan's southern Kyushu island offer a glimpse of how work and consumption may even be integrated. The auto plant lays claim to being the most automated in the world. About 20 percent of the work is now done by robots, and this is to rise to 30 percent by 1994. An environment has been created designed to appeal to young workers, complete with a landscaped "Central Park" for break-time recreation and attractively designed restaurants and gyms. Outside the plant, Nissan hopes to develop park and recreation areas that company sources say will make it more of "a holiday resort than a car factory."

To stimulate new consumption still further, Japanese retailing practices will also have to undergo significant change. One problem is that the long-standing "large store law" has blocked the full development of department stores, supermarkets, and shopping malls. Another problem is the monopolization of distribution channels by *keiretsu* and the resulting difficulty of introducing new products, obtaining trucking and warehousing services, and finding cost-efficient marketing opportunities.

Americans saw these problems in the case of Toys R Us, the U.S.-based toy retailing giant, which had to enlist the support of the U.S. president and the Japanese prime minister in order to get around barriers created by retailing laws. The eventual victory won by this foreign operation was the product of Japan's own internal consensus to allow the establishment of more consumption-inducing superstores, and to chip away at the protected status of 1.6 million small "mom-and-pop" retail shops. In the Toys R Us case, *gaiatsu* ("foreign pressure") was used by Japanese decision-makers as a tool to do that which Japan should do anyway, while blaming any downside effects on foreigners. The post-bubble economic squeeze is now helping by driving some of those "mom-and-pop" shops out of business and bringing the cost of real estate for retail use closer to earth.

Because the United States is the world's biggest and most aggressively consumption-oriented society—now actually consuming more each year than we produce, and financing the difference with debt—it is often assumed that consumption leads inevitably to *over*consumption and an ensuing loss of economic competitiveness.

But from 1945 to the late 1960s, the propensity of Americans to consume and the growth of massive consumer industries fueled extraordinary economic dynamism, fabulous increases in productivity, and a veritable revolution in quality of life. It was only when America attempted to maintain that sort of consumption and *add* to it a whole set of additional burdens that problems set in.

Japan is not likely to repeat American mistakes. Like everything else in Japan, the shift to more of a consumer society will be slow, gradual, and fine-tuned along the way to make sure that productivity doesn't fall and that the work ethic remains vigorous. While industry will almost certainly move more low-cost jobs offshore, economic planners will be careful to make sure that the best jobs stay onshore. Nor is Japan likely to engage in the kind of massive cost buildup in either defense spending or welfare state entitlements that has soaked up so much of America's capital resources in the last quarter-century. Japan is not oblivious to the challenges of global economic competition, as the United States was for so long. The development of a consumer society will not take place outside the framework of maintaining high levels of global competitiveness.

The Profit-Making Society

One of the hallmarks of Japanese capitalism has been the driving force of market share as a corporate goal unto itself. In many instances, Japanese businesses have been able to outmaneuver Western competitors, and eventually drive them out of business altogether, by engaging in an unrelenting battle for market share.

The Japanese willingness to sustain huge losses to build market share is legendary. It is the source of much envy among businessmen abroad, whose shareholders are far more interested in seeing regular quarterly profit growth than in how well the company is positioning itself for competition five or ten years hence. It is also the source of many antidumping actions brought against Japanese companies in North America and Europe.

Yet corporate Japan is running up against objective limitations on market share growth in global industries. In some cases, further growth has become politically intolerable—at least for the moment. More important, the post-bubble economy has placed new demands on companies, which can no longer raise capital as cheaply as before and are now being pressured to reduce working hours, expand benefits to employees, increase dividend payouts to shareholders, and even reward outstanding talent with higher salaries than has been the norm.

Obstructed by political considerations from exporting their way to greater growth, and bellying up to a bar of increased costs at home, Japanese businessmen are beginning to find the logical way out of the squeeze—the way that proves that Japan's system *is* properly classed as a form of capitalism: They are setting about raising the *profitability* of enterprises.

To say this does not mean that Japan is going to embrace American-style capitalism, seek American-style rates of return, or expect its industries to be managed for maximum profit in the American way. It only means that managers are beginning to take some thoroughly sensible steps to boost efficiency, cut costs, and become more profitable as a result.

In part because they have achieved such dominant market share positions in recent years, giant Japanese manufacturers now feel comfortable raising prices and profit margins, even at the expense of market share points. As a spokesman for electronics giant Matsushita explains the transition, "We are shifting from volume to quality. This is not a temporary move, but a permanent one. . . . The Japanese television industry produces 300 models. Only 100 can be displayed in the shops. Only 10 will sell. We can cut this waste without affecting consumers."[3]

With over 150 automobile models available in 1991—up nearly 50 percent from five years earlier—and as many as one thousand soft drinks thrown onto the domestic market each year, it is very possible that the Japanese have overinnovated. The *kaizen* techniques, flexible manufacturing systems, and other features of Japanese production may be generating significantly more innovation than the market can absorb profitably. Japanese managers are unlikely to abandon these techniques, but they will curtail some of this blizzard of changes in order to enhance profitability.

Japanese companies will also change in other ways. Cross-shareholdings will loosen. Investment decisions will be driven less by relationships than by the desire to buy shares of profitable companies. Management will raise its hurdle rates in considering new investments.

Price increases on Japanese goods will also be typical of the next few years. In an era when declining market share is a political *plus*, Japanese companies will at last be willing to do what most American companies would be only too glad to do: sell fewer units while making more money on each unit sold.

This trend poses new challenges for the U.S. side of the equation. As Japanese competitive pressure eases, will American companies be able to restrain themselves from raising their own prices and increasing their own profit margins? Will they be able to take a leaf from the Japanese playbook and increase market share by becoming the low-cost providers? Last time around—during the great runup of the yen's value in the late 1980s—most failed the same test. They tended to raise prices in line with the increases posted by their Japanese competitors. This fattened their own bottom lines briefly at the expense of huge losses in market share.

Now, Japanese companies are trying to give back a tiny slice of the marketplace, while enriching themselves in the process. Commenting on Japanese companies' price increases in the auto industry, Nissan executive vice-president Yoshikazu Hanawa says, "This is a good chance for the Big Three," and as of 1992, "they seem to be using it."[4]

The Creative Society

Can Japan use the post-bubble crisis of confidence to challenge some of its most traditional cultural influences? Can it finally make a breakthrough and become a more "creative" society? And can it develop as a more mobile, diverse, talent-and-idea-rewarding society, yet not lose its strong sense of teamwork and shared fate, which have proven such potent economic factors in a fraying world?

There are no certain answers to these questions. Clearly, the Japanese are more creative than many Americans think. The old shibboleth that "Americans create, Japanese imitate" is given the lie by the vibrancy of Japanese technological innovation in the last decade. In its aptitude for process innovation and its skill at commercializing new technological breakthroughs, Japan has developed a whole new dimension of industrial creativity. Even in basic scientific research, Japan has come a long way.

"Japanese scientists cannot match the U.S. or leading European countries in the breadth of their work," observes the *Financial Times*. Yet while the Japanese have few Nobel prizes, they are increasingly "acknowledged as equals by their foreign peers" in fields such as X-ray astronomy, lasers, and some aspects of quantum physics.[5]

In addition, Japanese methodologies in some creative pursuits may still prove more effective than, or at least competitive with, American approaches. "While the U.S. software industry is admired for its skills in creating and marketing new software packages, some say Japan has the edge in managing and developing massive software projects for large-scale information processing," reports *Investor's Business Daily*.[6] Michael Cusumano, an MIT professor and author of a book on Japanese "software factories," is one who believes the Japanese approach is working. Criticizing the one-sided emphasis of American software writers on invention over development, Cusumano says, "Japanese companies might represent the best practice in terms of managing the process of software development."[7]

Even so, it is clear to most Japanese thinkers that their society has not emerged as the innovative leader they would like it to be in many "creative" pursuits. This frustration is more than a matter of national ego. It has far-reaching business implications.

Nowhere is this more true than in the computer industry. The decade-long "fifth generation" computer project, undertaken in 1982 and funded by MITI to the tune of more than $400 million, planted fear in the hearts of top American scientists that Japan was going to win the computer wars as it had won the auto and consumer electronics battles. The project was enormously challenging. It attempted to orchestrate more creativity than most scientists could muster. But when it wound down in 1992, it was clearly a failure. Its only success was that it trained a cadre of personnel, who may go on to do other important work in such fields as expert systems, parallel processing, and artificial intelligence.

Meanwhile, American computer scientists, without the benefit of national technology policy or MITI-style resources, *lengthened* their lead in most areas of hardware and software for advanced computing systems during the last decade. To be sure, Japanese companies have come to dominate certain important parts of the computer industry, particularly the most "hardware"-intensive sectors such as computer memory chips, equipment for manufacturing semiconductors, and display and printing technologies. But American companies remain far ahead in the design of microprocessors that power computer systems, in developing the applications software that provides much of their use-value, and in organizing the networks that allow computers and other data-generating equipment to communicate.

A survey of leading computer industry experts in the United States, Japan, and Europe compared the strengths and weaknesses of the various "computer cultures" in the following ways (on a scale of 1–10, with 10 being best):[8]

Processor Design
U.S.   9.5
Japan   5.8
Europe   4.7

Software
U.S.   9.3
Europe   6.8
Japan   5.2

Displays and Printers
Japan   9.6
U.S.   6.0
Europe   4.1

Data Networks
U.S.   8.7
Europe   6.9
Japan   6.5

Chip-making Equipment
Japan   9.3
U.S.   7.5
Europe   4.3

Opto-Electronics
Japan   9.0
U.S.   7.0
Europe   5.1

With strengths and weaknesses distributed relatively evenly to Americans and Japanese, is the computer industry glass half empty or half full? The truth is that while American companies have frittered away their leadership in important areas, they have maintained leadership in a handful of the most "mission-critical" technologies that still drive and determine the way computer systems are developed and used.

While Japanese companies have at times appeared tantalizingly close to closing some of these gaps, the American system has developed a history of leap-frogging at the last minute and creating a new window of leadership. The development of Digital Signal Processing (DSP) chips provides a good example. In this niche, which is increasingly important to the marriage of computers, video images, and telecommunications gear, small American high-tech companies, using breakthrough designs and creative new applications, seized back leadership from Japanese giants that had once looked poised to dominate the market.

In a related vein, the evolution of High Definition Television (HDTV)—the benchmark issue for those debating industrial and technology policy in the late 1980s—underwent a dramatic change in the 1990s. Unexpected breakthroughs were made at American labs in figuring out how to broadcast HDTV signals in a next-generation digital format, rather than the present-generation analog format relied upon by the Japanese electronics industry.

It had always been assumed that creative American programming "software"—movies, videos, rock music, and so forth—would be needed to drive the global popularization of HDTV. That assumption was re-emphasized in 1991 when Japan began transmitting several hours of daily HDTV broadcasts. Even for those who had paid the exorbitant early adopters' price of thirty thousand dollars to have a brand-new HDTV set in their homes, there was virtually nothing of significance to watch. With the advent of the digital HDTV revolution spawned by American companies—and the new possibilities of linking digital signals to computers in the exploding world of "multimedia"—American entrants suddenly found themselves not just leaders in the race to dominate programming software, but back in the electronics hardware race as well.

In the wave of alliances that sprang up in the global electronics industry to pursue the development of multimedia products, some Japanese observers believed they were getting the short end of the stick, but had no choice owing to their lack of software expertise. "The biggest benefits go to Apple and IBM," one industry source noted of the Kaleida joint venture, which is licensing multimedia software.[9] The Japanese companies, which must bear the greatest costs for developing the hardware side of the projects, will get the least benefit.

Japanese businesses have enough historical perspective to understand that a few unexpected developments in technological competition will not necessarily deter them from increasing their global economic muscle over the long term. Although Americans continue to dominate the development of basic science and many kinds of basic technological research, there is no sign yet that the United States has reversed its long-standing difficulties in commercializing, manufacturing, and selling the fruits of its creative innovation. And some of the Japanese "failures" may be only temporary. Big failures, after all, are the product of big risks taken. The very fact that Japan is now willing to take such risks indicates a measure of success in changing old thinking.

Japan's economic visionaries also know that elegant, exciting, and promising as American "creative" breakthroughs may be in areas such as computers and software, biotechnology, space exploration, entertainment, and financial services, these fields are far from mature. They are just now unfolding on a global scale, and there is plenty of time to catch up, if through no other means than buying into American companies that are leaders in these fields.

But will Japan catch up? So far, the profound changes needed are barely being proposed, let alone seriously considered. To go beyond where rhetoric about "becoming more creative" has been able to take them, the Japanese need, at a minimum, a revolution in their educational system, a restructuring of reward mechanisms for talented people, and a rejection of the deep-seated social mechanisms that now mitigate against diversity, mobility, experimentation, and novel thinking.

It would be the height of American arrogance, as well as dangerous naivete, to think Japan could not change in these respects. *Time* magazine analyst Pico Iyer, invoking William Manchester, reminds us that certain cultural characteristics that appear im-

mutable are instead only products of time, place, circumstances—
and our perceptions:

> It may be that every nation . . . acquires certain habits at certain
> moments of its growth. One of the best descriptions of Japanese
> "conformity," as stereotype conceives of it, was given by William
> Manchester in *The Glory and the Dream*. Believing, he wrote, that
> "leadership came from the group, that progress lay in something
> called problem-solving meetings, [they] had no use for drive and
> imagination. Above all, they distrusted individualism. The indi-
> vidual sought prestige and achievement at the expense of others.
> He was abrasive; he rocked the boat; he threatened the corporate
> One, and they wanted no part of him." The only trouble is, Man-
> chester was describing Americans there, in the "silent generation"
> of the '50s.[10]

That Japanese society possesses the right stuff to become far
more creative and dynamic is unquestionable. The issue is
whether the entrenched, ossified forces of political and social
power will let it out.

As Yoshimichi Yamashita, the president of the Japan office of
Arthur D. Little, points out, "Japan has all the wide-awake brains
it needs, many of them trapped below the top management
level. . . . As the need becomes evident, the Japanese talent for
adaptability will push these brains up into the corporate skull
where they belong." When the brains of the future start running
Japan, Inc., he argues, they will immediately grasp the need to
give up feudalistic, top-down thinking. They will encourage diversity, "recognize individual talent in the company and rally
around the creative spirits," and put an end to the still-prevalent
practice of hammering down mavericks.[11]

Inside Japanese society, forces supportive of such change are
growing. As of now, however, they remain outmatched by their
opponents.

The Leading Society of the Pacific Rim

Many new, emerging markets attract the attention of business
people today: the European Community with the increased scale
and scope of its single market, Mexico and Latin America, which

appear resurrected from bankruptcy and ready to boom, and for those with long-term capital and an appetite for big risks, there are the opportunities being created in Eastern Europe and the former Soviet Union.

Yet no area of the world has such a demonstrable track record of growth and such excellent prospects for the future as the East Asian edge of the Pacific Rim, which happens to be Japan's backyard, geographically and culturally.

In the 1980s, the Asia/Pacific region enjoyed two and a half times more economic growth than the United States, three and a half times more than Europe, and nearly twice as much as Japan itself. Forecasters believe the growth will be just as brisk in the '90s, with economies like Malaysia, Thailand, Hong Kong, Singapore, Taiwan, and South Korea expected to post 8 percent annual *average* increases in GDP. This is about twice the best-case scenarios hoped for in North America, Europe, and Japan. While economists expect per capita GDP to rise only 14 percent in the United States during the '90s, it may rise as much as 93 percent in the Asia/Pacific region.

China, with its 1.2 billion people and its long-term potential to be the hugest of all markets in the world, remains a political enigma. But, three years after the massacre in Tiananmen Square, international investors are pouring back in. The Japanese never left. Despite the human tragedy of what happened in China, Deng Xiaoping and other Chinese leaders have succeeded, at least up until now, in their goal of keeping the country together and moving forward to economic reform. They have avoided the chaos that has transpired in some countries of Eastern Europe and the former Soviet Union.

New consumers are being created in the Pacific Rim faster than anywhere else in the world. Birthrates are higher than in North America, Europe, and Japan. At the same time, the demographic picture of education, skills, infrastructure, income, and savings is much superior to other high-birthrate regions. As East Asia augments its population, it adds new markets and new industries, not poverty and hunger.

In the years leading up to 2025, the developed world as a whole will add 400 million new consumers. Some 55 percent of them will live in the Asia/Pacific region. It is therefore hardly surprising that Japan has positioned itself for this boom.

The United States has long been a leading investor and trading partner with most East Asian countries. But Japanese outinvested Americans in Asia by 200 percent to 300 percent each year from 1987 to 1990. After a recent tour of Japanese global investments, Harvard scholar Ezra Vogel concludes that the United States "simply isn't regarded as a first-rate economic power in Asia anymore."[12]

Tokyo's bursting bubble has diminished the flow of Japanese capital. For a long time, "the Japanese were taking 90% of many deals," says Hong Kong loan packager John Muncy in 1992. "Now it's hard to get them to participate."[13] Some Japanese real estate investors have moved to liquidate holdings in Hong Kong and other Asian centers. (Alone among major world property markets, East Asian real estate could still be sold at a profit in 1992 over the sums paid in the late 1980s.)

But Japan's expansion into the region is still on the upswing, even if it is tempered by short-term capital problems. Asia is particularly attractive relative to other places where Japanese companies can manufacture. Although quick profits were never the goal of Japanese industrial investment in the United States, the fact is the profits have generally been painfully slow in coming. Wall Street analysts estimate that Japanese auto companies lost more than $2 billion in North America during 1991. Indeed, the biggest single complaint of Japanese executives doing business in the United States is not protectionism, political friction, or labor unions. The number-one complaint of 64 percent of them is "low profitability."[14]

In Pacific/Asia, however, where land is cheap and skilled workers are paid about 10 percent to 15 percent the wages of their Japanese or American counterparts, investments have yielded fast-track paybacks. Pretax profits from all Japanese direct investments in Asia reached $3.7 billion for the 1991 fiscal year, compared to a loss of $394 million experienced by Japanese companies in North America.[15]

While much of the rest of the world worries about industrial overcapacity, the Pacific Rim's appetite is nearly insatiable for consumer products as well as the technology and know-how that will allow their economies to continue moving up the development ladder.

Japanese investment is also more welcome in most of Asia than it is anywhere else. A few governments, as well as intellectuals and social critics almost everywhere, still cling to reservations about Japanese intentions. But in Asia, Japanese companies do not have to factor in the political concerns that affect most of their U.S. investments.

"The color of our economy is blue, because that is the color of the 1,000-yen note," says Malaysian economist Stephen Wong. "That is fine with us, because that is the reality."[16]

In Thailand, Japanese companies have created an estimated three hundred thousand jobs. Although there are complaints of Japanese "overpresence," most people understand it is Japanese investment that is driving Thailand into the modern age. Paisal Srisirichanya, editor of the *Bangkok Post*, emphasizes the extent of Japanese influence on Thai life today: "You have your breakfast from a Japanese rice cooker, you go to work in a Japanese car, your office is cooled by a Japanese air conditioner, and at night you may go to a Japanese restaurant for dinner."[17]

South Korea, Taiwan, Singapore, and Hong Kong are such economic dynamos that it is questionable whether they should still be classed as "Newly" Industrializing Economies. The degree of industrialization is certainly higher in these countries than it is in parts of Europe, as are the living standards. In each case, the flow of Japanese capital, technology, and trade is crucial to continued growth.

Asia looms as the centerpiece in the next round of global competition in the auto industry. Nine of the seventeen new auto plants in China are Japanese, and the vehicle market there is expected to double in annual size to 1.5 million units by 2000. "A great game of 'go' is taking place in Asia," says one Japanese market analyst. "By dominating the one true growth market of the world automobile industry, Japanese companies are denying growth opportunities to their international competitors."

No corner of Asia is uninteresting to Japanese investors. Now, there is even "Vietnam fever," says Toshio Oda, a manager with Sumitomo. Having developed a billion-dollar annual trading business in Vietnam during the U.S. trade embargo, many Japanese businessmen see the country as "the last frontier."[18]

Fifty years ago, Japan's "Greater East Asian Co-Prosperity Sphere" was a code phrase for Japanese imperialism, exploitation, and plunder. On the fiftieth anniversary of Pearl Harbor, *The New*

York Times observed that contemporary Japanese expansion across East Asia held the prospect of "real co-prosperity, with the power of the yen, not the military, bringing Asia into its own." Pointing out that Japan had already succeeded in turning Asia into its "manufacturing and merchandising backyard," and is even displacing American political influence in the region, the *Times* added:

> To travel through Southeast Asia today is to hear government officials and industrial leaders talk enthusiastically about their one-time invader as their teacher and financier. In contrast, the United States is often described as the region's absentee ally, a continuing military presence but an increasingly marginal player in the most dynamic, booming economies in the world today.

> Piece by piece, corporate Japan has created a startling replica of itself, not only in look and feel but also in culture. . . . The shift is most vivid inside the giant factories [in Malaysia] of the Matsushita Electric Industrial Company [whose] operations account for more than 3% of Malaysia's gross national product. Every morning, 17,000 Malaysian workers pour through the gates wearing uniforms nearly identical to those at Matsushita's headquarters in Osaka. They start the day by singing the Matsushita song—in Malay— and spend 45 minutes discussing Japanese-style manufacturing technique with their managers before heading to their posts on sparkling, highly automated production lines.[19]

Off the record, Japanese officials sometimes acknowledge that the issue of how they harness Asia's energies and markets may ultimately determine whether Japan's economy will overtake that of the United States in the next century. In this century, however, Japan still has delicate political problems to overcome as it increases its presence in Asian economies where old memories and nationalisms still breed resentment, and where a fine line exists between investment and exploitation.

So far, however, the Japanese have done a remarkably successful job of expanding their interests in the very part of the world where they are most disliked and feared. Official Japanese government aid has bolstered the benefits brought by private sector investment. Some 60 percent of Japan's annual foreign aid budget—the largest such budget of any country—is pouring into Asia. Most of those funds go to China, Indonesia, and the Philippines, the countries where Japanese companies need to see more development of infrastructure, schools, telecommunications, and power resources before they can invest further.

"Backyardism is becoming an increasingly important pillar of Japanese foreign economic policy," acknowledges the *Nikkei Weekly*.[20] MITI and other powerful forces in government are turning more of their energy, attention, and resources to Asia.

Yohei Kono, a Diet member who chairs the LDP's research commission on foreign affairs, hopes Japan will learn from Germany's example. By this he means his government should be more forthcoming in dealing with its wartime past and take more active measures to make amends to Koreans, Chinese, and others who suffered so many still unacknowledged atrocities at the hands of Japanese invaders. As Germany succeeded in healing the wounds it had left behind in Europe, Kono believes Japan can help weld the Asian region together on issues of the future after dealing more thoroughly with the problems of its past.

Japan is not about to retreat to an "Asia-only" strategy, nor are the world's three major regional trading groups likely to become exclusive fortresses forbidding penetration by those outside the region. Nevertheless, even as the European Community and the North American Free Trade Area develop as relatively open, liberal trading systems, it is worth remembering that Asia holds the most short-term profit potential as well as the greatest possibilities of market enlargement over time.

If the United States and Japan forge closer ties and work toward harmonizing their economies along the lines suggested in Chapter 8, the benefits will be powerful and mutual with regard to the rest of the Asia-Pacific region. A Japan more closely connected to the United States will be a more welcome leader in Asia, with American democracy leavening old fears of an overbearing Japan, and American military muscle making Japanese rearmament unnecessary. A Pacific economic framework that includes the United States, Japan, and the major Asian economies will stimulate trade and investment throughout the region. And any structure that anchors the American economy more firmly in the world's largest growth region can only be beneficial to American interests in the future.

The Global Society

The biggest challenge Japan faces is to define its long-term place in the world. A new, rising power always inspires a certain amount of international fear and mistrust. But Japan has engendered too much concern, particularly in North America and Europe, for this to be a healthy trend. It is not in Japan's interests, nor in the interests of a stable world environment.

Japan can be a critical force in the world's effort to chart a successful transition out of the Cold War era and into a new multipolar future. Of all nations, Japan has the most extensive recent experience in building international relationships with the tools of the future—capital, trade, and technology—rather than the military, ideological, and political tools of the past.

To look at Toyota's success in replicating its Japanese production methods in Kentucky, or Matsushita's success in doing the same thing in Malaysia, is to understand the new universality of what Japan has to offer. The proliferation of Japanese consumer products in everyday life tells the same story from another angle. So too, in an ironic way, does the international debate about Japan itself.

If Japan is ambivalent about being a world leader, most of the world is equally ambivalent about being led to any significant degree from Tokyo. Periodically, the outside world encourages Japan to take more initiative and responsibility on global issues. But when Japan takes a tentative leadership step in response, the chorus of criticism is unavoidable.

In the Gulf War crisis of 1991, most American political leaders wanted Japan not just to contribute to "checkbook diplomacy," but to commit troops to the multinational forces and share part of the "blood risk." Yet the discussion of sending Japanese military forces beyond the country's borders—even in limited roles as UN-commanded peacekeepers—immediately triggered opposition throughout Asia. Singapore's former prime minister, Lee Kuan Yew, likened the idea of small Japanese military deployments abroad to giving a chocolate liqueur candy to an alcoholic.

On more prosaic issues of international economics, the same pattern can be seen. Recalling the situation in the late 1980s, former vice-minister of finance Makoto Utsumi says, "The United States asked us to do more on the debt crisis. So we proposed what became known as the 'Miyazawa Plan' for LDC debt relief. Then Washington was furious that we made such a proposal. Eventually, after much discussion, both sides came to agreement with a plan that was almost identical to the Miyazawa Plan. Except this time it was called the Brady Plan. The truth is, without U.S. agreement, Japan cannot press its initiatives alone. The number-two power can only move forward together with number one."

It is easy to imagine the bold strokes an imaginative, globally committed, leadership-oriented Japan might ideally take: a massive package for the republics of the former Soviet Union, complete with cadres of talented young managers to provide technical know-how . . . a unilateral opening of Japanese agricultural markets to stimulate world trade and promote global progress through the GATT process . . . funding of a center to provide resources needed by the world scientific community for research on global warming, alternative energy sources, and other critical environmental issues . . . the establishment of a global engineering brigade to help war-torn countries get back on their feet . . . a major new initiative on refugees, such as a plan to resettle, educate, train, and employ several hundred thousand Indochinese or other displaced Asians . . . a substantive effort to do something for Africa and other parts of the "left behind" world . . . new programs to reduce trade imbalances dramatically with the United States and Europe, and so forth.

In small, low-key, piecemeal ways, Japan is doing most of these things. It is contributing some modest aid to Russia, even though the Russians have yet to meet Tokyo's long-standing demand for improved relations by returning the northern islands occupied at the end of World War II. JETRO, a Japanese government agency, is helping small American companies find markets for their products in Japan, while MITI is working on opening up direct investment opportunities for foreigners. Rather than engage in further quarrels with the European Community, Tokyo officialdom has nudged the major carmakers to accept proposals on limiting Japanese cars in the European Community. At the Rio environmental summit in 1992, Japan pledged the largest and most concrete aid package aimed at solving international problems related to development and the environment.

All these initiatives represent steps forward from Japan's previous provincialism and reluctance to involve itself with issues that didn't affect its immediate mercantile interests. Yet they all smack of too little too late. At the very best, they appear to be out of sync with Japan's true resources and talents.

The Gulf War provided a case in point. Although Japan eventually bore a heavy share of the financial burden for the war— $13 billion—most of the world remembers only that Tokyo waffled, delayed, and acted indecisively. The initial reaction of Masamichi Hanabusa, Japan's consul-general in New York, was perhaps a better indicator of Tokyo's true opinion than the billions of dollars in support for the U.S.-led coalition later supplied. Japan was a rich country that could afford to pay high prices for oil, Hanabusa said. Therefore, Japan was not particularly interested in supporting a war against Saddam Hussein. It is because of such views that the outside world continues to see Japan as a self-absorbed island, rather than a global partner and international leader.

In a world where international "peacekeeping" increasingly involves economic and environmental issues as well as the traditional agenda of military and security matters, it is interesting to look at what might be called the "global peacekeeping" budgets of various countries. The United States spends about 6 percent of its GDP to these ends. Although the vast majority of that staggering sum of money goes to the military budget, the post–Cold War world has generally judged the U.S. armed forces to be a global public utility of a kind, and it is therefore appropriate to consider U.S. defense spending as a contribution not just to American national interests but to the global good. European countries generally spend between 3 percent and 5 percent of their GDP on a combination of defense and foreign aid. But Japan spends considerably less than 2 percent of its GDP in these ways.

Most of the world does not want to see Japan become a major military power again. The majority of the Japanese people have made it equally clear they want to continue the pacifist tradition that has worked so well for them. But why won't Japan, a country that benefits so heavily from a stable world order, spend at American or even European levels for international peacekeeping, and put its yen to work on economic development projects and technical aid, rather than military deployments?

In 1992, when the G-7 economic summit was held in Munich, the world's leading powers were clearly in disarray and could agree on almost nothing. Pressing issues of what to do about the growing economic crisis in the former Soviet republics, how to save the Uruguay Round of the GATT talks, and how to enliven despondent economic growth worldwide all cried out for Japanese leadership, since none was to be found elsewhere. But Japan was not about to step into the breach. Observed Deutsche Bank economist Kenneth S. Courtis:

> The challenge Japan faces is not economic. It is at once more general and pervasive, and resides in the very ability of the country to assume a broader and bolder role on the world stage, a role commensurate with its economic might and geopolitical potential. When confronted with pressing issues of critical international importance, the country's leadership appears frequently in a quandary, indeed paralyzed, somehow unwilling or unable to project positively its enormous power into the realities of a more complicated world. . . . On all [the issues of the Munich summit], the world would benefit immensely, as would Japan itself, were the country to assume an active and positive leadership role.[21]

The conditions for Tokyo to influence world affairs in a positive way are improving. Just as detente is likely to prevail between the United States and Japan in the years ahead, detente is also the growing trend between Europe and Japan. Post-bubble, the Japanese seem less fearsome in Europe, just as they do in the United States. Europe was at one time paranoid about Japan— so much so that the EC was tempted in the late 1980s to build a "Fortress Europe" to keep the Japanese out. Today, however, most of Europe wants Japan in. They want the jobs, technology, and capital investment Japanese companies have to offer. This is true even if they also want to be sure Europe maintains control over certain of its biggest industries, and even if Europeans tend to be more strategic in their thinking than Americans when it comes to using reciprocity as a lever for gaining market access in Japan.

In Latin America, Eastern Europe, and other emerging markets, the zeal for economic reconstruction has put out the welcome mat for the Japanese almost without reservations. Mexico's president Salinas sends his own children to the Japanese school in Mexico City.

It can be said, therefore, that most of the world is coming to adequate terms with Japan. The question remains, are "adequate terms" sufficient? In Tokyo, the government appears ambivalent. Sometimes it behaves as if it would like to get away with doing as little as it possibly can for the rest of the world. At other times, its most thoughtful figures appear to understand that Japan should and must do more.

Japan need not take responsibility for world leadership in the way the United States or Britain did in prior eras. The future will be multipolar, rather than unipolar. The United States will continue to be a major world leader, even if it cannot commit the same measure of funds, vision, or energy as before. Unlike Japan, Europe's vision is grander than its practice. But even so, its practical contributions to world leadership are greater than Japan's and are likely to remain large.

What will Japan do? More than at any previous time, the conditions exist today for the world to accept a greater role for Japan. International leadership, even though it has a significant short-term cost, also has a way of proving at least as beneficial to the long-term economic interests of the leaders as to others. America's Marshall Plan not only rebuilt Europe, but made Europe safe to become a great arena of American business opportunity. In like manner, the very best thing Japan could do for its own economic vitality would be to blaze the frontiers for new businesses and industries in the new, emerging markets of the world.

The new world order could be one of growth, opportunity, and problem solving. Or it could degenerate into a new world *disorder*—an era of slow growth globally, bickering between developed nations, and nightmarish nationalism and war in many corners of the globe. Leadership will make the difference, and right now there is precious little of that.

An intellectual debate is now taking place on whether world peace and prosperity can make genuine advances in an era that lacks a single global hegemon to act as steward, rudder, economic engine, lender, and peacekeeper of last resort. History is not a hopeful guide: World War I broke out in a Europe in which Britain's decline had left a leadership vacuum. World War II broke out when the United States had already emerged as the world's strongest economy but had not yet faced up to other international leadership responsibilities.

Japan, of course, cannot solve the world's problems by itself.

But it can make a difference if it breaks through its own political gridlock over its international responsibilities and begins to chart a bold, activist path. If it does so in the context of joint initiatives with the United States, its role will not only be more easily accepted by much of the world, it may help reawaken America's now-dormant global leadership vision. In the vision of the two countries acting in concert lies the best hope that multilateralism will succeed, that world order can be managed, growth supported, and conflict minimized.

7

Heading Toward the Millennium: The Next America

The Real Reason Why Johnny Can't Compete

"Competitiveness" is one of those terms that has managed to transit from "obscurity to meaninglessness without an intervening period of coherence," says *The Wall Street Journal,* invoking a witticism from one of the co-coiners of this particular buzzword.[1] Whirring through the word search function of Washington databases, the *Journal* determined that halfway through the 102nd Congress, 547 "competitiveness bills" had already been introduced, handily in reach of the record of 611 set by the 100th Congress. Most had more to do with the self-interest of a particular congressman's district or campaign contributors than with America's genuine national interests; those that had any glint of national interest were often completely in contradiction with each other. As for the *Journal* itself, it admitted to publishing more than twice as many articles mentioning competitiveness in 1991 as in 1984, and that 1992 was running well ahead of 1991's pace.

Amid this blither of blather, it is important at least to try to insert some coherence into the discussion of "competitiveness," especially if we are to have any hope of finding real answers and solutions to the problems America faces.

Although the issues associated with the debate are often discussed in apocalyptic terms, no immediate apocalypse lies on the horizon. No matter how flawed the American system may be, it is not going to collapse any time soon. And no matter how well-adapted the Japanese model of capitalism may be, it is not going to take over the world in the short run, if ever.

What lies ahead is not an impending crisis of the 1930s type, but a *slowly* metastasizing cancer. The emphasis is on the word *slowly* because even today, two decades after showing the first signs of this cancer, America remains a phenomenally wealthy and robust country, with greater competitive prowess in many economic endeavors than is known anywhere else in the world. Even in the context of an American society that is continuing to fragment and break apart—and in some measure because of that process—innovative new businesses and industries continue to be born in the United States that countervail at least some of the losses suffered in other sectors. And leading competitor nations, such as Japan and Germany, no matter how successful they have been up until now, face significant problems of their own.

The nub of the problem is that the United States is emerging as the most conflict-ridden and polarized of all developed capitalist democracies. While others have opted for policies that are improving the incomes and living standards of citizens more or less across the board (very much in the manner of the once-expanding American middle class), the United States has allowed itself to move backward toward a society that is increasingly polarized between haves, have-littles, and have-nots.

Whether the outlook for the future is good or bad depends in large measure on where you fall along that spectrum. Americans with college educations have seen their real income rise steadily since 1980. But those without have experienced the sharpest real income contraction in fifty years. In much of Europe and in Japan, by contrast, real wages for manufacturing workers rose steeply in recent years. Although German production workers made only about one-third the wages of Americans in 1960, today they make slightly more—and the gap is widening.

According to a study by UCLA economist Edward E. Leamer, expanded international trade added $33 billion to the wages of American professionals during the period 1972–1985, but subtracted considerably more—$46 billion—from the wages of nonprofessionals. Similarly, forecasts on the effects of a U.S. free trade agreement with Mexico suggest ordinary manufacturing workers will be big losers, even though skilled workers and those in service businesses may be big winners.

American life is thus increasingly splintering into several entirely distinct societies.

One America is where the "Bill Gates–Biotech" factor predominates. This is the America of unmatched entrepreneurship, innovation, and competitive corporate excellence and vision. It is best seen in fields like biotechnology or computer software, where a uniquely American character like Bill Gates is able to drop out of college and found a company like Microsoft that goes on to lead the world in a revolutionary new business such as personal computer operating systems and applications software. Here, the best and brightest of the society dream the incredible and impossible dreams that have always inspired American entrepreneurs. They then tap their own talents and capture the benefits of the best-functioning features of the nation's educational and financial systems to make their dreams come true. In the end, they are spawning new global industries of the future. This is the America that is expanding exponentially, brimming with upside potential. It is the America that is fully aware of the global competition, is still ahead of the rest of the pack, and has intelligent strategies for staying there. This is an America not only of advanced technology but of advanced products and services of all kinds. Here dwell not just Microsoft and Amgen, but Wal-Mart and Home Depot, Dell Computer and Fidelity, a revitalized Intel, a resurgent Xerox, and an increasingly globally competitive Ford. Here, corporate profits are fat, young people are reasonably well educated and well trained, and institutions like MIT or Cal Tech are the envy of the world. This America is where the world's best-paid CEOs live, as well as the best-paid senior managers, scientists, technologists, engineers, designers, athletes, entertainers, doctors, business consultants, investment bankers, lawyers, journalists, software writers, and scriptwriters. The 1980s were very, very good to most of them, and even the '90s have not been particularly bad. Here, the American Dream is still widely shared, believed, and lived.

Then there is the economic middle of America, where businesses struggle and mostly survive, but not as handily or as profitably as a generation ago. In part, the problem is a loss of global competitiveness and easy superprofits raked in from global sales of once world-beating products. In larger part it is a more generalized inability to adapt to changing economic and social conditions. The wage-earners of this tier live well by general world historical standards but slightly less well than they used to—and considerably less well than they had once hoped. Here, the 1980s saw some small declines in income and some large declines in quality of life. And here, the prospects are dimmed by a steadily weakening educational system, which is not equipping American youth to be fully competitive with the skills of young people in other countries. The American Dream is still within grasp for the brightest and most ambitious of this group. But for many others, it is fading into institutionalized pessimism and bitterness as the once-great American middle class is slowly hollowed out.

And then there is the bottom tier of American society, where the loss of American economic strength is most viscerally felt. It is here that those historically drawn in by the centrifugal force of American economic dynamism are now increasingly spun out instead, not just excluded from the American Dream but living in nightmarish conditions. This America will be seen and felt more intensely in the years to come. It is the America of big-city school systems where literacy rates are falling and math and science test scores would be unacceptable even by the standards of some third-world countries. This is the America of the Los Angeles riots of 1992, where violence is routinized and its dangers spill out of the once-defined boundaries of ghettos and barrios to threaten almost everyone. True, that particular episode of rioting is over, and the country at large has managed to digest and almost forget about the experience. But Los Angeles in 1992 was only a warning sign. The fires next time will be still greater. In the meantime, conditions of life deteriorate for many Americans and the cost to the system in both economic and moral terms rises daily.

The increased polarization of American society has economic origins. But economic polarization has its corollaries in moral, social, and political fragmentation. The inability of the society to move forward as a whole has fractured the melting pot, not only of race, ethnicity, and class, but of values, beliefs, and interests. It is on the plane of social cohesion that the "competitiveness crisis" may actually be most intense. The tension bred by a fraying society is the chief force sapping America's strength and eroding its productivity.

Pollster Dan Yankelovich has synthesized these realities based on in-depth surveys of American opinion. His summary is as instructive as it is frightening:

> Our faltering competitiveness is undermining the foundation of America's social stability: the ability of the society to offer genuine equality of opportunity through the mechanism of economic growth. The success of the traditional American strategy—advancing equality of opportunity—depends on broad-based growth in manufacturing as well as services. If the American dream becomes a mockery for tens of millions of vigorous young Americans, the nation can expect rising levels of violence, crime, drug addiction, rioting, sabotage and social instability. The stakes for addressing the nation's competitive flaws are broader than economics. *They go to the heart of America's viability as a democratic society.*

Instead of the top tier of the American economy regularly bringing those from below into its ranks—as was the process in the nineteenth and most of the twentieth centuries—the top tier is now being walled off in protective isolation. The companies, business sectors, and people of the top tier will continue to thrive for a long time to come, but not forever. As the gulf widens between those with education, skills, talents, and capital and those without, the ranks of the have-nots slowly begin to cannibalize the ranks of the haves.

Francis Fukuyama (best known for his "end of history" argument) acknowledges that even if, in a general way, liberal democratic capitalism has proven itself to be the pinnacle and endpoint in civilization's long quest for the ideal social order, the shades of difference among capitalist societies are significant:

> Beyond the economic decline is a clear-cut deterioration in our moral life. If there is any broadly felt sense of malaise in the U.S. today it has to do with the decline of community—from the breakdown of the family to the prevalence of crime, to the loss of any meaningful sense of neighborhood, to the fragmentation of national purpose. . . . The retention of a society in which the moral bonds linking individuals have not been so badly frayed may in the end be *a more important strength of contemporary Asian societies than their economic efficiency.*[2]

The economic value of the social cohesion enjoyed by Japan or other countries that possess this particular virtue is hard to quantify precisely—but it is surely immense. The cost of its absence in America is equally hard to quantify, yet no less large.

The cost to American society sneaks up semi-invisibly, or at least invisibly to those who aren't looking for it. It can be seen in the length of time it has taken the debt-burdened, low-productivity society of the early '90s to lift itself out of recession—and all the losses of jobs, homes, businesses, and communities that has entailed. It is in the crisis-ridden public educational system, the decaying network of public infrastructure, the increased homelessness, and the growing prison population. It is in the inability to address satisfactorily the new challenges posed by issues such as AIDS or environmental cleanup. It helps explain why, after an expenditure totaling $10 trillion to win the Cold War, there is now neither will nor wallet for a new Marshall Plan for the former Soviet Union that would consolidate the new peace.

The high cost of social fragmentation lies behind the fact that Americans no longer believe that theirs is a land of such opportunity that it can afford to offer health care to all who need it, or the possibility of a college education to all who have the aptitude for it. It is in the rising structural joblessness, lower real wages, and increased pressures on two-income families, all of which combine to leave Americans feeling downwardly mobile.

Even Federal Reserve chairman Alan Greenspan, long one of the chieftains of the rose-colored-glasses school, admitted to Congress in 1992: "There's a deep-seated concern out there, which I must say to you I have not seen in my lifetime . . . about whether the current generation will live as well as the previous one."

An increasingly dysfunctional American society is regularly forced to try to absorb new and more incredible burdens: A half-trillion-dollar bailout of corrupt savings and loans . . . a tort system that now costs close to $200 billion a year and consumes more than three times more of our GDP than the legal system does in our next-most-litigious competitor nation . . . a generation of crack babies destined to become wards of the welfare state . . . disability legislation that will force American business to make sure that any person with any disability can work in any workplace, without a thought to the untold billions required to make that high-minded principle a reality . . . an energy policy under which Americans are entitled to put gasoline in their cars at about one-third of the industrial world's market prices, sub-sidized by Washington's refusal to consider the obviously nec-essary, conservation-enhancing, deficit-reducing gas taxes . . . and on and on.

No real debate is ever held on such issues, not even in an election year. Even well-informed Americans are steered into debating the "character" flaws of politicians and their sex lives, gimmicky generalizations such as "no new taxes" or "middle-class tax cuts," and inflammatory personal issues such as the "right to life" versus the "right to choose." The frenzy of concern about the biological rights of the fetus is not matched by any comparable concern about the economic or social environment into which today's yet-to-be-born children will arrive.

"America is going nuts. But we're getting used to it." So says columnist Morton Kondracke, commenting on themes from the 1992 film *Grand Canyon*.[3] Precisely because the American system has such vast wealth and creativity within it, we come close to being able to manage these awesome new burdens and still com-pete—to get used to it, in effect. But with each passing year, we lose a little bit of our national energy, our productivity falls a bit further, our savings rate dips lower, our aggregate debt mounts, and what it will take to pull the nation out of this structural dysfunction grows.

Even so, there will be no single, galvanizing moment of truth, no dramatic day of reckoning. No apocalyptic event will force decisions upon a system that now fails to take decisive action on most of the important issues and reserves its frail ability to make any decisions at all for false and trivial matters. In this age, the economic world is diverse, complex, heterogeneous. We could go on this way for a generation or more, just as Britain did in its era of decline. What is more, the United States could well ex-perience sustained economic and social crises and still maintain its leadership in certain niches of technology and industry.

The lack of a visible, direct cause-and-effect relationship be-tween today's self-destructive orgy of laissez-faire and tomorrow's vanished economic vitality allows the Hallelujah Chorus of free marketeers to claim that large trade deficits, budget deficits, or the absence of government leadership are not producing any ill effects at all. The chaos around us is dismissed as nothing more than Schumpeter's "creative destruction" of capitalism at work, clearing the path for the finest flowerings of next-generation American businesses, from Bill Gates to biotech.

The tragedy is that the United States still has plenty of assets to deploy in pulling society together and generating a new competitive edge. But the lack of social cohesion has generated a situation in which the system cannot reach a consensus on *how* to deploy these assets. Ours has become what Peter G. Peterson has called "the choiceless society." It is not that we have no choices, but that we refuse to make the important ones—cutting the budget deficit, investing in R&D, overhauling our educational system, and so forth. And, as Peterson observes, "the failure to choose is in itself the most damaging choice of all," because it allows the unkind forces of history to choose our destiny for us.

This choiceless drift has been especially rampant in the last dozen years when the most important and visible of leaders, American presidents, have publicly embraced a belief system that holds that government ought *not* serve as activist and catalyst in national problem solving.

Meanwhile, other countries with fewer national assets—Japan and most of East Asia, Germany and much of the European Community—do not find the national consensus process so elusive. Certainly, they have difficulties of their own. But on the whole, they are able to make the choices necessary to use the more limited assets they have relatively efficiently and productively.

Viewed in this light, it is resoundingly clear that the long-term erosion of American competitiveness has little or nothing to do with unfair trade practices of the Japanese or others. It has everything to do with what we have done and continue to do to ourselves.

American Assets—Use Them or Lose Them

Yes, America still has many of the right assets: world-leading basic science and research, world leadership in many new technologies, world-leading service businesses, some important world-leading manufacturing industries, a huge domestic market, vast supplies of raw materials, plenty of open land, a strong position in export industries, a world-leading university system, the world's most efficient capital markets, the world's only viable global military-security capability, and a social system that for all its problems still brings out the best in many creative, talented people.

If we continue to use these assets as we are doing at present, however, some of them may depreciate and even waste away. If we were to use them strategically, on the other hand, they would form the basis for overcoming much of what ails American society. They could help the United States turn the corner toward a new forward vision of productivity, investment, innovation, renewed community, and a renewed American Dream.

Let us listen, for a moment, to the measured, reasonable, and wise voice of one of those world-leading American technology entrepreneurs, W. Daniel Hillis. He is the chief scientist of Thinking Machines, a Cambridge, Massachusetts, company that pioneered the booming field known as "massively parallel" computing. Even from his rarefied perspective in the world of top computer talent, Hillis worries that the United States is "sliding toward technological incompetence." Says he:

> These are painful words, but the painful reality is that the United States no longer leads the world in the exploitation of technology. Except for a few bright spots, such as computers, aircraft, and certain types of biotechnology, U.S. products must increasingly compete with technologically superior products from overseas.
>
> *The problem is not how well we invent new technology but, rather, how we turn our ideas into an economic advantage.* It is tempting to blame our problems on competitors. The U.S. system of encouraging innovation and funding basic research has become so effective that the rest of the world has come to depend on it, which leaves countries such as Japan free to concentrate on the development and exploitation of ideas that have originated in the United States. . . .
>
> In the first decades following World War II, the U.S. economic and technological base was so much stronger than that of other countries it was safe to assume that economic success would follow naturally and painlessly from our technological innovations. However, in today's world, where many nations have the technological, educational and economic infrastructure to exploit technology, success requires long-term investment and steady commitment. . . . When it comes to this long-term global perspective, U.S. industry falls short.[4]

In high-technology industries, Hillis argues, there is a particularly strong relationship between high volume and low cost, which favors the long-term investor. The startup costs for a new technology are inherently high and only justifiable by long-term volume. The best strategy for exploiting high-technology is to outspend the competition at the outset and outlast them during initial unprofitable market building—a strategy most U.S. investors find unattractive. But, says Hillis:

> It is difficult to imagine a U.S. appliance manufacturer, for example, announcing that it plans to lose money for the next five years in order to regain a technologically competitive position in consumer electronics. Yet that's what is required to compete successfully in that industry.[5]

America is still the world's leading laboratory for basic research and basic innovation in technology, even if the Japanese and others are beginning to close the gap. These assets should be of phenomenal value to us as a society, both short-term andlong-term, especially in a globalizing economy that is becoming ever more driven by advanced technology. The U.S. business-industrial marketplace environment, however, is not set up to maximize the benefits from the strategic advantages we possess. Indeed, it is other cultures, particularly the Japanese, that have found some of the best ways to optimize the assets of the American system.

This story is told over and over again in the realm of advanced technology: American researchers make the initial breakthroughs, but others reap most of the economic benefits from commercializing them. Something similar is happening across the length and breadth of the American system. From the openness of our markets to the extent of our financial resources, to the power of our military resources, even to the value of our natural resources, American society is failing to benefit fully from our own indigenous assets. In many cases, others are benefiting more than we ourselves.

The Strategy Gap

Tokyo: January 1992. It is an embarrassing scene most Americans would like to forget. President George Bush, nearing the end of a trade mission to Asia that the press has already dubbed a "disaster," "fiasco," and "failure," collapses at a state dinner in his honor.

It is only a case of the flu. It could have happened to anyone. Within twenty-four hours, Bush has resumed most of his schedule. Yet one doesn't have to go too far out on a psychological limb to wonder about the possibility of a psychosomatic influence.

Perhaps the pressure finally got to the cool, unflappable George Bush. The pressure of being the wrong president, accompanied by the wrong delegation, on the wrong trip to Japan for the wrong reasons at the wrong time. The pressure of being the president who presided over the final historic moments when America had its last chance to restore itself to global economic leadership—and failed to take it. The pressure of having been a Pacific war veteran and victor, a Cold War victor, a Gulf War commander-in-chief and victor, and now suddenly representing a vanquished America in an appeal to the Japanese victors for a few crumbs—a few jobs to improve the political situation in a recession-gripped United States.

As a news event, the Bush trip to Tokyo is ancient history. Yet it is worth reanalyzing, because of what it tells us about America's way of dealing with Japan. The annals of U.S.-Japan relations, both government-to-government and within the private sector, are filled with strategic failures on a par with the Bush visit of 1992. Some have even been much worse. But because of the high visibility of this particular presidential trip, and because it proved to be a turning point in recent U.S.-Japan relations, it is worth examining as a case study in our national failure to understand and meet the challenges of the new global era and the new global economy.

Recall, for a moment, the basic facts: In November 1991, with a visit to Tokyo impending, George Bush faces a stubbornly deepening U.S. recession, which he had previously declared over. The unprecedented popularity he enjoyed in the heady days after the Gulf War has evaporated. Now, he is being stung by well-targeted criticism that he has focused on foreign geopolitical affairs to the exclusion of domestic and economic issues. On Pennsylvania's senatorial election night, Bush watches a nightmarish curtain-raiser for the 1992 presidential election year: Populist Democrat Harris Wofford, running a strong campaign focused on health care and the domestic economy, handily defeats the Republican incumbent (and Bush administration veteran) Dick Thornburgh.

Bush's advisors realize a political crisis is brewing. They urge him to cancel his scheduled visit to Japan in order to dampen further criticism that the president is gallivanting about the world while the American economy burns. Impetuously, Bush agrees to the postponement and thereby commits *strategic blunder number one:* If Washington is to be taken at its word that it is serious about cooperation in mutual problem solving with Tokyo, an American president ought not cancel a visit over domestic political concerns. This is especially true when dealing with a country as sensitive to signs, gestures, and symbols as Japan.

Moreover, in Kiichi Miyazawa, Japan had only weeks before chosen the most international-minded and cosmopolitan prime minister in its history. Miyazawa was Japan's first fluent English-speaking chief of state, and he was eager to be a part of Bush's "Rolodex diplomacy." Yet Japan was headed into recession, Miyazawa's grasp on power was weak, and he could have used all the support he could get from Bush for his own domestic political needs. Instead, he got the rug pulled out from under him.

The agenda of the Bush-Miyazawa summit had been designed to focus on the lofty goal of a U.S.-Japan "global partnership." Theoretically, this should have been fertile ground for the two leaders, since both are viewed by their own domestic political cultures as strong on foreign affairs and global issues.

Although it is not well known or widely understood, Washington was actually enjoying relative success at the time in getting Tokyo to accept more global responsibilities. Americans remember Japan's role in the Gulf War chiefly for Tokyo's maddening reluctance to support the U.S. position. Yet the fact is that the Gulf War was an instance where American pressure on Japan *actually worked.* While it is true that the Japanese dithered for far too long, it is also true that Japan ultimately bankrolled Bush's anti-Saddam coalition by contributing $13 billion to the multinational forces—a contribution larger than that of any other country except Kuwait and Saudi Arabia. In fact, when all the accounting was done, Japan's $13 billion was even more than the United States itself spent on the war. And that was for a cause Japan never fully supported for some intelligent, if infuriating, reasons. In reality, Tokyo moved faster, did more, and lived up to its commitments better on the Gulf War than on any of the negotiations over trade or other matters that have dominated the U.S.-Japan bilateral agenda of recent years.

All this illustrated an underlying trend: Strategically speaking, an internal dynamic was at work in Japan driving it toward more internationalist positions. Americans could have leveraged this to the benefit of U.S. interests if they played their cards right. But in abruptly canceling his November 1991 visit to Tokyo, Bush let die on the vine the very real possibility that Japan could have been drawn into a much broader scheme for global burden sharing with the United States. That burden sharing, as we shall discuss in the next chapter, is critical to reducing the U.S. budget deficit and allowing more resources to be devoted to the domestic U.S. economy. Yet Bush allowed the opportune moment to slip away.

In Tokyo, the unilateral and sudden cancellation of the expected Bush visit was humiliating to Miyazawa and his men. "It is a slap in the face," said one Miyazawa confidant. The reply made by the Japanese elite to Bush would be classically Japanese: Say nothing, accept the shock stoically, and remember until next time. Whatever Bush's needs would be on his next visit to Tokyo, the Japanese side would be unlikely to find themselves able to comply. But no one in Washington realized this. After all, it is difficult to understand what the Japanese are thinking when the best and brightest in the administration are still working on the old agenda of U.S. foreign policy (such questions as What to do about Yeltsin? How to handle the Serbian crisis? What about Israeli settlements?), and when not a single person on the White House staff even reads Japanese.

By December, Bush had rescheduled the trip to Tokyo for January 1992. In doing so, however, he committed *strategic blunder number two* in openly declaring that the focus of his trip would be on cracking open the Japanese market for U.S. exports in order to create what he termed "jobs, jobs, jobs" for Americans. Attempting to make up for not having fought the recession with bold actions at home, Bush advisors led by then–Commerce Secretary Robert Mosbacher argued that the president could regain his faltering popularity by appearing to take bold actions against the Japanese. In pretrip publicity, Mosbacher even blamed the U.S. recession on Japan.

Yet the idea of George Bush going to Tokyo in the role of

"trade hawk" was as much a non sequitur as a nonstarter. The Japanese side knew Bush had an eleven-year-long record in Washington of opposing tough measures on trade. Like Ronald Reagan before him, he vociferously opposed anything that smacked of "managed trade," "industrial policy," or other efforts to put the weight of the American government behind the interests of American business. Predisposed to be unhelpful because of the cancellation of the previous Bush trip, the Japanese decided to stonewall Bush, reinforced by the knowledge that the agenda he brought with him was pure posturing and no substance. Once Bush returned home empty-handed, he would be unlikely to raise the same issues again.

In choosing a symbol for Bush's newfound (and short-lived) concern about trade, the president stepped into *strategic blunder number three:* He chose to focus on an area of American weakness rather than strength, namely, the automobile industry. Two decades earlier, Charles de Gaulle disparaged Japanese leaders as nothing more than a bunch of "transistor salesmen." Now Japan was shocked to find George Bush cast in the role of an auto salesman. "The difference," said a wry Japanese journalist, "is that our transistor radios were cheap, useful, breakthrough products."

In wrapping America's interests up with the fate of the auto industry, Bush walked into a trap. He was pleading the case for an industry that even many *Americans* believe to be uncompetitive.

By mid-December, the Japanese began telling American reporters in private briefings that they had trouble accepting blame for the difficulties faced by an American industry that was laying off thousands of its own workers while heaping fat bonuses and salaries upon its top executives. The same briefers were quick to point out that no American manufacturer even made right-hand-drive cars for the Japanese market—a market where almost 98 percent of all cars sold are right-hand drive. It wasn't long before stories started showing up in the American press about bungling, overpaid American auto executives trying to sell cars to the Japanese that were not even designed for driving on the proper side of the road. "Three whine mice" was one of the nicer epithets used by media to describe the CEOs of the Big Three auto companies along for the ride with Bush.

Within the erroneous focus on automobiles, Bush committed *strategic blunder number four* by focusing on the issue of Japanese barriers to American car *exports*. While the barriers are real, the notion that American competitiveness will be enhanced and large numbers of American jobs gained by opening the Japanese market is patently absurd. The Japanese are now far ahead of most of the rest of the world's automotive engineers. If there is one product area where Japan has substantial comparative advantage, it is in automobile production. The best American car companies can hope for in the 1990s is the kind of niche market in Japan that German car companies have obtained there—a few percentage points of the total market—*if* Americans can deliver top quality or particularly attractive premium features as the Germans have done.

Carrying coals to Newcastle by exhorting the Japanese to import more American cars, Bush ignored much more useful ground to explore. If his goal were truly "jobs, jobs, jobs," he might have focused his efforts where jobs can really be created and where the political *and* economic case is compelling: encouraging Japanese auto companies to bring more manufacturing and more advanced technology to their production facilities in the United States. Instead of beseeching Japan to buy more Chryslers, he should have been asking Japanese auto companies what they were prepared to do to help reopen the U.S. facilities being shut down by General Motors and perhaps even using his good offices to broker a deal along those lines.

MITI's vice-minister Noboru Hatakeyama was correct when he declared that what ailed America's economy was not insufficient car exports to Japan, but a crumbling manufacturing base. Bush and other American leaders "have not faced reality yet," he said.[6]

In a showdown meeting of the heads of the "Big Eight"—America's Big Three plus Japan's Big Five—the U.S. side made little progress on its demands for greater access to the Japanese market. The Japanese side, recognizing the political urgency of the situation, finally made a few meager concessions. Loosely— very loosely—they offered a vague formula for doubling imports of American auto parts.

The Japanese also made a loose best-efforts commitment to increase imports of American cars to about twenty thousand units by 1994. *If* they meet that target, they will be responsible for creating at most a few thousand new American jobs. Other crumbs flung in Bush's direction included the purchase of a grand total of two symbolic Pontiacs for official use by the Japanese Diet and an agreement by the Japanese automobile industry to lower its "voluntary restraint" levels on U.S.-destined exports. It was a thoroughly costless gesture, since Japanese exports have already fallen well below prior voluntary restraint targets as a result of transplanted manufacturing inside the United States.

Just the same, Bush said he was satisfied with the outcome of the talks and that "clear and measurable" progress would be forthcoming.

The central problem in all this was *not* primarily George Bush. After all, the trends have been evident for a long time. Throughout three decades of structural change in the global auto industry, American presidents and trade missions went to Tokyo, made demands for more equitable treatment for U.S. car companies, and came back to Washington declaring progress and even victory.

As far back as 1972, for example, Richard Nixon declared, "There is now an unfavorable balance of trade between Japan and the United States of $3.4 billion a year. Naturally, this is not healthy for the United States, but responsible Japanese leaders do not believe it is healthy for Japan. What will happen if that kind of imbalance continues?"[7] *Today, the U.S. trade deficit with Japan is 1200 percent greater than when Nixon worried about how unhealthy this tendency was.*

In 1980, it was a Democratic president, Jimmy Carter, who said, "I have expressed concern to the Japanese about the level of Japanese imports and I have stated quite clearly that the United States does not intend to abandon any portion of our share of the domestic auto market."[8] *Since that time, domestic U.S. auto manufacturers have lost an additional 25 percent of the domestic market to Japanese competition.*

In 1987, Ronald Reagan made this forecast: "Both Japan and the United States recognize that the current trade imbalance is politically unsustainable and requires urgent action. Prime Minister Nakasone described to me the measures his government intends to take and I am optimistic we will soon see the situation begin to improve."[9] *But the 1992 U.S. trade deficit with Japan is almost as high as that of 1987.*

What was new about the Bush visit was not its content, but the era in which it took place—an era when it is increasingly recognized that economic competitiveness is the new fulcrum of world power. "He doesn't understand that international power now depends on domestic economic strength," wrote *New York Times* foreign affairs columnist Leslie Gelb of the president:

> He went to Japan in the worst possible position—to bash on bended knee. . . . Neither he nor his advisors know the first thing about Japan, perhaps the country that will have the most profound impact on American interests. . . . He doesn't get the point that he ought to be fighting to open up markets for American industries that can compete, not those that don't. . . . He hasn't begun to tailor his Government toward the new agenda in world politics, namely the issues of trade and competitiveness and the connections between foreign and domestic affairs.[10]

Thus, the ill-fated Bush trip underscored perhaps the biggest competitive disadvantage America faces in dealing with Japan: the *strategy gap*. Japan has a well-developed strategy for dealing with us. It is centered on seeking the maximum benefits from America—maximum access to our market, maximum access to our advanced technology, maximum use of our financial system, maximum protection from our military-security system, and maximum value from our role as leader of a world order that has been very good to Japan—all at minimum cost. As Japan has become richer and more successful, the cost has invariably gone up in terms of the concessions Japan has had to make to keep the relationship workable. And, as America has become weaker and more troubled, the benefits have gone down somewhat. Nevertheless, this Japanese strategy is still basically sound. Honed and refined for years, it is now practiced to near-artistic perfection. What is more, there is nothing wrong or shocking about this. Nations have no enduring friends, only enduring interests, the political scientists remind us. This has never been more true than in the new era shaped by global economic competition.

Washington, however, has lost sight of its interests. It has lost the only Japan strategy it has known for the past four decades— the Cold War strategy of the State Department, Pentagon, National Security Council, and ultimately the White House. That strategy involved supporting Japanese economic development and even turning a blind eye to Tokyo's egregiously unfair trade policies and protectionisms of the 1950s, '60s, and '70s, and the more complex and subtle protectionism of the early 1980s. The bargain here was a Faustian one, although it has come to be understood as such only in the last few years. Japan was allowed and even encouraged to use any means necessary to become economically successful. A strong Japan would be a bulwark against communism in Asia and a pliant forward military base for the United States in the dangerous waters of the Pacific.

By the late 1980s, many in Washington came to understand that American Cold War strategy vis-à-vis Japan had perhaps worked *too well*. While American policymakers were focused on geopolitical scenarios and Soviet missile throw weights, Japan had become an economic superpower, competing directly with the United States for global economic leadership. But even as Japan policy became more conditioned by economic issues—and even as Washington agencies from the Commerce Department to the Office of the Trade Representative demanded more of a say— the old Cold War strategy was never decisively abandoned.

The result was a strategic vacuum in the Reagan-Bush era. As Thomas L. Friedman, chief diplomatic correspondent for *The New York Times*, reported in 1992,

> What is American policy toward Japan? Such a simple question. Ask American diplomats about policy toward Russia or Israel or China and they will immediately tick off several highlights. But ask what is Japan policy and who makes it and the most common answer you get around Washington is: "Beats me."

> Despite the importance of Japan–United States relations, policy making toward Japan is characterized by conflicting strategies, uneven coordination and a shocking indifference among senior decision makers. The truth is we have no Japan policy.[11]

Constant internecine argument between Washington agencies further undermined any consensus. The State Department and Pentagon—joined by the ideological chorus of Washington's free-traders—played their traditional Cold War role of opposing tough negotiating positions toward Japan. The Commerce Department and the Office of the Trade Representative tried to answer to their constituencies by positioning themselves as "getting tough with Japan"—although usually this vaunted toughness was only on specific issues of concern to major lobbies, not necessarily the key issues affecting U.S.-Japan business and trade.

A telling anecdote is recounted by Glen Fukushima, a former deputy assistant U.S. Trade Representative. In 1988, he tried to get a copy of a State Department paper analyzing negotiations he himself was involved in with the Japanese on importing more American beef and oranges. The State Department refused to let him have it. By the time the State Department finally decided to release it to him, they had already given it to the Japanese foreign ministry.

As for George Bush, he served only as a "sort of referee, trying to balance the competing wings of his Government." He "flip-flop[ped] between advocating managed trade one week, free trade the next and subtle Japan-bashing the next."[12] In the Bush admin-istration, as in most prior administrations, Japan was considered politically unsexy and unrewarding. Bush himself was raised on the notion that China is the real powerhouse in Asia, and had a hard time focusing on Japan. Secretary of State James A. Baker III spent more time visiting Mongolia than Japan. And the admin-istration spoke volumes about the importance it assigned to Japan policy by making Vice-President Dan Quayle its point man on Japan issues.

Washington's lack of a Japan policy in recent years is not all that surprising, given the lack of coherent strategy in confronting most of the other economic challenges faced by the United States. In fact, an absence of strategy was the byproduct of the strong ideological impact of laissez-faire economic theory. Developing a strategy requires a certain belief in the possibility of planning for desired ends and using the combined weight of government and business to achieve them. In a political-economic culture that opposes government participation, let alone leadership, in a con-certed process of economic planning, strategy itself is anathema. Laissez-faire thinking encourages a "let the chips fall where they may" bravado, fearing no downside from a future in which Amer-icans sell potato chips to the Japanese, while they sell computer chips to us.

Laissez-faire attitudes—antistrategy and antiactivist—were not just the province of a handful of ideologues among the president's economic advisors. They became the dominant mode of thought throughout American government, as is made clear by the sad, seminal lament of a senior Republican staffer who spent the last decade in the Reagan and Bush administrations:

> There has developed in Washington a ruling ethic that national good will flow simply from embracing platitudes in the guise of principles. . . . Deregulation and *laissez-faire* "empowerment" are relied on, like states of grace, to insure a better America.
>
> In this view, America is not a nation but a "market." . . . Those who work, buy homes, and raise families are not American citizens but production and consumption resource factors in an economic model. . . . They are on their own to solve their problems. Traditional government initiatives . . . are no longer a manifestation of a nation's pursuit of health and general welfare, but merely interference with omniscient market forces. . . .
>
> It is worth remembering that our national highway system was not built by the Kiwanis Club. The Chamber of Commerce did not send astronauts to the moon. Social Security was not a neighborhood project. Contrary to folklore, the U.S. computer industry, now deeply troubled, began and rose to world pre-eminence out of the Pentagon, not someone's garage. The U.S. aerospace industry was an economic winner picked long ago by the Federal government. These and other accomplishments were the products of leadership that energized a nation.[13]

In short, economic strategy, planning, and activist leadership used to be the American way in another era. It is only rather recently that we have been told government has no business being involved in business.

Curiously, there were a few exceptions to Washington's anti-strategy in recent years. Curiouser and curiouser, such areas have proven to be precisely the ones where government still continues to reach its highest levels of functionality, at least within the framework of stated goals.

One is agriculture. True, there are outlandish subsidies and boondoggles of all kinds, as well as thousands of family farmers who have lost their land needlessly and tragically. But on the whole, American farm policy is a success. Government resources are lavished upon it; long-term policies have long-term payoff. The same government that disdains "picking winners and losers" in high-technology actually micromanages farming. Washington controls pricing and land use, provides funding for infrastructure building, makes low-cost capital available to farmers, and backs special education and training initiatives to enhance agricultural productivity. The same government that sliced manpower training funds in the manufacturing sector by 50 percent since 1980 put *increased* funds to work in the agricultural sector. A recent study found an excellent 27 percent return on government investment in agricultural research and training.[14] The bottom line: The American farmer remains the most efficient and competitive in the world by far, even though he is competing against farmers in many countries where labor and land are dirt cheap.

Similarly, the defense sector is a success story, in spite of its well-known costs and corruption. There can be no question but that the United States has developed the world's most "competitive" military system. Indeed, it is the most advanced and capable military force ever assembled in world history. Through careful planning and strategy as well as generous funding, the Pentagon has also been highly successful at developing advanced, breakthrough technology. In the experiences of DARPA, the advanced research arm of the Defense Department, which has helped develop critical fields from data networks to new materials, we can see some of the best examples of how to seed new technologies. The U.S. armed forces are also institutional leaders on another key front: manpower training. The Pentagon oversees what is in effect the largest and most successful government-sponsored job training initiative. It is particularly successful at the hardest part of such efforts—training personnel from disadvantaged backgrounds.

One of the few experimental initiatives with technology policy reluctantly authorized during the Reagan years is Sematech. Basically a Japanese-style government-business consortium, Sematech is charged with developing designs and processes for next-generation equipment to manufacture advanced semiconductors. This venture into technology policy snuck through during the days when Ronald Reagan was still worried about the "Evil Empire." Washington's last Cold Warriors could be sold on the danger to national security posed by lost American leadership in semiconductors, since semiconductors are at the heart of missile guidance technology and other "smart" weapons systems. As a result, Sematech was allowed a dollop of Pentagon funding. However, as the Cold War has subsided, it has become clear that Sematech's real relevance to American security is "only" in economic terms. Sematech's future is now in doubt. Pressure is mounting cut to cut its budget even though Sematech has been successful in leapfrogging some state-of-the-art Japanese chipmaking techniques.

One would think these success stories might have speeded the diffusion of strategic planning to areas of public life where it was more desperately needed: education, health care, savings and investment, environmental protection, and of course, industry, technology, and trade.

But not so. Just as the need for a strategy became more urgently obvious, the Reagan-Bush approach to government became more intransigent in opposing long-term planning, arguing, as laissez-faire enthusiasts typically do, that the marketplace would generate the proper strategic direction spontaneously.

The leaders of America's best companies, many of them life-long Republicans, came to worry about what they saw happening. Particularly eloquent was George Fisher, CEO of Motorola, a company widely noted for its ability to compete head-to-head with Japan's best:

> The American people are asking, "Where is our economic vision?" and "Where is our national strategy?" . . . Other countries noted years ago that international rivalry has shifted from military power to economic strength, and they have adjusted their economic, technology and industrial policies accordingly. The United States government, unfortunately, is still trying to make up its mind what to do, and as a result is losing ground to the competition, day by day.[15]

Although business builders like Fisher understood that an economic strategy is an imperative, the supposedly probusiness Reagan-Bush governments refused to hear the message from what they should have known to be their core constituency. Even when Congress has been able to push through some meaningful "competitiveness" legislation, it was usually undermined by the administration.

Such was the case, for example, with the National Advisory Committee on Semiconductors, a government-industry group established under the provisions of 1988 trade legislation. Chaired by one of the country's leading experts on technology policy, Ian Ross, president of Bell Labs, the committee made ambitious proposals. It argued for the establishment of a public–private sector partnership to get America back into consumer electronics and urged Washington to adopt a plan called Micro Tech 2000, an all-out, put-a-man-on-the-moon-type program to ensure U.S. leadership in semiconductors.

By 1992, however, Ian Ross said he saw no point in continuing. Everything the group proposed had been shot down by the White House, no matter how much support the ideas enjoyed from important figures in business and industry. A typical news report on the group's demise said it all: "A government advisory panel charged with drafting a strategy to help the American semiconductor industry issued its final report yesterday and prepared to shut itself down, its numerous recommendations having gone largely unheeded."[16]

Closing the strategy gap does not require huge new government deficits. In a $6 trillion economy, America has all the resources it needs. But it does require us to do some things that have eluded us in recent years. To close the strategy gap, we must think long, hard, carefully, and critically. Then, once we have a clear understanding of our long-term interests and the nature of the world we now live in, we must be willing to act decisively. Both steps are certainly more difficult than mindlessly practicing the art of laissez-faire and consuming the next generation's share of our national wealth. Yet neither represents anything Americans have not done incredibly well in the past.

Bill Clinton speaks the language of strategy and, seemingly, the right mix of government and the marketplace. But can he and his team restart the rusted strategic machinery of national policy and planning?

That America would prefer to avoid the arduous process of self-reinvention is obvious from the number of tailor-made opportunities to get started that have been passed up in the last few years. As we saw in Chapter 2, "the Japan metaphor," as it developed in the 1980s, had all the makings of a Sputnik-type incentive for America to do whatever was necessary to become more competitive. Some leading U.S. corporations responded appropriately, but the U.S. government and the society as a whole did not. Now, the full force of the Japanese challenge is dissipating.

The aftermath of the 1987 stock market crash on Wall Street was an ideal opportunity for a strategic shift in public policy, especially because it injected a twinge of fear that an economic crisis lay ahead—perhaps even a 1930s-style depression affecting pocketbooks across the board. It highlighted the rapacious greed and short-term thinking that had come to dominate the American business system. Yet aside from a few technical modifications in the way the New York Stock Exchange operates, no changes in the overall economic environment emerged.

Next came the 1988 presidential election campaign. Party professionals, pundits, and voters alike understood that after eight years of Reaganomics, it was time for a political campaign whose substance would serve as a referendum on the nation's economic future. Yet the debate over economics was shoved aside by passion-inflaming issues such as flag burning and the furlough of an obscure prisoner named Willie Horton.

Again in the spring of 1991, the moment was ripe. The Gulf War victory had engendered a rare sense of patriotism, collective destiny, and national self-confidence. Strong leaders might well have found the way to translate this new American pride into a force aimed at solving problems on the domestic agenda.

The collapse of the Soviet Union provided yet another defining national moment. The president could have declared victory in the Cold War and proceeded to refocus national priorities on economic issues. But this too was not to be.

For those wishing America would see the light, the 1992 presidential campaign offered hope. The deep-seated public desire for substantial political change was the only consistent trend of the long campaign. The early successes of candidates like Pat Buchanan, Paul Tsongas, and Jerry Brown—and the far more significant movement built around Ross Perot—all signaled that Americans want change and are willing to accept new leaders as well as new ideas. Tsongas built his early strength around an eighty-page booklet that offered some of the best ideas ever discussed in an election campaign about changing the role of the U.S. government and renewing the American economic system. Later, the Perot campaign reflected some of the same perspectives.

Although Perot was criticized by partisan professionals for having "no ideas," the businessman-candidate actually espoused some excellent and even revolutionary ideas, albeit not fully formed. Perot was able to gain the widest audience yet for the importance of strategic thinking and government leadership in economic, industrial, technology, and trade policies. His meteoric rise in popularity reflected the public's willingness to consider some of these ideas. But the quick collapse of his campaign before it even got off the ground reflected his own lack of courage in trying to convince a plurality of voters of the need to do the right things. Once Perot realized that restoring the American economy to health was not just a matter of "sweeping out the barn" (as he initially said), he had no stomach for selling Americans on the tough medicine required. Re-entering the presidential race in its final weeks, Perot lacked the credibility he had at first enjoyed.

Bill Clinton became the last agent of change left standing in 1992. "Clintonomics," with its focus on infrastructure building, "human capital" initiatives in education and job training, and government support for advanced technology projects, represents the closest thing Americans will see to the right economic direction for the country in the nation's real political life. But even Clinton's plan represents only half the battle. Without credible means of cutting the budget deficit, improving capital formation, and refocusing numerous other priorities in American economic life, it is questionable how many of Clinton's best initiatives can be realized.

In the Reagan-Bush years, it was easy for those troubled by America's lost competitiveness to blame the president's wrong-headed vision or lack of vision altogether. But while the president is the key figure in setting the nation's direction, no one person, not even the most capable visionary, can do everything.

Getting the ideas out in the open is the first step on a long road. That finally happened in 1992, at least to a degree. Changing Washington's antistrategy bias, developing long-term thinking in public policy, and recapturing government's role as a leader and activist in the process of American renewal—these goals represent deep institutional transformation that will require years of groundwork. Incremental, workable change in the right direction must come before the needed revolution can take place.

Part III

SOLUTIONS AND CONCLUSIONS

8

Turning the Tables: Toward a Japan Strategy for the Future

Getting Started: Practical Proposals for the Mid-'90s

The development of a coherent American strategy toward Japan is only a modest piece of a much larger jigsaw puzzle involving the component issues of U.S. economic renewal that have been discussed throughout this book. Yet the Japan piece is a particularly intriguing one.

For one thing, Japan policy is a discrete world unto itself, where changes can be made without having to change America's entire national thought process and political mechanisms. Even so, Japan is a kind of benchmark, "litmus test" issue, because it has such close associations with so many key domestic policy questions. Therefore, changing the thinking about Japan can be an important step on the road to making the larger strategic shift America must eventually make. As Michael H. Armacost, U.S. ambassador to Japan, notes:

> You cannot sit here in Tokyo and observe the way they deal with economic fundamentals—the level of savings, the level of investment, the level of research and development spending—without being concerned because we are not doing as well. It doesn't take a genius to figure out how trends like that, if they persist, will show up in the marketplace.[1]

To thrive in a twenty-first century likely to be conditioned by global economic issues, as well as to deal with its intensifying domestic social crisis, the United States *requires* a new economic strategy. This would be true even if Japan did not exist. But especially because Japan does exist and is setting the example for twenty-first-century approaches in so many aspects of economics, the two issues have certain obvious interstices and synergies.

Most important, the changed circumstances of the early '90s over the prior decade present new opportunities for interweaving the issues of Japan policy and domestic American economic strategy in new and promising ways. "If American business is guilty of anything in the ongoing competitiveness battle with Japan, it is lack of imagination," says business writer William Taylor.[2] Executives have been mired in trench warfare, stuck in the same uninteresting, uninspired, and fundamentally unhelpful debates, about tariffs, dumping penalties, and quotas. Taylor's well-targeted advice: Now is the time to break out of the rut and claim the strategic high ground.

In that spirit, let us begin this chapter with a practical look at what could be done relatively easily over the next few years. These ideas are by no means a comprehensive list. They are merely illustrative of the new thinking needed, and some of the new opportunities possible in the mid-'90s. While offering concrete benefits in themselves the points below also lay the groundwork for the long-term strategic shift the United States would be well advised to make. That shift is detailed in the final sections of this chapter.

1. Shift Gears on U.S. Trade Negotiations on the Auto Sector

Precious American political capital should be expended where it can gain the most advantage for American jobs and for redeveloping the U.S. manufacturing base. Instead of making U.S. auto *exports* the focus of trade negotiations, Washington should be encouraging increased transfer of Japanese auto production to the U.S. market. Right now, the Japanese make roughly half their cars for the U.S. market at American plants and export the other half from Japan. The ones made in the United States, while featuring a steadily increasing local content, still use many high-value-added parts from Japan. The goal should be to bring at least 75 percent of the total Japanese nameplate production for the U.S. market to U.S. sites, with expanded local content for all

U.S. models. This orientation would bring real and immediate benefits to the American economy, whereas focusing on the fight to open the Japanese market to American-made cars, while long on rhetorical virtues, is quite short on positive economic impact.

Similar approaches should be taken toward other areas of industry. Wherever Japanese companies are willing to establish U.S. facilities, provide high-skilled jobs, transfer technology and manufacturing know-how, they should be welcomed. Indeed, special efforts should be made to continue attracting them, now that they are growing more circumspect about foreign investment and more interested in other markets of the world.

Is this realistic? Emphatically yes. The fact that 50 percent of the Japanese automobile export industry has already relocated across the Pacific is a key indicator here, as are the hundreds of transplants in other sectors. All told, Japanese companies have invested over $30 billion in new U.S. manufacturing operations. That is not window dressing, that is tangible and significant.

Sometimes Japanese business leaders seem more concerned about the importance of rebuilding America's manufacturing base than American political leaders do. No matter how hard they have competed against American companies, they understand that a strong, economically vibrant America is in Japan's own interests as a trading partner, a source of advanced research and ideas, and as the ultimate guarantor of stability in a dangerous world.

"Since Japan owes much to the U.S. for its economic rehabilitation after World War II, now it is Japan's turn to help U.S. industry," said MITI vice-minister Yuji Tanahashi on taking office in 1991.[3] He openly called on Japanese companies to enter into more joint ventures with U.S. partners and transfer Japanese production methods to revitalize the American industrial base.

Sony's Akio Morita went even further, offering a list of steps he would like to see more Japanese companies take to foster a spirit of partnership in renewing American industrial competitiveness. Morita asked his Japanese colleagues to consider steps such as:

> manufacturing more products locally in the United States . . . discovering and developing more parts and components suppliers among American companies . . . augmenting American "human capital" by training workers in the most advanced aspects of Jap-

anese production processes . . . doing more advanced R&D locally . . . [and] building business partnerships with like-minded
U.S. corporations, including technology exchanges and transfers.[4]

It's not just good politics for Japanese companies to step up
U.S. production, it's good business. Even the German luxury car
maker BMW has recognized this. Under no visible political pressure, BMW chose in 1992 to locate a car plant in Spartanburg,
South Carolina, because of massive cost savings that could be
realized by producing in the now low-cost U.S. marketplace.

2. Go Digital! And Focus on Technology Policy

It is unlikely that the United States will adopt an all-round strategic economic policy in the next few years. The political opposition is simply too great. However, it may be possible to zero
in on shifting the prevalent laissez-faire attitudes to a more strategic policy in the advanced technology sector. Particular projects,
such as the initiative to create a national "data highway," long
championed by Al Gore, and the human genome mapping project,
have been able to win the necessary votes in Congress. Political
support for this direction is already substantive, even if it isn't
yet the majority view. Certainly the Clinton administration will
find that aiding companies and industries aimed at the future is
economically more beneficial and politically sexier than trying to
deal with the problems of dying industries.

Every effort should be made to support U.S. efforts in promising technology directions such as the "digital revolution." In
this cornucopia of converging multimedia technologies, American
companies are leading the way in integrating computer hardware
and software, interactive video, and telecommunications. Several
huge global businesses loom at the other end of this rainbow.

To bolster efforts to develop a domestic technology policy,
American trade negotiators should make the removal of barriers
to high-tech trade the heart of their agenda with Japan. A U.S.
technology policy does not have to be nationalistic or protectionist, or to buck the trend of globalization. The emphasis should
not be on keeping advanced products out of the American market.
Rather, the emphasis should be on making sure the U.S. infrastructure for the development of new technology continues to be

world-leading, and that foreign markets are open to U.S. technological products and services.

As for the U.S. government–funded ventures into advanced technology that exist today, such as Sematech, and the increased efforts that may exist tomorrow, these should be open to the participation of all companies that have American operations and employ significant numbers of American workers and researchers, regardless of the headquarters nation of the parent company. At the same time, Washington should press for full, open American access to Japanese basic scientific work and equitable terms for American participation in Japanese government–sponsored technology projects as well as private-sector R&D.

Forget rice, beef, oranges, lumber, wood products, and countless other low-tech or no-tech items that have figured prominently in U.S.-Japan trade disputes of recent years. Let the natural momentum toward more of a consumer marketplace in Japan drive the desire to import more of these kinds of products. American trade negotiators should focus on promoting U.S. sales of semiconductors, computer systems and software, telecommunications and fiber optic products, biotechnology and pharmaceuticals, aircraft and satellites, and multimedia digital electronics devices and services. Substantial informal Japanese protectionism still exists in most of these areas. Lifting these barriers and winning leading positions in the Japanese market for U.S. companies will be far more consequential over the long term than selling rice.

What is more, the United States should abandon its agriculture-driven strategies for improving the world trading system and advancing the GATT (General Agreement on Tariffs and Trade) talks to include new areas. Let the Europeans and Japanese subsidize their agriculture! What American business needs now more than anything is a more liberal trading order in services, and most especially, a more liberal order backed by firmer protections for the trade in software and other high-technology "intellectual property" where American business excels.

3. This Is the Time to Invest in Japan

For the first time in recent memory, American companies are reasonably well positioned to invest in Japan, one of the world's largest and most dynamic markets. Real estate prices are coming back to earth, making it possible for American companies to think once again about buying offices, building plants, and settling into Japan for the long haul. Although dented by recession, the Japanese market has shown itself open enough to many kinds of products and services to allow American managers to recommend upgrading their corporate presence in Japan. And American companies willing to undertake the necessary efforts have been able to establish leading-edge R&D centers in Japan.

Certainly, Japan remains a difficult place for foreigners to invest. Japanese ratios of foreign investment to GDP are only one-twentieth to one-tenth American and European norms. Yet even so, the collapse of the bubble has made some Japanese companies more interested in access to foreign capital. Small deals typify the trend to date. In 1992, General Motors' EDS subsidiary acquired a $30 million interest in Japan Systems Corporation, a software developer. Pfizer made a similar-sized investment in Koshin Medical. Hasbro, the U.S.-based toymaker, purchased Nomura Toys, a small Japanese toy and game company, to improve access to the local market and distribution there. But bigger deals are in the offing. As some of the traditional cross-shareholdings of the *keiretsu* groups loosen, some Japanese companies may be more open to accepting foreign partners and investors into their families. Some companies may actually *need* to do so.

The establishment of local manufacturing in Japan is a key step American companies need to take for many reasons. To be world-class competitors, they need direct access to Japanese R&D, production methods, and other competitive factors of the marketplace. What's more, much of transpacific trade is intracompany— perhaps as much as two-thirds, according to Harvard Business School professor Dennis Encarnation. Japanese companies operating in the United States import many parts, components, and materials from Japan; U.S. companies operating in Japan have similar buying patterns. But because the Japanese manufacturing presence in the United States is so much greater than the other way around, the U.S. trade deficit with Japan is likely to remain stubbornly high and "may worsen if U.S. companies don't establish a stronger presence in the Japanese market," says Encarnation.[5]

4. It Is Also the Time to Invest with Japan

In the heady 1980s, Japanese companies often bought out the interests of their long-time American joint-venture partners. Now, with weaker balance sheets in Japan, Americans are in a better position to create joint ventures and negotiate terms. Ford, which has long had a 25 percent stake in Mazda, was able to take a controlling interest in Autorama, a joint venture responsible for importing Ford vehicles to Japan, as well as to negotiate for a 50 percent interest and greater production control at the two companies' shared auto plant in Flat Rock, Michigan.

"Ford is getting more control and will have more input in a plant that is very important to them," declared Christopher Cedergren, auto analyst for the AutoPacific Group.[6] Mazda, hard-pressed by Japan's recession, needs the money.

Hosts of new alliances and joint ventures have been formed across the Pacific in the electronics industry. Indeed, what American high-tech companies can't find at home because of the absence of a domestic technology policy, they are sometimes able to find in Japan. AT&T has teamed up with NEC to develop next-generation computer chips, for example. Their agreement to share R&D on thirty different process technologies has been hailed as a "marriage of equals with each giving the other access to superior technologies."[7]

Among the most significant of the new alliances is the expansion of an existing IBM alliance with German electronics giant Siemens to bring in Toshiba's expertise and resources as well. The trilateral project will focus on developing next-generation computer memory chips. The IBM-Siemens alliance had originally been seen as a response to Japan's relentlessly accelerating leadership in semiconductor development; the three-way alliance suggests an acceptance of rough parity and new incentives to share costs and breakthroughs as the technology globalizes. Perhaps most important, the headquarters for the trilateral research will be in the United States at IBM's East Fishkill, New York, facility.

Similar opportunities for American companies to build more equal, balanced relationships with Japanese partners are opening up in a variety of industries—and now is the time to take them.

5. *Internationalize the* Keiretsu *System*

The *keiretsu* system of interlocking companies and monopolized distribution channels has been correctly identified as an obstacle to the full entry of American companies into the Japanese market. But the American demand to break up the *keiretsu* groupings and enforce U.S.-style antitrust policies is unlikely to ever gain acceptance in Japan.

Since the system of production *keiretsu* actually works quite efficiently in the manufacturing sector, the focus of American negotiations should be on integrating U.S.-based companies into *keiretsu* as partners and suppliers. At the same time, business should continue to press for easements in U.S. antitrust law that will allow American companies to collaborate in the same ways their Japanese competitors do, especially in establishing shared R&D activities.

As for the distribution *keiretsu*, American trade negotiators should keep the pressure on to change the outmoded and *inefficient* nature of this system. The Japanese consumer, the Japanese economy as a whole, and American business will all benefit from less monopolized market channels.

6. *Resist the Temptation to Raise Prices*

As Japanese exporters ease up a bit on their relentless drive for U.S. market share, American corporations will be sorely tempted to raise their own prices and boost profitability. But U.S. companies have a great opportunity to win back market share in both the domestic and global markets, and they should try not to blow it this time! At GM's Saturn division, for example, prices have been creeping up as Saturn's chief competitor, Toyota, has raised its prices. This trend, if continued, would be a big mistake—a classic example of short-term profits at the expense of long-term interests.

Saturn has a chance to be fully competitive with Japanese product offerings. But it can succeed only if it lures value-oriented American consumers to buy the car, not just in a short-term burst of fashion, but over a sustained period. Like Japanese cars in the 1970s, American cars today must not only be as good or better, they must also be cheaper. Hold the line on prices, and profitability will improve in time.

7. Don't Backslide on Product Development Times

Just as Japanese companies are going to be raising prices, they are also going to be introducing fewer new products and slowing the fiery pace of new product development they sustained from 1985 to 1991. American companies, which have only recently begun striving to improve product development times, must be very careful on this score. Some auto executives openly question whether American companies should continue pressing to close the development time gap with their Japanese competitors. "I personally believe that five to seven years is right," says one, even though such norms are still about twenty percent slower than the slowed-down Japanese schedule.[8]

Maybe American manufacturers can save some short-term money by cutting back on efforts to speed development times. But remember, the Japanese *know* how to introduce products rapidly, even if they moderate the pace for a while. American companies in most cases have never matched Japanese standards in this area and should not backslide now. Otherwise, they will find themselves at the mercy of the Japanese later in the decade, when the Japanese side next decides to pick up the pace.

8. Turn the Guns of Japanese Industrial Policy Around

A number of Japanese government programs have been developed in the last few years designed to spur imports into Japan as well as foreign investment. These efforts are substantial enough to be more than mere tokenism. They are the beginnings of genuine affirmative actions to facilitate the breaking down of barriers and the full entry of foreign business into Japan. JETRO (Japan External Trade Organization) offers a number of programs, including one to advise U.S. small businesses on how to export to Japan. In its first two years of operation, it has introduced three dozen American companies to the Japan market for the first time. It also operates offices in the United States and elsewhere that offer information and aid to foreign companies wishing to invest in Japan.

MITI has developed a package of tax incentives for foreign investors that will allow them to write off startup costs against later-stage profits over a decade. It is also organizing the construction of nearly two dozen "access zones" around Japanese airports and harbors to smooth the flow of imports.

Japan should promote the goal of "business global partnership," says MITI—and to do that, the ministry has begun pressuring major Japanese companies to "establish cooperative relationships on the international level by intensifying their efforts to expand imports at home, increase local production abroad, and help foreign firms establish themselves in the Japanese market."[9] On another tack, MITI's export insurance division is working with the U.S. Export-Import Bank to cofinance the insurance needs of U.S.-based exporters, and the Japan Development Bank has indicated a willingness to finance warehouse construction and other needed facilities for U.S. companies importing their products into Japan.

Meanwhile, the U.S. Commerce Department as well as a number of American states now have in place market research and promotional activities for would-be exporters. These efforts, although unfortunately peripheral and poorly funded, represent the beginning of what the United States must do at home to raise consciousness about exports and foreign markets.

The Japanese private sector is taking some steps as well. Most trading companies have special programs to identify appropriate foreign products for introduction to Japan; industrial companies are creating procurement and training centers with special mandates to try to increase the imported content of Japanese-made products. Toyota has set up a special office to help inform and train potential American suppliers.

These efforts are all partial solutions to bringing down Japanese barriers. They are not enough, to be sure. The American side should keep up the pressure for Japan to do more—to become the "importing superpower" MITI has said it should be. Having so rationally and strategically crafted the industrial policies that led Japan to become an exporting giant, Japanese government agencies are perfectly capable of designing and introducing the incentives that will encourage the Japanese system to absorb much higher levels of imports.

Rather than fighting over every sectorial issue, the American position should be to encourage the Japanese side to turn its industrial policy planning guns around and take aim at achieving specific levels of increased imports over a set time. A zero trade balance, while politically attractive, is hard to achieve, especially in one gulp. But a $5-billion- or $10-billion-a-year improvement is not—especially if Japan will commit itself to such a goal.

9. Maximize the Advantage of Low-Cost U.S. Capital

With American capital costs temporarily on a par with Japanese, and with the dollar locked into long-term structural weakness, American companies should be expanding productive capacity and investing in new manufacturing technology. That they are doing so only slowly and reluctantly says much about the debt burdens of the 1980s that remain with corporate America and about the legacy of absent economic vision in Washington.

A strategy-conscious U.S. government would be taking special initiatives to seize this historic, low-cost moment to rebuild the U.S. manufacturing base. Even without an all-embracing strategy, it is reasonable to hope that lawmakers will see the virtue in maintaining and expanding existing R&D tax credits, bringing back the investment tax credit (targeted to investment in new plant and equipment), and perhaps at last reaching consensus on a targeted capital gains tax reduction as well. Perhaps they will even take some deficit-reducing measures and some policy initiatives to raise the savings rate—and thereby help institutionalize our currently moderate interest rates.

As we wait for such policies to develop at the national level, smart companies should be out front in the effort to make sure they have the capacity to benefit from the global market share they can regain now that American costs in many industries are internationally competitive.

10. Help Japan Do the Right Thing on Burden Sharing

As one of the world's largest foreign aid donors, one of its top five military spenders, a contributor of $13 billion to the Gulf War coalition, and a country that pays at least half the costs of keeping U.S. troops stationed within its own borders, Japan can hardly be criticized anymore for getting a "free ride" on defense and international security. Yet while Japanese spending has increased significantly in these areas, it remains far below the standards of other leading industrial democracies as a percentage of its huge GDP.

Japan is already moving in the direction of assuming more global responsibilities. But Washington should encourage Tokyo to accelerate the pace—both because so much of the world could well use Japanese aid and because every 120 or so yen the Japanese spend for such purposes can be one less dollar the United States government has to spend.

The United States should push Japan particularly hard on aiding the emerging market economies of Eastern Europe and the Soviet Union. The best hope for curing the world's slow growth climate is to enlarge the total economic pie. And the best hope for averting a new era of international instability is to ensure that new democracies have access to the investment capital, know-how, and technology that will help them expand economically. Japan has a deep vested interest in both goals, but is not yet carrying its weight.

On military security, Japan is understandably reluctant to expand its self-defense forces further. Certainly, the United States should not be pushing Tokyo toward full-scale rearmament. What Washington *should* seek is (1) Japanese assumption of the whole of the cost for the American troops they host and (2) a dialogue about how Japan (as well as European countries) can contribute more directly to sharing the burden of maintaining the U.S. global defense network. Such a dialogue would naturally include discussion of how America's allies can have more direct input into the military-security policies of the defense network they are helping to underwrite.

The way to continue making significant cuts in U.S. military spending without precipitously eliminating defense capabilities that may someday be needed lies along this line of reasoning. Because the specter of American troops becoming "mercenaries" for Japan, Germany, and other countries touches many sensitive nerves, American policymakers must find ways to ensure that foreign allies share the "blood risk" of any actual fighting that has to be done. But the fact is that American military power is one of our most potent national assets. Its technical excellence as well as the firm democratic checks and balances on its use has turned American military forces into a kind of global public utility. Military power is an area of American comparative advantage— and it should be used as such. That means it should not be run at a financial loss to the American economy and U.S. taxpayers, when it is at the service of much of the world. Japan, with its huge current account surplus and far-flung global interests, should be asked to make more sizable contributions to ensure the continuing security provided by the U.S. armed forces.

Reich's Dilemma

Political economist Robert B. Reich tells an interesting story about a "test" he gives to various groups of Harvard students, business executives, government bureaucrats, ordinary citizens, and professional economists.[10] He offers them two scenarios. In the first, the American economy grows by 25 percent over the next decade, but the Japanese economy grows 75 percent over the same period. In the second scenario, the U.S. economy grows 10 percent while Japan's does only fractionally better at 10.3 percent.

Asked to choose which future they prefer, all the groups choose the second scenario except the economists, who choose the first. The economists undoubtedly think they are smarter than the public by recognizing that 25 percent growth of the American economy will make Americans far better off than 10 percent growth, even if Japan's economy grows simultaneously by phenomenally greater percentages. But the laymen may actually be smarter than the economists in choosing more balanced growth between the world's two largest economies.

Wealth, after all, is always *relative* wealth—relative to socially conditioned norms. Today's Americans who live below the poverty line often have cars, TV sets, washing machines, microwaves, hot and cold running water, heat, and other conveniences that even the richest king of a few centuries ago could not enjoy. Today it is possible to have all these things and still live in grinding, oppressive poverty.

If Japan races ahead of the United States economically, American society will feel it in many respects, even if our own economy continues to grow at rates better than present. The kind of unbalanced growth suggested by Reich's first scenario would ultimately undermine all the major strengths of the American economy and pass leadership to Japan. America might really become a techno-colony under such circumstances.

The right answer to Reich's test is neither the first nor the second scenario. The right answer is to find the ways to match the complementary strengths of the two economies to overcome their weaknesses, with the net result that *both* countries grow robustly and in relatively balanced ways.

The Next Step: Aikido Thinking

Of all the Japanese martial arts, *aikido* is perhaps the most intellectually interesting. Although its founder once cautioned that "words and letters can never adequately describe Aikido,"[11] a feeble attempt to do so would include highlighting these elements:

- Aikido aims to win by using the attacker's energy and momentum, rather than one's own.
- It emphasizes subduing attackers rather than killing them; it is, according to its founder, "not an art for defeating others; it is for the unification of the world."[12] Harmonization with natural forces in the world is extremely important: aikido itself translates very roughly as "the way of harmony."
- To the extent that aikido encourages a "fight to the death," that fight is said not to be with one's attacker but inside one's self—between the constantly competing tensions of the lower and higher selves.
- Every aikido technique presupposes multiple attackers and the movements remain the same regardless of the number of opponents.

Conceptually and philosophically, aikido serves as an apt metaphor for the new strategy America needs in dealing with Japan. The first point above is the most important. While it would be nice, from an American point of view, to hope that the U.S. economy could develop its own force and momentum to outcompete Japan's, that prospect is unlikely, at least in the visible future. More realistic is the possibility that the United States can turn

Japanese economic strength to American competitive advantage, not by opposing it with brute force and "get tough" measures, but by judiciously leveraging it.

The other points are also relevant: What we must seek is a way of making U.S.-Japan economic interactions not zero-sum games, but positive-sum games where both sides win. The road to doing this lies in harmonizing the two economic systems, which are now at sharp odds on many points, and in harmonizing both systems with the global economy. The energy to revitalize the American economy must ultimately come not from tapping America's desire to bash Japan—we are running out of steam there, anyway—but rather from arousing the higher purpose of America out of the lower depths that now dominate our economic and political decision making. The same approach is needed in thinking about our "multiple attackers"—the other major economic competitors in Asia and Europe.

In Search of a Bold Vision

No serious student of U.S.-Japan relations can fail to be impressed by the complementary nature of our two unique societies. If one were to grow an "ideal" variety of capitalism in a hothouse, it would certainly have features from both systems—and seek to have none of either side's problems. The list of qualities that could be considered American national virtues reads like a list of Japanese weaknesses and problems. The same is true the other way around: Japan seems to lead the world in many kinds of "hardware"; the United States leads in software. Japan has little global clout either militarily or politically; the United States is a superpower on both counts. America is a melting pot thriving on diversity; Japan has been an inward society thriving on homogeneity . . . and so on. Inside out, mirror images, opposite poles attract, synergies—all are apt descriptions of the relationship of Japanese and American societies.

For all our oppositeness, the United States and Japan have somehow managed to construct what is, in today's world, the most economically consequential relationship of any two nation-states. The substance of the relationship—imports and exports, capital flows, technology flows, knowledge flows, business deals,

human interchanges—grows steadily, in spite of political acrimony. We are indeed "interdependent," as the academic experts
on U.S.-Japan relations never fail to point out.

Until quite recently, only the United States seemed to face
daunting economic challenges, while Japan's possibilities seemed
unlimited. Now, concern about the future is somewhat more
equally shared, although Americans, on the whole, are more fearful of the future than the Japanese—as well they should be. But
the fact is that both societies face certain obvious limits and certain
acute problems. Both societies are politically gridlocked on at
least some key questions. Both are virtually inert in the face of
at least some badly needed adaptations.

Now that Japan is a bit less fearsome in the American mind,
now that the bursting of the bubble has sobered a previously
arrogant Japan, now that the interdependence is a bit more balanced, perhaps we can look at each other more realistically. Perhaps both sides can even dare to think about expanding and
building on our interdependence for mutual benefit. Perhaps we
can begin to see each other as holding at least some aspects of
the solutions to our separate problems.

Every expert on U.S.-Japan relations will tell you that Cold
War assumptions—specifically, a mutual interest in containing the
Soviet Union—provided the glue cementing America and Japan
together even during the worst trade disputes. Today, those same
experts will tell you that the two sides "lack a vision" about the
future. Now that the Cold War is over and security links can no
longer be considered decisive in underpinning the relationship,
what next? As one blue-ribbon panel composed of top American
business and government officials put it:

> America's relationship with Japan is coming to the end of an
> era. . . . In the past, a common overriding interest in containing
> the threat from the Soviet Union sheltered U.S.-Japan ties from
> the effects of trade and other economic frictions. In the post–Cold
> War period, however, a new basis for the relationship will have to
> be established or economic conflict could bring the alliance to an
> end.[13]

Yet no one seems to know exactly what the new basis or new
vision for the alliance should be. Nor is there much certainty

about the future of a U.S.-Japan global partnership in light of the efforts to create a multilateral framework for international decision making that includes the European Community and others.

Conventional wisdom among foreign policy cognoscenti correctly senses that there is something special and unique about U.S.-Japan synergies and that efforts should be made not only to prevent devastating clashes, but to capture the benefits of these synergies. Thus, we frequently hear that the two countries should work for more amicable relations, expanded economic, technological, and intellectual ties, and greater global cooperation in fields like environmental research, basic science, or development aid to emerging democracies. But little new is happening along these lines.

Official talk in both Washington and Tokyo glibly asserts that both nations are building some sort of "global partnership," yet the concept remains a vague generality, hostage to domestic political considerations. A formula widely accepted on both sides of the Pacific in word if not in deed is that the United States should focus on putting its economic house in order while Japan should focus on opening its markets and assuming greater global leadership responsibilities. Perhaps there is progress in these directions, but it is glacial.

For all the talk of closer cooperation, U.S.-Japan ties at the leadership level are cooler and more distant than they have been in a long time. Richard Holbrooke, the former East Asia specialist for the Carter administration's State Department, wrote of the crisis in U.S.-Japan relations provoked by the Bush trip to Tokyo in 1992:

Everyone knows—and has paid rhetorical lip service for years to—the proposition that these two mightiest of economies (together amounting to 40% of the world's gross national product) have a responsibility to address pressing world problems that during the Cold War received insufficient attention.

But just when the Cold War has finally ended and the moment arrived to put substantive flesh on those rhetorical bones, two weak leaders allowed domestic politics to turn them away from their original (and worthy) game plan and toward pandering to their own protectionist constituencies. In a word, political weakness drove President Bush and Prime Minister Miyazawa into positions with which neither man could possibly feel comfortable—and from which they must extricate themselves. Both men . . . should tell the people of both nations the truth: while we have many problems to resolve, we have even more opportunities before us if we work together.[14]

Well, Bush has lost his chance to tell the people the truth, but Clinton still has that opportunity. Yet he is unknown in Japan, and his own Japan policy is torn between the contradictory expertise of different advisors. The situation calls for the presentation of a big, bold, dramatic vision to end the drift and jolt both sides into action. And here is one proposed starting point for such a vision: *a joint project to construct a Trans-Pacific Community.*

The Trans-Pacific Community would link the two economies in maximally synergistic ways. An economic community in the broadest sense—concerning itself with cross-border trade, investment, finance, technology, and the macroeconomic framework—it would be more than a free trade zone and less than a political union. It would resemble today's European Community in that it would be a conscious, legal, specific effort to blur boundaries and create the dynamic of a single economy. But it would not share the EC's troubling ambition to achieve federalism on the political front.

The Trans-Pacific Community would require shared institutions and structures capable of making, implementing, and enforcing economic policy. It would be energized by a variety of public-private partnerships to promote cooperation in sharing resources, technology, and the burdens of global development aid and peacekeeping.

Pioneered by the United States and Japan, the Trans-Pacific Community should be open to other members as it evolves. Indeed, it would provide a strategic beginning to the ultimate task of linking the world's various economic communities—the European Community (EC), the Asia/Pacific Economic Cooperation group (APEC), the North American Free Trade Agreement (NAFTA), the Latin American group (Mercosur), and others— under one global economic umbrella.

The effort to construct such a community could be one that lifts both our economies out of what may otherwise be long-term torpor and low growth and provides a liberalizing kick to trade, investment, and competition. It would help Americans capitalize on the economic vitality of Japan and help the Japanese open up and internationalize. It would facilitate the efforts of people in both countries to get more of the much-heralded boom effects of the globalizing economy, while suffering fewer of its problems.

The Trans-Pacific Community's benefits would extend beyond the realm of the economic. Such a community could provide a new frontier for two postindustrial societies and define many of the new ways of doing business in the twenty-first century. One should be mindful of Jacques Delors's sagacious understatement about the European Community's 1992 project: "No one can fall in love with the idea of a single market—there's nothing romantic or sexy about it." But the effort to pioneer a new postnational economic order on the basis of the combined strengths of the United States and Japan would, if nothing else, be a refreshing tonic poured over the fabric of our exhausted and cynical cultures. It might even hold the possibility of awakening the spirit of daring and of experimentation which is now so sorely lacking throughout the developed world.

In a certain sense, such a community is already arising as a result of spontaneous forces of the marketplace. As IBM president Jack D. Kuehler said after rejecting a go-it-without-the-Japanese approach in computer memory chips and announcing his firm's new alliance with Japan's Toshiba, "Companies need to be able to compete globally to survive. Survival is the first priority. Nationalistic factors are second priority."[15]

The political, social, and economic changes of the last few years have confirmed what the marketplace had already been indicating for a long time: There is no going it alone, there is only going global. Even so, the process of going global will be smoother if it is intelligently conceived rather than simply the product of laissez-faire benign neglect.

"We are past the point where the U.S. can do all this on our own," observes political economist Michael Borrus of the economic challenges of the twenty-first century. "The question is how to reorganize ourselves so that we can get what we need from abroad while safeguarding the values we hold most dear."[16]

A structured partnership with Japan is increasingly necessary as the economic stakes grow. One of the key problems the two countries face right now is their lack of collective institutions.

Negotiators and diplomats may work out deals, but there is no real enforcement mechanism aside from the clumsy international proceedings of the GATT and the theater of the absurd that now passes for antidumping legal procedures in American courts. No structured way exists to carry out the horse trades necessary for achieving harmonization and balance in the two economies. And few institutions exist to expand the shared long-term interests of the two countries. In fact, the most historically prominent such institution, the U.S.-Japan security relationship, is rapidly declining in importance.

What is needed is not so much the *creation* of a Trans-Pacific Community, because a de facto U.S.-Japan economic community is already taking shape. Instead, what is needed is the political *organization* of it, the determination of a framework for it, the setting of a conscious direction for it so as to get the greatest benefits and minimize the chaos. Going in such a direction requires the kind of strategic thinking on the part of government that has been absent for twelve years. But the exercise of trying to figure out how best to cooperate with Japan may allow the breakthrough in Washington that trying to figure out how to compete with Japan has not.

A Postindustrial Organization

Although our world is witnessing spectacular social sea changes, most people—and particularly most political leaders—are turning out to be conservatives and traditionalists. The end of the Cold War has not yielded the creative, innovative ideas demanded by the new realities.

It is therefore no surprise that most of the regional economic groupings that have arisen are based not on the needs and requirements of postindustrial society, but on the *preindustrial* logic of geography and culture. Indeed, today's existing economic groupings bear very specific resemblances to old empires, ancient trading routes, and historical spheres of influence.

Clearly, immediate tangible economic benefits can be reaped by amalgamating the economies of countries that share borders, truck routes, ocean littorals, languages, and business cultures. The single market enjoyed by the *United* States of America is perhaps the pre-eminent expression of this fact. Europe, although it may never be as unified a market as the United States, is also demonstrating that a bigger, more integrated economy is better than several smaller ones. There is certainly nothing wrong in principle with the Free Trade Agreement with Canada, or the efforts to create a similar arrangement with Mexico—although NAFTA could surely benefit from much more strategic thought and planning about jobs, investment flows, and economic and environmental impact than it was given in its formative stages.

The United States, however, should not limit itself to structured economic partnerships with its immediate neighbors. An economic zone shared with Japan presents more opportunity, greater potential for synergy, and more long-term benefits than any other single economic relationship the United States could forge today. In an age when data and capital flow as instantaneously to Tokyo as to Toronto, Americans need not limit our partnership horizons to the old logic of physical geography.

The Trans-Pacific Community is inherently a postindustrial phenomenon—a new kind of organization for a new age. While it requires governments to establish the skeleton of its operations, the essence of it is a lean, loose business-oriented organization. Its purpose is not to micromanage the U.S.-Japan economy. Rather, it is to macromanage the broad parameters of competition and cooperation, in order to give full play to the free flow (and clash) of economic forces in the marketplace and the social system.

The concept of a Trans-Pacific Community provides some of the answers to pressing American problems: where the United States is going to get some of the investment capital and technology to renew its manufacturing base; how the United States is going to exploit to maximum advantage its continuing areas of economic leadership; how Americans are going to learn the new skills needed for the new economic era; how competitive pressures can best be marshaled to force the necessary changes in the U.S. business system; how the American economy can best capture the benefits of the booming growth markets throughout the Asia-Pacific region; and how the United States can bring down the cost of its massive defense budget without jeopardizing genuine security considerations.

At the same time, it also answers some of the key questions

Japan faces: how Japanese business can find symbiosis in a global world; how Japan can transit from its current isolation to the center of world leadership; how Japan can shape the Asia-Pacific region into a coherent economic zone without itself appearing to be an overbearing leader; how the Japanese domestic policy gridlock can be broken, consumption stimulated, and a more consumer-oriented society evolved; and where Japan can get some of the creative "software" resources it needs to reinvent its society.

In short, many of the elements of what both sides need most critically at this juncture in history are possible in this deal. Japan, which may be reaching the limit of how much it will change out of fear that the United States may turn protectionist, gets *positive* benefits in this deal, which should provide greater motivation for change. The United States, meanwhile, capitalizes on some of Japan's strengths, leverages its own to greater value, embraces the dynamism of the Pacific Rim as a leader rather than a mere participant, and sets up a framework through which it can be the leading force in designing the new global economic system.

Closer cooperation between the United States and Japan, while it could be seen as a threat by others in Europe or Asia, does not have to be antithetical to the interests of multilateralism and globalism. This is especially true if the Trans-Pacific Community, whatever its shape, makes clear its openness to others and its desire to interconnect with others.

Arthur Dunkel, the relentlessly negotiating chief of the GATT talks, points out, "I don't see any contradiction between developing large free trade areas or economic associations and making progress on the global trading order through GATT." The GATT article that concerns itself with free trade areas has been recently reinforced, he says. "One can argue that greater regional harmonization of economic policy will make the GATT process less full of conflict on a global basis."

Sometime in the twenty-first century it is possible that a single economic community, with a harmonized set of business rules and technological standards, will embrace much or even all of the globe. As the two most future-oriented societies in the world at this late stage of the twentieth century, the United States and Japan would be well advised to follow the visionary path the Europeans have charted and take the next big step toward a truly global economic system: the creation of the first formal economic union that leaps oceans and time zones.

Half a millennium ago, Christopher Columbus set out from Europe to find Asia—but found America instead. Now, the circle uncovered by his discovery can be completed. The two new economic worlds of America and East Asia can be connected as a precursor to a linkage with the revitalized old world of Europe. Then the Triad can set about the even more daunting task of bringing in the developing world as well.

U.S.-Japan, Inc.: The Deal of the Next Century

Let us step out into the future and imagine an optimistic best-case scenario: A Trans-Pacific Community (TPC) has come into existence in the late 1990s, launched at the initiative of the U.S. president and the Japanese prime minister, chartered by both the U.S. Congress and the Japanese Diet, presided over by a bina-tional executive body, with shared policy-making and enforce-ment institutions.

The broad goal of the TPC would be to ensure the free move-ment of people, capital, goods, services, technology, and infor-mation between the two countries. Naturally, this would not take place immediately, but on a defined timetable. The early phase of the community's institutional life would be largely devoted to harmonizing the structural differences between the two econ-omies in order to make such interpenetration truly free and max-imally beneficial.

In putting together a shared economic community, everything gets put on the table, and the hands of negotiators are no longer tied as they are today by the narrow, compartmentalized nature of the issues. It allows the kind of big-picture, *realpolitik*, geo-economic horse trading that is necessary: If the Japanese want continued American military security, then they must either be willing to pay for it directly, or pay for it in the form of increased purchases of American goods. (The portion of the "services" rendered by the U.S. military to Japan that are not paid for by Tokyo has been calculated at about 75 percent of the U.S. trade deficit with Japan—and much more if one includes a global def-inition of Japanese security needs, rather than a local territorial one.)

The TPC would feature an affirmative action system to break through trade and investment barriers, as well as a court or an

arbitration system to enforce open markets and suggest remedies
to specific problems of access. Just as the European Community
has done, the Trans-Pacific Community would make exceptions
and develop specific policies for particularly critical matters.

The key goal of the TPC during its early years would be to
promote higher levels of sustainable growth in both economies.
To do this, TPC policies would focus on supporting the renewal
of America's industrial base and competitive infrastructure, and
the internationalization, opening, and liberalization of the Japanese economic system.

Japanese companies—which are short of land for expansion and
increasingly short of labor at home—would be vigorously encouraged to locate new facilities in the American market. Instead
of today's patchwork of American state and local governments
outbidding each other in trying to attract Japanese factories, there
would be a centralized binational system of tax credits and other
incentives to promote the twin goals of Japanese companies moving production to the United States and American companies
developing deeper roots in the Japanese market. A joint U.S.-
Japan panel would review cross-border investment with the aim
of encouraging it and maximizing its positive impact on American
economic security. This would be a significant departure from
today's Cold War–oriented U.S. review process on foreign investment, whereby the official Committee on Foreign Investment
in the United States (CFIUS) sits in judgment on foreign acquisitions of American companies using traditional "national security" criteria.

The right questions to ask in the future will have increasingly
less to do with worries about vital war-making technology slipping
into the hands of our Japanese or European economic partners.
Instead, what political representatives should be asked to consider
is whether or not a specific foreign investment will add skilled
jobs, open up new markets, expand the local tax base, and otherwise stimulate economic growth.

On automobiles, semiconductors, or other hotly contested
products—assuming these areas are still bones of contention by
the time such a community could be developed—the TPC would
offer Japanese companies free access to the U.S. market, provided
the emphasis was on local American manufacturing.

The United States would take special measures to assure Japan a supply of oil and other resources, as well as agricultural crops. Japan would thus be free to reduce its farmland and reap all the benefits for consumption entailed in that shift. With special access to American resources, Japan's *need* to run large trade surpluses would be curtailed.

In addition to general market-opening measures, Japan would be particularly encouraged to use advanced technology and services from American companies through joint ventures, partnerships, and cross-shareholdings of various kinds.

Under these circumstances, many U.S.-Japan business alliances that are now unthinkable could be promoted. For example, the U.S. aircraft industry, one of America's crown jewels of technology, is currently hesitant to develop extensive tie-ups with Japanese companies, and the Japanese side is hesitant to invest, because of the industry's close connection to the defense sector and other political misgivings. Thus, McDonnell-Douglas floundered around for over a year seeking to put together a re-capitalization strategy involving Taiwan, when a tie-up with a Japanese company would have been an obvious solution to McDonnell's financial problems.

The same has been true for other troubled American companies in high-profile industries from automobiles to computers: Even when the American side can think past the competitive problems to develop a vision for collaboration with a deep-pocketed Japanese partner, the Japanese side has become reluctant to make investments that could become politicized and negatively regarded. A CFIUS-type organization, with a mandate to base itself on *economic* security concerns rather than *military* security concerns, would be instrumental in encouraging transpacific corporate marriages.

As to matters of market access within the TPC, business lobbies would no longer have to try to get government attention to press their case with the other side. Instead, American companies or industry groups (or Japanese companies or industry groups, as the case may be) could go directly to a binational arbitration panel. Arbitrators would then rule on questions such as whether products were being systematically kept out of the market and detail the remedies to be taken. While the arbitrators would be citizens of the two countries, they would follow a code of conduct designed to make them as independent of their nationality and government

policy as possible. The experience of European Community institutions again shows that it is possible for individual decision-
makers to rise above the narrow confines of nationality, in much
the way the justices of the U.S. Supreme Court have a reputation
for rendering decisions that confound those who appointed them.

The TPC would also have a system such as Europe's "structural
funds" scheme. In the EC, contributions from wealthy countries
are recycled to the weakest regions in an effort to narrow the
grossest disparities of economic development. In the TPC, structural funds might be raised either through direct national contributions, very modest corporate income taxes, or a joint system
of value-added sales taxes. The funds would then be used for
infrastructure building, education and training, R&D, and other
means for expanding and harmonizing the competitive capabilities of both countries.

TPC structural funds could also be used to back efforts to
promote imports in Japan or rebuild America's manufacturing base
by providing low-cost loans or seed equity investments to private
sector companies engaged in such efforts. Funds could also be
made available to support new transpacific technology consortia
and environmental research projects, or targeted to other goals
such as supporting the creation of collaborative industries.

Eventually, the TPC might merge large parts of Japanese and
American government budgets for scientific research and technology development. Companies taking active measures to create
transpacific links might benefit from special tax treatment and
incentives.

Perhaps no issue is more central to long-term economic balance
than macroeconomic and financial policies. The shift to free-
floating currency exchange rates of the 1970s has been a major
negative for the world economy. It has promoted speculation and
the narrow interests of the financial services sector at the expense
of rational strategies for well-rounded economic growth. The damage has been visible in all developed world economies.

Today, currency rates typically fluctuate by 10 percent to 20
percent each year, and sometimes even more. Even in the most
stable years, fluctuations are sufficient to turn a product that was
originally priced profitably into one being "dumped" in another
market. Europe's drive toward a common currency has been a
highly intelligent response to the destructive chaos of the last

financial generation. Common currencies, or at least closely targeted exchange rate zones, not only help remove economic distortions, they represent one of the best uses of the invisible hand of the marketplace to harmonize economies.

If harmonization in a Trans-Pacific Community is to be achieved in part by Japan becoming more of a consumer society and the United States becoming more of a producer society, then the macroeconomic environment must encourage those directions. Just as German fiscal discipline has been brought to bear on the once-profligate French, the TPC would have a shared financial authority, perhaps even a shared central bank, which would work to pressure the United States to become more fiscally prudent. A shared macroeconomic policy would also seek to get Japan to reduce savings rates and consume more. Special incentives would be built in for consuming imported goods and services.

Ideally, the two countries could join Europe's efforts to put an end to the international exchange rate casino by agreeing on standardizing the value of the dollar against the yen. (Accomplishing such a breakthrough in calming international financial chaos would also provide the basis for creating a standardized world system linking the dollar, the yen, and the European ECU.) With a stable exchange rate, businessmen compete against one less major unknown in an uncertain world. Long-term cross-border investment ties would be enhanced. The present temporary global victory against inflation could be consolidated.

The TPC would use U.S.-Japan synergies to address a multitude of challenges. A single combined patent system, for example, could be designed to address the increasing inadequacies of both American and Japanese patent law and ensure better respect for sophisticated new kinds of intellectual property than is the current norm. A joint U.S.-Japan environmental research corporation could not only help develop clean energy sources, electric cars, and pollution control equipment, but could share the commercial benefits of what Peter Drucker has predicted will be one of the few large growth markets of the twenty-first century for private sector business: environmental cleanup.

The Japanese, who produce nearly 2.5 units more of finished goods using the same amount of energy as U.S. manufacturers, could transfer some of their know-how in this crucial area. The two countries could find ways to explore and tap new energy

sources in the Americas, East Asia, Russia, and China, thus promoting economic growth in those regions and reducing reliance
on Middle Eastern oil.

Through the framework of the community, initiatives could be
launched to narrow the structural differences between the two
business systems on such mundane yet crucial competitive matters as antitrust law, environmental regulations, accounting procedures, banking and financial service regulations. It is in these
areas where the international business playing field is often at its
least level. While it is not necessary to create universal standards,
the approach used by the European Community of "harmonization"—narrowing the differences without trying to eliminate
them completely—would allow business and technological competition to take place in a freer, more positive, more productive
fashion.

Unlike today's European Community, the initial phase of a
Trans-Pacific Community would be focused on economic and
business issues, without seeking to create a political union. (Indeed, European efforts to move fast on creating a political union
have been responsible for triggering new opposition to previously
accepted agreements on economic union.) However, a certain
spillover of economic issues into the realm of politics would be
inevitable—and positive. The Japanese Diet and the U.S. Congress might exchange official observers, who would be able to
comment on matters of mutual concern; both countries might
create cabinet-level Offices of Trans-Pacific Cooperation; the mass
media of the two countries would become more interlinked.

Forums within the community could be created to consult,
fund, and dispense development aid jointly to other countries,
particularly newly emerging democracies. The recycling of Japan's
vast current account surplus—which in the last few years has
represented the lion's share of *all* net new funds for cross-border
investment on a global basis—would become a subject of binational discussion, rather than unilateral Japanese strategy.

As the functions of economic and military peacekeeping blend
more closely together, the two countries might also consider initiatives to converge their expenditures and consult about their
allocation. Assuming the United States continues to be the world's
principal superpower in maintaining military security, and Japan
focuses its human and financial resources on economic aid to less

developed countries, each country should be sharing relatively equal portions of the total burden.

As the Cold War fades and the classified uses of defense technology become less significant, the two countries could establish a consortium to commercialize the treasure house of leading-edge technology now under Pentagon wraps. The Japanese private sector could lend its particularly skilled hands in this process not only to commercializing defense-related research, but also to helping American companies reap the benefits from the research findings of more than five hundred other government-funded labs.

In the context of an overall U.S.-Japan deal, the American side would help Japan grow into its full-fledged role as a world leader. Washington would carry the ball on the effort to get a permanent Security Council seat for Japan at the United Nations, as well as obtaining fuller Japanese representation in other multilateral bodies from the Conference on Security and Cooperation in Europe (CSCE) to the IMF and the World Bank.

Having laid the groundwork for a viable Trans-Pacific Community and shaped its original institutions, the United States and Japan could then welcome the membership of other countries on both sides of the Pacific. Eventually, a structural link to the European Community could be forged. By then, the EC will have brought into its orbit much of Eastern Europe and some of the former Soviet republics. The linking of the Trans-Pacific Community with the Atlantic community would form the basis for an economically harmonized Triad. This new organization would govern the process of meeting the challenges of the developing world and drawing more of the globe out of the age of nationalism and into the borderless age that will follow.

Is all of the above too idealistic a path for the hard-headed, highly politicized world of U.S.-Japan relations? Going in such a direction is obviously an enormous challenge. Yet we are headed that way, even though few have dared to put a name to the process.

As a matter of fact, the U.S.-Japan dialogue known as the Structural Impediments Initiative (SII), which has been going on since 1989, has already provided the basic outline of the Trans-Pacific Community's initial agenda. This can be seen in the following summary, which is distilled from the SII's binational "working group" report:[17]

What the United States wants Japan to do

- Reduce high savings rate, stimulate consumption.
- Liberalize and open the distribution system to foreign companies.
- Develop more rational land use policies.
- Reform the *keiretsu* system so that foreigners can have better access to the Japanese economy.
- End exclusionary business practices.
- Increase public spending.

What Japan wants the United States to do

- Raise the savings rate and curb excessive consumption.
- Augment corporate investment.
- Lengthen the time horizons of business.
- Devote more effort and investment to civilian R&D.
- End protectionist government regulations.
- Promote export-consciousness among domestic companies.
- Improve the system of education and training.

The working group of SII negotiators includes high-level officials from Japan's Ministry of Foreign Affairs, MITI, MoF, and the Economic Planning Agency, as well as the U.S. State Department, Treasury Department, Commerce Department, and Office of the Trade Representative. In three years of SII talks, almost all of the right problems have been identified. SII negotiators have even proposed some innovative solutions.

At one point, the two sides exchanged what former MITI vice-minister Makoto Kuroda admitted were "a bunch of very crazy ideas" for reforming each other's systems.[18] The Japanese side suggested that the United States limit the number of credit cards citizens can have in order to reduce consumption and debt; forbid junk bonds; place more emphasis on teaching the fundamentals of manufacturing in business school curricula; impose high gasoline taxes to get gas-guzzling cars off the road; build a network of high-speed trains; end the mortgage interest deduction for expensive homes; reduce the American corporate pay gap norm of forty to one between executives and skilled workers to something more like the Japanese norm of eleven to one; and require public companies to report financial information semiannually instead of quarterly, to try to break the short-term influence on management thinking of quarter-to-quarter reports.

The American side, meanwhile, proposed that Japan increase public spending from 6 percent of GNP to 10 percent; repeal the large retail store law that makes it so difficult to open department stores and shopping malls; and require businesses to disclose the minutes of *keiretsu* group meetings.

Crazy? Maybe, but also quite interesting and very much to the point. The reality is that the two sides are emerging as each other's conscience. They are often more right about what the other side should do than they are in their own domestic policy making.

The idea of the Trans-Pacific Community assumes that the Japanese and American practice of capitalism will remain very different, but that balance and benefit can be achieved by coordinating the interplay of the two systems and matching strengths and weaknesses. The TPC is not by any means a substitute for America's domestic competitiveness agenda. Rather, it is a vehicle for improving the conditions for working on the problems of American competitiveness and enhancing the benefits once those problems are successfully resolved by enlarging the theater of the American economy and marketplace.

It is said that the United States is Japan's only effective opposition party. Ever since Commodore Perry's "Black Ships" forced Japan to open its door to the outside world in the nineteenth century, *gaiatsu* ("foreign pressure") has been used by Japanese leaders as one of the best excuses to make needed changes. This has been especially true in the last decade. Almost every major change in Japan's economic and political life made nominally in response to "American pressure" has been a net positive for Japan.

What is new in the last few years is that the United States has begun to feel the heat of Japanese *gaiatsu*. Occasionally, this reverse *gaiatsu* is political, as when MITI responds to American calls for opening Japan's markets by issuing reports documenting all the ways the United States protects *its* markets. But more often Japanese pressure is economic. It is *gaiatsu* of the Darwinian, adapt-or-die type. Much of America's industrial revival of recent years is directly attributable to companies being forced to take necessary steps to stave off Japanese competitors. This has been profoundly healthy for the United States economy.

Jonathan Rauch put it well in *The Outnation*, his recent book of observations on Japan and the Japanese: "As for Americans, what is our own best hope? The only pressure that works on so stubborn and strong a people is steadfast economic competition. We will have it from Japan and it will improve us."[19]

In short, the possibility now exists for large-scale "mutual *gaiatsu*"—and for having it work for the betterment of both societies.

The SII process is a virtuous intellectual exercise. But it is all talk and no action. It has no teeth for mutual enforcement of each other's commitments. The Japanese side has said that its touchstone question for whether the United States is living up to its commitments under SII is whether the federal budget deficit is being cut. Clearly, there is no progress on that score. The same is true the other way around: American negotiators have said the key test of whether Japan is truly breaking down its structural barriers is whether prices in the domestic consumer market are equalizing with foreign prices—which, so far, they are not.

Under the shared framework of a Trans-Pacific Community, these issues would be handled in a very different way. We would have binational institutions capable of deploying carrots as well as sticks to see that timetables are set and the goals of harmonization are, in fact, achieved.

Many thoughtful voices are beginning to make soundings around the edges of the concept of a formally structured U.S.-Japan symbiosis. The Commission on U.S.-Japan Relations for the Twenty-first Century, a group composed of distinguished American business and government leaders, issued a report at the end of 1991 calling on the two countries to launch a movement to create a "Pacific Community . . . aimed at evolving rules and structures to make the Pacific economic regime genuinely open and inclusive."[20] To begin the process of constructing a Pacific Community, the commission called on Washington and Tokyo to issue a Pacific Charter, which would seek to rally all the countries of the region around fundamental principles such as free trade and investment, open markets, and human rights.

A U.S.-Japan free trade area is perhaps the most concrete proposal actually getting serious political consideration on both sides of the Pacific. In various ways, important political leaders in both countries have come forward to endorse such a concept.

Stephen J. Solarz, the former chairman of the Asia Pacific Subcommittee of the U.S. House of Representatives, and Nobuo Matsunaga, former Japanese ambassador to the United States, have explicitly called for a free trade association between the United States and Japan, which would ultimately be open to other participants. Looking at the troubled, compromised nature of the GATT process, they argued that a U.S.-Japan free trade area would be a complement to GATT if the Uruguay Round succeeds, and a healthy alternative if it continues to flounder:

> Whichever way GATT goes, the United States and Japan should begin discussions on creating an open economic association or free trade association that would include all other countries of Asia and the Pacific Rim for consultation and participation. By the sheer size of the two economies and their joint share of world trade, others would have powerful incentives to abjure protectionism and participate.[21]

C. Fred Bergsten, director of the Institute for International Economics, suggests what he has dubbed the "G-2" approach of "collective economic management" between the United States and Japan. A "G-2" relationship would help America address its post–Cold War economic agenda at the same time as it would provide Japan with what it most wants: "a natural route to the larger, proactive rather than reactive, world role that is widely sought but not yet conceived."[22]

Bergsten sees G-2 as the beginnings of a Triad-wide system that would manage international monetary affairs and promote free trade and a free investment climate among the world's leading economies. He also addresses the issue of why the United States should pursue such a dialogue bilaterally with Japan, rather than trilaterally with Europe included:

> A central question for the United States–Japan relationship at this time is whether a tripolar response to these historical transformations is essential or whether the G-2 should proceed on its own. There are at least three arguments for starting with the bilateral approach. First, it will be some time before Europe can complete its regional economic and monetary unification and thus be able to play a full global role. Second, the intensity of U.S.-Japan pressures requires the two countries to move ahead to deal with their problems as rapidly as possible. Third, bilateral negotiations (à la

SII) are simply more practical and likely to succeed on such complex issues. . . . Any new G-2 efforts would presumably leave the door open for subsequent partnership with Europe.[23]

In a survey of economists, high-tech entrepreneurs, and futurists in California, the *San Jose Mercury News* found a number of trend-spotters talking about various policies a G-2 relationship might engender. Some spoke of the need for a Japanese "Marshall Plan of the '90s" to help rebuild the American economy:

What's needed is the U.S. government putting together a plan for economic redevelopment, then asking the Japanese to play a role in it with money, manufacturing expertise and technology. . . . Although conventional American wisdom sees Japanese investment as a negative, experts argue that if it is controlled, it can bring jobs, expertise and technology back into the United States, and actually help nurture struggling industries.[24]

Former U.S. defense secretary Harold Brown has elaborated a proposal for organized U.S.-Japan interchanges that would seek to use each country's main strength to overcome the other's main weakness. As he sees the future, "Japan transfers advanced manufacturing technology and organization techniques for commercialization to the United States. Through deeper scientific collaboration, Japan learns (from the United States) to promote more creative basic research."[25] But Brown is explicit in suggesting that without conscious, structured efforts, such mutually beneficial scenarios for interdependence will not happen. In fact, he is one of those warning that without specific new initiatives to bring the two countries together, either Japan will continue to get more economic benefit from its relationship with the United States than vice-versa, or the relationship will become decoupled.

In Japan, the search is also on for new forms to accelerate and institutionalize interdependence. The current campaign of Keidanren, the Japanese business federation, is to promote something called *kyosei*, which translates roughly as economic symbiosis. Keidanren's appeal for *kyosei* solutions to U.S.-Japan problems has led to many new articulations of how best to link the two economies.

Toshihiro Kiribuchi, managing director of Omron, argues for

"Japanese perestroika" to help move Japan more toward the openness, creativity, and individuality of America—without going to the extreme. Kiribuchi also has a long-term idea about global convergence. The EC, NAFTA, and Pacific Rim Community will coexist for a while, he says. But they are only "interim stages in the formation of a globally unified economy and culture," which, according to Kiribuchi, will be based largely on the American model, and include wide use of the dollar and the English language. The new world system will also "incorporate elements of many cultures" around its "Anglo-Saxon core." Japan, he believes, should welcome this change and try to contribute the positive aspects of its economic and social culture.[26]

Even Shintaro Ishihara, the Japanese "hawk" best known in the United States for what is perceived as "America-bashing" on his part, sometimes speaks of the two nations achieving some sort of "economic synthesis in the near future." The new world order, he says, "will be created by a blending, rather than a confrontation of East and West. The leaders, I believe, will be America and Japan."[27]

All of these comments and proposals are mere straws in the wind of change. But they all point to a set of new truths: The era of direct U.S.-Japan confrontation on trade and other matters has ended. The era when some Americans hoped their country would emulate Japanese strategies and win a head-to-head competition across the gamut of economic excellence is likewise over, because that goal is neither desired nor attainable by present-day American society. The era of imagining that Japan would continue uninterrupted along its trajectory of economic expansion has also closed. It is now clear that neither America nor the world will be "Japanized" at the rate of the late 1980s.

If and when America develops a national economic strategy, the right question will no longer be, "How can we outcompete Japan?" Rather, it will be, "How can we best leverage Japan's strengths and gain the most advantage from our increasingly symbiotic relationship?" In the meantime, looking at U.S.-Japan economic relations as an asset rather than a liability will help lead Washington closer to an intelligent national economic strategy for a global age.

Many will argue that a formal Trans-Pacific Community is an impossibly optimistic proposal for the future, given the antagonisms between the two countries. But as we have seen in this book, a growing linkage of American and Japanese economic interests is occurring anyway. To oppose this trend is to fight a rearguard, Luddite battle against history. As Machiavelli reminds us, the wise man who "adapts his policy to the times prospers, and likewise, the one whose policy clashes with the demands of the times does not."[28]

But those who merely accept or welcome the trend without thinking about how to organize, tame, and control the forces it unleashes are also making a serious mistake. Here, too, Machiavelli is instructive.

The Europe that Machiavelli knew was one of rapid change, much like our own. "Great changes and variations, beyond human imagining" were becoming features of daily reality. This was fostering a new belief that future events were beyond the control of men. Yes and no, averred Machiavelli, comparing political history to a river. When enraged, the river could violently flood the land, destroy buildings, and force everyone to flee. Yet the possibility of such violence does not make attempts to control the river fruitless. When a river is flowing quietly it is precisely the time to build embankments and dikes to protect against possible flooding.

"So it is with fortune," concludes Machiavelli. "She shows her potency when there is no well-regulated power to resist her, and her impetus is felt where she knows there are no embankments and dikes built to restrain her."[29]

Whether or not progress is made in vivifying a Trans-Pacific Community, or even just a free trade area, this is the decade to build "dikes and embankments"—the structures that can harness the powerful flows of U.S.-Japan economic relations to mutual benefit, rather than mutual adversity.

Notes

Introduction

1. Niccolò Machiavelli, *The Prince*, translated by George Bull, London: Penguin Books, 1981.

Chapter 1

1. Karen Elliott House, "Japan's Decline, America's Rise," *The Wall Street Journal*, April 21, 1992.
2. James J. Cramer, "We're Back! The Unsung Revival of American Manufacturing," *The New Republic*, April 27, 1992.
3. Howard Banks, "The World's Most Competitive Economy," *Forbes*, March 30, 1992.
4. A. Gary Shilling, "Wounded Giant," *Forbes*, April 27, 1992.
5. *Marketplace* radio broadcast, American Public Radio, April 15, 1992.
6. Alan Reynolds, "Fear Japan's Feeble Economy," *Wall Street Journal*, March 24, 1992.
7. Robert L. Bartley, *The Seven Fat Years and How to Do It Again*, New York: The Free Press, 1992.
8. Richard I. Kirkland, Jr., "What If Japan Triumphs?" *Fortune*, May 18, 1992.
9. David Warsh, "The Man from Mars (but Not Bob Bartley) Visits Kankakee," *Boston Globe*, April 5, 1992.
10. Maureen Dowd, "Voters Want Candidates to Take a Reality Check," *New York Times*, January 17, 1992.
11. Paul F. Horvitz, "CIA Study Warns that Japan Seeks Economic Domination," *International Herald Tribune*, June 8, 1991.
12. Andrew Dougherty, *Japan 2000*, unpublished draft, 1991.
13. Gene Koretz, "Economic Trends," *Business Week*, February 10, 1992.
14. Steven R. Weisman, "Stunned Japanese Offer Sympathy as Some Are Struck by Symbolism," *New York Times*, January 9, 1992.

15. T. R. Reid, "Tokyo Official Calls U.S. 'Subcontractor' to Japanese Economy," *International Herald Tribune*, January 21, 1992.
16. Jim Carlton and Neil Barsky, "Japanese Purchases of U.S. Real Estate Fall on Hard Times," *Wall Street Journal*, February 21, 1992.
17. Gale Eisenstodt, "Guessing Game," *Forbes*, May 11, 1992.
18. Robert Neff, "Japan: Will It Lose Its Competitive Edge?" *Business Week*, April 27, 1992.
19. "Now Hear This," *Fortune*, April 20, 1992.
20. "For the Record," *Business Tokyo*, June 1992.
21. Akio Morita, "A New Paradigm for True Partnership," text of speech delivered in Honolulu, Hawaii, January 3, 1992.
22. John J. Curran, "Why Japan Will Emerge Stronger," *Fortune*, May 18, 1992.
23. Karen Lowry Miller, "How Can You Call This a Recession?" *Business Week*, April 27, 1992.
24. Mortimer B. Zuckerman, "Washington's Nasty Addiction," *U.S. News & World Report*, May 4, 1992.
25. Gene Bylinsky, "A U.S. Comeback in Electronics?" *Fortune*, April 20, 1992.
26. Robert McGough and Richard Wrubel, "Second Chance," *Financial World*, April 28, 1992.
27. Mark Stahlman, "Is Mighty Japan Ready to Topple?" *Upside*, April 1992.
28. Peter Passell, "End of the Game for Motor City?" *New York Times*, October 23, 1991.
29. Carla Rapoport, "Why Japan Keeps On Winning," *Fortune*, July 15, 1991.

Chapter 2

1. Don Oberdorfer, "U.S.-Japan Relations Seen Suffering Worst Downturn in Decades," *Washington Post*, March 1, 1992.
2. Robert J. Samuelson, "The Loathing of Japan," *Washington Post*, February 19, 1992.
3. Lee A. Iacocca, "O.K., O.K., Call Me a Protectionist," *New York Times*, February 10, 1991.
4. Barnaby J. Feder, "Blunt Talk by Iacocca, Just Back from Japan," *New York Times*, January 11, 1992.
5. Lucy Soto, "Hollings-Japan Bashing," Associated Press, March 4, 1992.
6. Quentin Hardy, "Financial Markets Turmoil in Japan Leads to 'Jewish Conspiracy' Article," *Wall Street Journal*, July 3, 1992.

7. George Friedman and Meredith Lebard, *The Coming War with Japan*, New York: St. Martin's Press, 1991.
8. "Looking for Leadership," public opinion survey by Council on Competitiveness, Washington, D.C., November 1991.
9. Richard I. Kirkland, op. cit.
10. Paul Krugman, *The Age of Diminished Expectations*, Cambridge, Mass.: MIT Press, 1990, pp. 9–12.
11. Carla Rapoport, op. cit.
12. Christopher Farrell and Michael J. Mandel, "Industrial Policy," *Business Week*, April 6, 1992.
13. Steven Greenhouse, "The Calls for Industrial Policy Grow Louder," *New York Times*, July 19, 1992.
14. Machiavelli, op. cit.
15. Laurence Hooper and Jacob M. Schlesinger, "Pragmatism Wins as Rivals Start to Cooperate on Memory Chips," *Wall Street Journal*, July 14, 1992.
16. Ibid.
17. "MCC Abruptly Decides to Seek Cooperation by Japanese Firms," *Japan Digest*, October 31, 1991.
18. John Markoff, "Rethinking the National Chip Policy," *New York Times*, July 14, 1992.

Chapter 3

1. "Shoveling It," *San Jose Mercury News*, December 11, 1991.
2. Sam Nakagama, "Is Japan a Drag on the U.S. Recovery?" *New York Times*, May 10, 1992.
3. Sylvia Nasar, "Tokyo Slide Has No Shock Wave in the U.S.," *New York Times*, July 9, 1992.
4. Thomas F. O'Boyle, "Under Japanese Bosses, Americans Find Work Both Better and Worse," *Wall Street Journal*, November 27, 1991.
5. Paul Ingrassia, "Detroit Welcomes Japanese Investment," *Wall Street Journal*, May 8, 1991.
6. Gary R. Saxonhouse, "Sony Side Up: Japan's Contributions to the U.S. Economy," *Policy Review*, Spring 1991.
7. Doron P. Levin, "Toyota Plant in Kentucky Is Font of Ideas for U.S.," *New York Times*, May 5, 1992.
8. Sheldon Weinig, "The Guys in White Hats from Sony," *New York Times*, June 10, 1990.
9. Robert B. Reich, "Who Is Us?" *Harvard Business Review*, January–February 1990.

10. Richard Morin, "U.S. Gets Negative About Japan," *Washington Post*, February 14, 1992.

11. Stephen W. White, "The Global Marketplace," *National Forum*, Spring 1992.

12. David E. Sanger, "U.S. Tariff Appears to Backfire," *New York Times*, September 26, 1991.

13. Steve Lohr, "A Split over Machine Tool Imports," *New York Times*, October 7, 1991.

14. Claire Smith, "Baseball Will Allow Sale of Seattle Team to Japanese Group," *New York Times*, June 10, 1992.

15. T. R. Reid, "Wilder the Conciliator," *Washington Post*, October 10, 1991.

16. David Sanger, "U.S. Companies in Japan Say Things Aren't So Bad," *New York Times*, June 12, 1991.

17. Ibid.

18. James C. Morgan and J. Jeffrey Morgan, *Cracking the Japanese Market*, New York: Free Press, 1991.

Chapter 4

1. "The 1992 Cars," *Consumer Reports*, April 1992.

2. "Lexus Named Best Car," *New York Times*, May 28, 1992.

3. Alex Taylor III, "Why Toyota Keeps Getting Better and Better and Better," *Fortune*, November 19, 1990.

4. Winston Churchill, speech in the House of Commons, November 11, 1947.

5. James P. Womack, Daniel T. Jones, and Daniel Roos, *The Machine that Changed the World*, New York: Rawson Associates, 1990, pp. 12–15.

6. Ibid.

7. Ibid.

8. Ikujiro Nonaka, "The Knowledge-Creating Company," *Harvard Business Review*, November–December 1991.

9. "The Quality Imperative," *Business Week*, October 25, 1991.

10. "The Cracks in Quality," *The Economist*, April 18, 1992.

11. William J. Broad, "Japan Seen Passing U.S. in Research by Industry," *New York Times*, February 25, 1992.

12. Fujitsu advertisement, *Wall Street Journal*, June 1, 1992.

13. Council on Competitiveness, *Gaining New Ground*, Washington, D.C., 1991.

14. Peter Drucker, "Japan: New Strategies for a New Reality," *Wall Street Journal*, October 2, 1991.

15. Neil Gross, "This Man Really Knows How to Clean Up His Room," *Business Week*, October 25, 1991.
16. Marie-Louise Caravatti, "Business Needs More 'Dull' R&D," *New York Times*, October 6, 1991.
17. Ford S. Worthy, "Japan's Smart Secret Weapon," *Fortune*, August 12, 1991.
18. Brian Dumaine, "Closing the Innovation Gap," *Fortune*, December 2, 1991.
19. Gary Hamel and C. K. Prahalad, "Corporate Imagination and Expeditionary Marketing," *Harvard Business Review*, July–August 1991.
20. Ibid.
21. Fumio Kodama, "Flexible Manufacturing Frees Industry to Concentrate on Visions of the Future," *Japan Economic Journal*, May 25, 1991.
22. Council on Competitiveness, op. cit.
23. "Future View: Manufacturing Management in Crisis," *Manufacturing Engineering*, January 1992.
24. Carla Rapoport, "Why Japan Keeps Winning," *Fortune*, July 15, 1991.
25. Ibid.
26. Alan S. Blinder, "A Japanese Buddy System that Could Benefit U.S. Business," *Business Week*, Octoer 14, 1991.
27. Yoshio Tsurumi, "Don't Beat the Keiretsu. Join Them," *New York Times*, August 2, 1992.
28. Joseph T. Gorman, "Comments on Japan," *Japan Close-Up*, March 1992.
29. Interview with Masasuke Ide, *Nihon Keizai Shimbun*, May 11, 1992.
30. Alan S. Blinder, "How Japan Puts the 'Human' in Human Capital," *Business Week*, November 11, 1991.
31. Ibid.
32. T. J. Rodgers, "An Industry that Doesn't Need Saving from Japan," *Wall Street Journal*, January 2, 1992.
33. Cypress Semiconductor Corporation press release, May 13, 1992.
34. American Electronics Association press release, May 27, 1992.
35. William M. Bulkeley, "The Videophone Era May Finally Be Near, Bringing Big Changes," *Wall Street Journal*, March 10, 1992.
36. Lester Thurow, *Head to Head: The Coming Economic Battle among Japan, Europe and America*, New York: William Morrow & Co., 1992, pp. 248–49.
37. "Asia Ascending," *Newsweek*, December 9, 1991.
38. Steven Greenhouse, "Attention America! Snap Out of It!" *New York Times*, February 9, 1992.

Chapter 5

1. Jonathan Peterson and Sam Jameson, "The Banker Behind Japan's Rising Rates," *Los Angeles Times*, March 16, 1990.
2. Robert Neff, "The Man Who Said 'The Bubble Has Burst,' " *Business Week*, April 27, 1992.
3. Stefan Wagstyl, "The Big Squeeze in Japan," *Financial Times*, April 27, 1992.
4. Yukio Noguchi, "Asset Price Inflation and Its Aftereffects," presentation to Japan Society of New York, May 28, 1992.
5. Hidetaka Tomomatsu, "Fall in Asset Values Seen Having Little Effect on Economy," *Nikkei Weekly*, June 20, 1992.
6. John J. Curran, "Why Japan Will Emerge Stronger," *Fortune*, May 18, 1992.
7. Paul Bluestein, "This Time, a More Modest Economic Revival for Japan," *Washington Post*, June 22, 1992.
8. Akio Morita, "A Critical Moment for Japanese Management," *Bungei Shunju*, January 10, 1992.
9. Akio Morita, speech to the Trilateral Commission, Lisbon, April 1992.
10. Akio Morita, speech to Japan America Society of Alabama, February 20, 1992.
11. "Why Japan Must Change," *Fortune*, March 9, 1992.
12. Reuters, "Sony's Morita Says Japan Can Change and Compete," April 16, 1992.
13. James C. Abegglen, "Morita's Argument Misses Bigger Issues," *Tokyo Business Today*, April 1992.
14. Masaya Miyoshi, "Restructuring Japan's Market Economy," *Tokyo Business Today*, April 1992.
15. Shoichiro Toyoda, "Japan's Role in the World Community," speech to the Japan Society of New York, October 16, 1991.
16. Christopher J. Chipello, "Japan's Leaders Urge Businesses to Shift Their Focus to Improve Quality of Life," *Wall Street Journal*, January 28, 1992.
17. "Is a Richer Life on the Horizon?" *Japan Times*, January 20, 1992.
18. David E. Sanger, "Shoguns' Foe Takes a Page from Past (and Perot)," *New York Times*, July 14, 1992.
19. Yoshio Terasawa, "Running for a New Life in Japan," *Washington Post*, July 12, 1992.
20. Takeshi Sasaki, "LDP's Grip on Power May Be Loosening," *Nikkei Weekly*, July 27, 1992.
21. Kenichi Ohmae, speech to the Japan Society of New York, February 6, 1992.

22. Clay Chandler, "Japan's Woes Stir Talk Its Firms May Modify Time-Honored Ways," *Wall Street Journal*, April 30, 1992.

Chapter 6

1. Kenneth S. Courtis, "Dear Mr. Prime Minister: Your Country Needs to Shift Gears," *International Herald Tribune*, January 8, 1992.
2. Naoto Omi, "Labor Sets Its Sights on the 1,800-Hour Year," *Economic Eye*, Spring 1992.
3. Stefan Wagstyl, "The Big Squeeze in Japan," *Financial Times*, April 27, 1992.
4. Kathleen Kerwin and James B. Treece, "Detroit's Big Chance," *Business Week*, June 29, 1992.
5. Stefan Wagstyl, "The Science of Superiority," *Financial Times*, December 3, 1990.
6. Brian Deagon, "Can a Factory Approach Work in Creative World of Software Development?" *Investor's Business Daily*, June 19, 1992.
7. Neil W. Davis, "Japan Underrated on Software," *Nikkei Weekly*, June 20, 1992.
8. David Kirkpatrick, "Who's Winning the Computer Race," *Fortune*, June 17, 1991.
9. Yuko Inoue, "Americans Seen Gaining Edge from 'Multimedia' Alliances," *Nikkei Weekly*, July 4, 1992.
10. Pico Iyer, "What Oscar Wilde Knew About Japan," *Time*, May 25, 1992.
11. Yoshimichi Yamashita, "Japanese Executives Face Life Out of the Next," *Wall Street Journal*, December 16, 1991.
12. Bill Powell and Peter McKillop, "Sayonara, America," *Newsweek*, August 19, 1991.
13. Paul Bluestein, "Sitting It Out in Asia," *Washington Post*, June 7, 1992.
14. Hirotomo Nomura and Eri Kudo, "Litigious U.S. Worries Japanese Executives," *Nikkei Weekly*, June 20, 1992.
15. *Wall Street Journal*, May 7, 1992.
16. Powell and McKillop, op. cit.
17. Urban C. Lehner, " 'Things Japanese' Permeate Thailand," *Wall Street Journal*, June 24, 1991.
18. Urban C. Lehner, "Japanese Prepare for Vietnam Gold Rush," *Wall Street Journal*, February 21, 1992.
19. David E. Sanger, "Power of the Yen Winning Asia," *New York Times*, December 5, 1991.

20. Hiroshi Yamazaki and Bill Clifford, "MITI Sharpens Asian Focus in Policy," *Nikkei Weekly*, June 20, 1992.
21. Kenneth S. Courtis, "Japan at the Summit," Deutsche Bank Group global strategy research paper, July 6, 1992.

Chapter 7

1. Bob Davis, "Competitiveness Is a Big Word in D.C., Just Ask the V.P.," *Wall Street Journal*, July 1, 1992.
2. Francis Fukuyama, "Is America on the Way Down? (Round Two)," *Commentary*, May 1992.
3. Morton Kondracke, "Washington Diarist," *New Republic*, April 20, 1992.
4. W. Daniel Hillis, letter to the *Harvard Business Review*, May–June 1992.
5. Ibid.
6. James Sterngold, "It's Not Just Some Cars, It's the Future," *New York Times*, January 12, 1992.
7. Senator Carl Levin, unpublished briefing paper, "Two Decades of White House False Optimism on Trade with Japan," January 1992.
8. Ibid.
9. Ibid.
10. Leslie H. Gelb, "Three Whine Mice," *New York Times*, January 13, 1992.
11. Thomas L. Friedman, "Fractured Vision," *New York Times Magazine*, June 28, 1992.
12. Ibid.
13. Anonymous, "Our Do-Nothing Government," *New York Times*, March 30, 1992.
14. Joseph J. Romm, "The Gospel According to Sun Tzu," *Forbes*, December 9, 1991.
15. George Fisher, speech to the Japan Society of New York, February 19, 1992.
16. Andrew Pollack, "Frustrated, Chip Group May Disband," *New York Times*, February 12, 1992.

Chapter 8

1. Thomas L. Friedman, op. cit.
2. William Taylor, "Stop Playing 'Catch Up' with the Japanese," *Wall Street Journal*, March 9, 1992.

3. Paul Bluestein, "Japanese Advocates Sharing New Technology with U.S.," *Washington Post*, June 17, 1991.

4. Akio Morita, "Partnering for Competitiveness: The Role of Japanese Business," *Harvard Business Review*, May–June 1992.

5. Robert Neff, "Japan Opens the Export Spigot," *Business Week*, June 29, 1992.

6. Jacqueline Mitchell, "Ford Agrees to Buy 50% Stake in Mazda's Car Factory in Michigan," *Wall Street Journal*, April 16, 1992.

7. Jacob M. Schlesinger, "AT&T, NEC Unveil Alliance to Make Chips," *Asian Wall Street Journal*, April 23, 1991.

8. Alex Taylor III, "Chrysler's Next Boss Speaks," *Fortune*, July 27, 1992.

9. "Measures for Promoting Foreign Direct Investment in Japan," *News from MITI*, February 1992.

10. Robert Reich, "Do We Want U.S. to Be Rich or Japan Poor?" *Wall Street Journal*, June 18, 1990.

11. John Stevens, *Aikido: The Way of Harmony*, Boston: Shambala, 1985.

12. Ibid.

13. "Final Report," Commission on U.S.-Japan Relations for the Twenty-first Century," Washington, D.C., November 1991.

14. Richard Holbrooke, "Bashing Is Dangerous and Avoidable," *New York Times*, February 22, 1992.

15. John Markoff, "Rethinking the National Chip Policy," *New York Times*, July 14, 1992.

16. Ibid.

17. "Joint Report of the U.S.-Japan Working Group on the Structural Impediments Initiative," June 28, 1990.

18. David E. Sanger, "Japan to U.S.: Tighten Up. U.S. to Japan: Loosen Up," *New York Times*, March 27, 1991.

19. Jonathan Rauch, *The Outnation: A Search for the Soul of Japan*, Boston: Harvard University Press, 1992.

20. "Final Report," Commission on U.S.-Japan Relations for the Twenty-first Century," Washington, D.C., November 1991.

21. Stephen J. Solarz and Nobuo Matsunaga, "Open a Freeway for Pacific Trade," *Los Angeles Times*, June 24, 1992.

22. C. Fred Bergsten, "The United States and Japan in the Post–Cold War Era: Forging a New Partnership for the 1990s and Beyond," speech in Tokyo, March 9, 1992.

23. Ibid.

24. Valerie Rice, "U.S. and Japan: Allies or Adversaries," *San Jose Mercury News*, December 15, 1991.

25. Harold Brown, "Crossroads for U.S.-Japan Relations," *Issues in Science and Technology*, Winter 1992.

26. Toshihiro Kiribuchi, "Japanese Culture, Management and Economic Friction," unpublished paper, 1992.

27. Shintaro Ishihara, "Forget Pearl Harbor," *The Economist*, November 30, 1991.

28. Machiavelli, op. cit.

29. Ibid.

Acknowledgments

This book was written during a period of extraordinary upheaval and fluctuation in the events that form its context. Supportive editors and publishers were enormously important to me under those circumstances. I am particularly grateful to Fred Hills, my editor at Simon and Schuster, and to Jack McKeown, publisher at S&S, for their unflagging encouragement, their patience, and their many good ideas along the way. I am similarly and equally indebted to my editors and publishers in Japan, including Yoshihiro Mita, president of Mita Industrial Co., and Akio Etori, executive director at Mita Press.

A great many experts on U.S.-Japan relations shared their thinking and stimulated my own as I was working on this book. In addition, I have borrowed extensively from the reports of many outstanding journalists and from the intriguing and useful ideas of a wide range of writers, business leaders, and political figures. Although most of the specific citations are footnoted, I would like to salute these people for the intellectual work they are doing in analyzing the difficult issues involved in U.S.-Japan affairs and related matters of the new global economy. Many other friends and colleagues have been of special help to me. A very partial list of those to whom I would like to say some special words of thanks includes:

James C. Abegglen, Kiyoshi Asano, Makoto Asano, Seale Ballenger, Dave Barbor, C. Fred Bergsten, Alan S. Blinder, Paul Bluestein, Michael Borrus, Harold Brown, Craig Buck, Marie-Louise Caravatti, Jonathan Colby, Laureen Connelly, Kenneth S. Courtis, John J. Curran, Arne J. deKeijzer, Peter Drucker, Arthur Dunkel, Martin Edelston, Leslie Ellen, Glenn W. Erickson, Michele Farinet, George Fisher, Kathy Franco, Thomas L. Friedman, Jeffrey E. Garten, Leslie H. Gelb, Grace Glassman, Joseph T. Gorman, Steven Greenhouse, Gary Hamel, W. Daniel Hillis, Richard Holbrooke, Koichi Hori, Junji Ito, Kenichi Ito, Pico Iyer, Toshihiro Kiribuchi, Fumio Kodama, Paul Krugman, Katsura Kuno, Makoto Kuroda, Shawn Layden, Doron P. Levin, John Markoff, Nobuo Matsunaga, Victoria Meyer, James C. Morgan & J. Jeffrey Morgan, Akio Morita, Robert Neff, Yukio Noguchi, Ikujiro Nonaka, Joan

O'Connor, Kenichi Ohmae, Takeshi Ohta, Peter Passell, Peter G. Peterson, Bill Powell, C.K. Prahalad, Carla Rapoport, Jonathan Rauch, Robert B. Reich, T. R. Reid, Ian Ross, Kei Sakaguchi, Masakatsu Sakomoto, David Sanger, Gary R. Saxonhouse, Kunio Shimazu, Stephen J. Solarz, James Sterngold, Chikara Suzuki, Alex Taylor III, Yoshio Terasawa, Lester Thurow, Alvin and Heidi Toffler, Shoichiro Toyoda, Yoshio Tsurumi, Ezra Vogel, Stefan Wagstyl, David Warsh, Steven R. Weisman, James P. Womack, Yoshimichi Yamashita, Daniel Yankelovich, John Young, Mortimer B. Zuckerman, as well as the Commission on U.S.-Japan Relations for the Twenty-first Century, and the Council on Competitiveness.

My family rallied around this effort with enthusiasm, understanding, patience, and grace. David, my four-year-old son, not only put up with my difficult work schedule, but helped persuade me to reject a rather poor title I had earlier contemplated.

My wife Julie was there, emotionally and intellectually, every one of the more than five hundred days it took to finish this project. Some of her unique insights and ideas about Japan, America, and the future of the Pacific Rim are reflected in this book. Through the late nights and endless worries that go with the territory of writing a book such as this, I was certain that no writer could ask for more loving support, or for a deeper partnership with another human being.

Index

Abegglen, James C., 154
Advanced Micro Devices, 66
aerospace industry, 205, 237
AIDS, 55, 191
Akers, John, 116
Amaya, Naohiro, 32
Apple, 173
Armacost, Michael H., 213
Asia:
  Japanese influence in, 88, 100,
    133, 174–79
  social structure in, 190
  U.S. influence in, 176, 178
asset inflation, 141, 143, 144, 145,
  146, 147
AT&T, 41, 74, 129, 219
automobile industry:
  in Asia, 177
  Big Three of, 31, 43, 65, 94,
    199–200
  "bubble" collapse and, 35–36,
    37
  Bush's Tokyo visit and, 31,
    199–201
  competitiveness in, 67
  defect ratios in, 104
  domestic content in, 78, 214–15
  employment in, 199, 200, 201
  energy efficiency in, 95
  flexible manufacturing in, 111–
    112
  foreign trade and, 27, 31, 95
  global market for, 101–2

Japanese, 28, 35–36, 72, 132,
  168, 170, 176, 199, 200–201
Japanese market for, 49, 75, 77,
  199–201, 215
joint ventures in, 215–16
keiretsu system in, 120, 121
long-term investment in, 53–54
luxury market for, 94–96
managed trade for, 60
market share in, 38, 43, 96,
  201, 220
parts contracts for, 32, 58, 73
plants for, 28, 43, 75, 78, 91–
  93, 101–2, 201, 214, 215
price increases in, 72, 169, 220–
  221
profitability of, 176
quality in, 91–96, 200
robotization in, 43, 110–11, 166
trade negotiations on, 199–201,
  214–16
U.S., 60, 65, 72, 73, 214–16

Baker, James A., III, 204
banking industry, 13, 29, 33, 34–
  35, 122–23, 142–43, 146, 149
Bank of Japan, 140, 145, 146
Bank of Tokyo, 29
bankruptcies, 13, 33–34, 149
Bartley, Robert L., 24
Bell Labs, 74
Bergsten, C. Fred, 245–46
Bingaman, Jeff, 105

biotechnology, 41, 188
Blinder, Alan S., 121, 126–27
BMW, 94, 95–96, 216
Boeing, 41
bonds:
  Japanese government, 122
  junk, 30, 35, 242
  Treasury, 29, 70
  warrant, 35, 141
Borrus, Michael, 231
Brady Plan, 181
Brown, Harold, 246
Brown, Jerry, 209
"bubble" economy, Japanese:
  banking industry affected by,
    33, 34–35
  capital investment and, 29–30,
    35, 36–37, 40, 106, 112, 124
  collapse of, 22, 23, 28–36, 37,
    146–50, 160–61, 228
  economic impact of, 36–46, 63,
    142, 145, 146, 147–48
  foreign trade and, 140
  formation of, 139–46
  money supply and, 38, 39, 140–
    141, 146–47
  new era initiated by, 39–40, 70,
    71–72, 138, 147–50, 151,
    152, 166, 168, 176
  political impact of, 142, 143,
    144–45, 146, 147
  real estate values and, 33, 37,
    38, 142, 143, 146, 147
  stock market crash in, 33–34,
    37, 38, 40, 48, 122, 138,
    141–44, 146, 147
  U.S. response to, 41–46, 70
  see also economy, Japanese
bubei, 47
Buchanan, Pat, 83, 209
Bungei Shunju, 152
Bush, George:
  economic policies of, 14, 16,
    17, 30, 56, 58, 60, 62–63, 65,
    66, 69, 83, 137–38, 151, 199,
    205, 207
  government as viewed by, 12,
    199, 205, 207, 210
  Japan policy of, 203–4

  leadership of, 209
  Miyazawa's meeting with, 79
  "new world order" of, 151
  political agenda of, 196–97,
    200
  Tokyo visit of (1992), 31–32,
    48, 78, 195–202, 229–30
  trade policy of, 31
Business Week, 59, 82
"Buy American" movement, 77–
  79, 83

Canada, 51, 87, 88, 233
capital:
  availability of, 38, 50, 53
  cost of, 46, 223
  formation of, 122–24, 210
  "human," 54, 124–30, 215–16
  investment of, 25, 28–30, 35,
    36–37, 40, 54, 70–71, 106,
    112, 122–24, 148, 149, 168–
    169, 176, 233
  liquidity of, 46, 141, 144, 146,
    147
  productivity and, 44
capitalism:
  creative destruction in, 99, 192–
    193
  European, 100
  Japanese, 55–57, 59, 63, 97,
    119, 126–27, 161, 168, 187,
    227, 243
  "relationship," 117–22, 168–69
  revisionist critique of, 56–63
  U.S., 22, 56–57, 59, 63, 97, 98,
    99, 119, 168, 187, 190, 192–
    193, 227, 243
Caravatti, Marie-Louise, 109
Carter, Jimmy, 201
Cavuto, Neal, 149
Cedergren, Christopher, 219
Central Intelligence Agency
  (CIA), 30
Chamber of Commerce, Japan, 51
Chamber of Commerce, U.S., 85
China, People's Republic of, 175,
  204
Chrysler, 30, 73
Churchill, Winston S., 100

Clinton, Bill, 14, 17, 24, 55, 62, 64–65, 76, 138, 208
Cold War:
   ending of, 49, 180, 182, 191, 209, 232
   global economy and, 59
   U.S.-Japanese relationship in, 12, 30, 48, 56, 202–3, 228, 236, 241, 245
Columbia Pictures, 29, 30
Columbus, Christopher, 235
Commerce Department, U.S., 80, 222
Commission on U.S.-Japan Relations for the Twenty-first Century, 244
Committee for the Year 2010, 114
Committee on Foreign Investment in the United States (CFIUS), 236, 237
competitiveness:
   agenda for, 61–63, 65–67
   as concept, 45, 59, 153, 186
   domestic, 58, 243
   foreign investment and, 63–64
   Japanese, 12, 23–24, 40, 41, 67, 124, 134, 153, 187
   legislation on, 186, 207
   in semiconductor industry, 66, 127–28
   U.S., 23, 43, 51, 55, 57, 61–63, 65, 76, 82, 186–93, 202, 208, 214
computers, computer industry, 80, 114, 170–73, 194, 205, 214
   desktop, 165
   fifth-generation, 96, 170
   hardware for, 170–72
   software for, 41, 111, 170–72, 173, 188
Cooper, Robin, 109
corporations:
   acquisitions by, 28–29, 51, 70, 75–76
   affiliates and subsidiaries of, 73–74
   earnings of, 37, 44
   interlocking, *see keiretsu*

   middle management in, 54, 165, 168
   philanthropy of, 73, 152–53
Council on Competitiveness, U.S., 30, 106, 113–14
Courtis, Kenneth S., 40–41, 112–113, 183
Cracking the Japanese Market (Morgan), 86
Cramer, James J., 23
Cresson, Edith, 102
Cuban Missile Crisis, 49
currency, 27, 149, 151
   exchange rates for, 238–39
   weak, 13, 45, 46
   see also dollar; yen
Cusumano, Michael, 170
Cypress Semiconductor, 127, 128

Dai-Ichi Kangyo Bank (DKB), 34, 118
DARPA, 206
"data highways," 54, 216
debt crisis, international, 180–81
Defense Department, U.S., 66, 106
defense industry, 205, 206
defense spending, 62, 65, 167, 182, 223–25, 233
de Gaulle, Charles, 199
Delors, Jacques, 231
Deming, W. Edwards, 103–4
Deng Xiaoping, 175
Digital Equipment Corporation, 85
digital signal-processing chips, 41, 42, 172
discount rate, 38, 140, 145, 146
dividends, 72, 99, 123, 152
Doi, Takako, 156
dollar:
   devaluation of, 28
   strength of, 29, 50, 143, 223
   yen vs., 56–57, 149, 151, 239
Dow-Jones Index, 27, 33
Drucker, Peter, 106–7, 239
drug addiction, 55
Dukakis, Michael, 82
Dulles, John Foster, 94–95
Dunkel, Arthur, 234

economics:
  "bubble," 147–48
  demand-side, 163
  fashions in, 26
  Keynesian, 160
  laissez-faire, 16, 56, 57, 58, 60,
    192–93, 204–5, 208, 216
  macro-, 27, 87–88, 239
  planned, 98–99
  supply-side, 148, 163
economy, global:
  cross-border partnerships in, 59,
    66, 74, 240
  emerging markets of, 66, 110,
    129–30, 133, 174–75, 184
  interdependence of, 79–82,
    133, 184–85, 247
  strategy in, 27–28, 30, 130–34
  Triad in, 129, 133, 241, 245–46
economy, Japanese:
  access to, 58, 64
  "bicycle theory" of, 141
  core competencies of, 97–135
  efficiency in, 126–27
  as expansionist, 71, 130–34,
    247
  fundamentals of, 37–38
  governmental direction for, 56,
    57, 114, 130–32
  growth of, 12, 28, 148, 162–63,
    202–3, 225–26
  mercantilism of, 56, 71, 182
  money supply in, 38, 39
  post-bubble era of, 39–40, 70,
    71–72, 138, 147–50, 151,
    152, 166, 168, 176
  in recession, 13, 23, 26, 27, 35,
    39, 44, 137, 147–50, 197,
    218
  restructuring of, 13, 36, 38–41,
    44, 71–72, 150–59
  risk-taking and, 150–52, 173
  social values and, 14, 46, 97,
    150–59
  U.S. economy vs., 11–12, 25,
    26–27, 29–32, 178, 179, 195–
    210, 225–27
  see also "bubble" economy, Jap-
    anese

economy, U.S.:
  congressional action on, 14,
    235, 240
  financial services sector in,
    144–45
  governmental direction for, 29,
    44, 45, 54–55, 192, 193, 203–
    205, 210
  growth of, 225–26
  Japanese economy vs., 11–12,
    25, 26–27, 29–32, 178, 179,
    195–210, 225–27
  political impact of, 12–13
  Reagan-Bush policies on, 16,
    56, 60, 62–63, 65
  in recession, 13, 30, 149, 191,
    196, 198
  restructuring of, 13–14, 16, 39–
    40, 57, 61, 63, 130, 151,
    213–25, 233
  resurgence of, 23, 26, 27, 33
  self-correction by, 45
  social support for, 27, 46, 54,
    61, 129
  strategic approach for, 195–210,
    225–27
  vision for, 227–30
  wealth generated by, 98, 99, 137
Edelston, Martin, 27–28
education and training, 38, 53, 54,
  61, 62, 124, 191
  Japanese vs. U.S., 125–26,
    173–74, 189, 191, 193, 215–
    216, 242
electronics industry:
  competitiveness in, 67
  foreign trade and, 27
  Japanese, 38, 67, 120, 128, 170,
    172–73
  keiretsu system in, 120
  long-term investment in, 54
  as "low-tech," 116–17
  market share in, 38, 128
  U.S., 41, 42, 128, 129, 172,
    195, 207–8
employment, 43, 128
  assurances of, 38–39, 93, 126–
    127
  in auto industry, 199, 200, 201

employment (*cont.*)
  protectionism and, 64, 68
  structural unemployment vs.,
    12, 191
Encarnation, Dennis, 218
energy, 13, 95, 143, 151, 152,
    191–92, 239–40
engineers, 108
entrepreneurship, 188
environment, 155, 191, 239
Europe, Eastern, 175, 224
European Community (EC), 60,
    87, 100, 174, 179, 181, 183,
    229, 230, 231, 233, 234, 236,
    238, 240, 241, 247
Export-Import Bank, U.S., 222
Ezoe, Hiromasa, 144

Fields, Craig, 66–67
Financial World, 42
Fisher, George, 207
Forbes, 23
Ford, 30, 72, 219
fortuna, 15, 17, 248
Fortune, 38, 94
Friedman, Thomas L., 203
Fuji Bank, 34
Fujita, Shiro, 36
Fujitsu, 66, 70, 106, 118
Fukushima, Glen, 204
Fukuyama, Francis, 190

G-7 economic summit (1992),
    182–83
gaiatsu, 166, 243, 244
Gates, Bill, 188
GATT (General Agreement on
    Tariffs and Trade), 87, 181,
    183, 217, 232, 234, 245
Gelb, Leslie, 202
General Motors (GM), 30, 36, 37,
    44, 54, 70, 94, 110–11, 120–
    121, 200, 218, 220
Gephardt, Richard A., 82, 83, 119
Germany, 55, 179, 187
Glory and the Dream, The (Man-
    chester), 174
Goldman Sachs, 29
Gore, Al, Jr., 24, 54–55, 65

Gorman, Joseph T., 122
Great Britain, 98, 133, 184
Great Depression, 160
Greater East Asian Co-Prosperity
    Sphere, 177–78
Greenspan, Alan, 191
Grove, Andrew, 45
Gyohten, Toyoo, 141–42, 145

Hamel, Gary, 109–10
Hammer, Susan, 69–70
Hanabusa, Masamichi, 182
Hanawa, Yoshikazu, 169
Harkin, Tom, 69, 82
Harvard Business Review, 76
Hashimoto, Ryutaro, 146
Hatakeyama, Noboru, 200
health care, 61, 191
Hewlett Packard, 116
High Definition Television
    (HDTV), 42, 172
Hillis, W. Daniel, 194–95
Hiroshima bombing, 69
Hitachi, 70
Hitachi Metals, 73
Holbrooke, Richard, 229
Hollings, Ernest, 48
Honda, 72, 73, 95, 106
Hong Kong, 176
Hori, Koichi, 159
Horton, Willie, 209
Hosokawa, Morihiro, 157, 158
House, Karen Elliott, 23
Hussein, Saddam, 182, 197

Iacocca, Lee, 48, 85
IBJ Bank, 34
IBM, 42, 80, 116, 120, 173, 219
Ide, Masasuke, 124
industrial policy, 59–67
  governmental direction for, 57,
    59–60, 61, 62–63, 67, 216–
    217, 221–23
  Japanese, 12, 57, 132–34, 221–
    223
  Reagan-Bush opposition to, 12,
    199, 205, 207, 210
  U.S., 59–60, 61
Industrial Revolution, 67, 130

inflation, 38, 39, 141, 145
Intel, 45
interest rates, 27, 50, 143, 147
International Monetary Fund
    (IMF), 137, 241
Ishihara, Shintaro, 47–48, 154, 247
Ishihara, Takashi, 159
Isutani, Minoru, 33
Isuzu, 36
Iverson, J. Richard, 128
Iyer, Pico, 173–74

Japan:
    "access zones" in, 222
    agriculture in, 136, 163–65,
        181, 237
    Asian economic sphere of, 88,
        100, 133, 174–79
    budget surplus of, 39, 40, 123
    consumerism in, 72, 155, 157,
        161–67, 234, 239
    corporatism in, 155, 178
    corruption in, 124, 144, 146,
        147, 156, 157
    as creative society, 169–74
    Diet of, 155, 156, 158, 201,
        235, 240
    domestic market of, 46, 49, 51–
        53, 58, 85–86, 140, 181, 198,
        199–201, 202, 217, 221–23
    economy of, *see* economy, Japa-
        nese
    foreign aid of, 178–79, 181,
        182, 223
    foreign investment by, 25, 28–
        30, 35, 36–37, 44, 51–52,
        131, 143, 176, 215, 218
    GDP of, 39, 52, 123, 135, 137,
        162, 182, 218, 224
    "getting tough" with, 16, 60,
        79–82, 203–4
    global responsibilities of, 153,
        155, 156, 180–85, 198, 229,
        234, 241
    GNP of, 158, 243
    as homogeneous society, 97,
        190–91, 227
    imperialism of, 177–78, 179
    international influence of, 12,
        13, 71, 84–85, 99–100, 130,
        133–34, 160, 178–79, 198,
        247
    labor movement in, 38, 165
    land use in, 163–64
    living standards in, 72, 93, 100,
        148, 152–56, 157, 164
    as metaphor, 49–55, 59, 62, 208
    as military power, 182, 223–25
    as mirror image of U.S., 49–51
    natural resources of, 131, 132,
        134
    oil imports by, 13, 140, 143,
        182, 237, 240
    "overpresence" of, 143, 177
    in Persian Gulf War, 156, 180,
        182, 197–98, 223
    polarization in, 142
    political system of, 156–59
    as producer society, 56, 98, 142,
        155
    productivity in, 26, 28, 44, 97,
        134–38, 167
    as profit-making society, 167–
        169
    real estate values in, 13, 33, 37,
        38, 124, 142, 143, 146, 147,
        164, 217–18
    "reinvention" of, 45, 152–56,
        161
    reputation of, 14–15, 143, 177
    retailing practices in, 166
    social transformation of, 160–85
    suicide rate in, 48, 149
    trade surplus of, 25, 57, 62, 68,
        79, 82, 95, 123–24, 132, 136,
        140, 162, 201, 218, 235
    unemployment in, 38, 149
    U.S. as perceived in, 32, 47–
        49, 154
    U.S. investment in, 217–18
    U.S. occupation of, 117–18
    wages in, 46, 162
    women in, 39
    work ethic in, 38, 51, 97
    workforce of, 40, 44, 45, 93,
        102–3, 124–30, 152, 153, 155
    xenophobia in, 163
Japan Development Bank, 222

Japan External Trade Organization
  (JETRO), 132, 181, 221
Japan New Party, 157
Japan Systems Corporation, 218
Japan 2000, 30–31
J. D. Power & Associates, 91, 96,
  104
"just-in-time" delivery, 36, 104

Kanemaru, Shin, 157
Kawamoto, Nobuhiko, 36
Kawasaki Steel, 28
Kearney, A. T., 109
kee-wahdos, 152
Keidanren, 246
keiretsu:
  "bubble" collapse and, 35
  definition of, 117–18
  distribution, 49, 119–20, 121,
    166, 220, 242
  horizontal, 118–19
  internationalization of, 121–22,
    133, 220, 242
  as "relationship capitalism,"
    117–22, 168–69
  supplier, 74–75, 152
  U.S. interests excluded by,
    119–20, 218, 242, 243
  U.S. trusts compared with, 118,
    120–21
  vertical, 119, 120, 121
kenbei, 47
Kennedy, Paul, 24
Kerrey, Bob, 69, 82–83
Kiribuchi, Toshihiro, 246
Kodama, Fumio, 112
Komatsu, 78
Kondracke, Morton, 192
Kono, Yohei, 179
Krugman, Paul, 53
Kuehler, Jack D., 231
Kuroda, Makoto, 242
kyosei, 246

Latin America, 174–75
Leamer, Edward E., 187
Lexus LS400, 91–96, 111–12
Liberal Democratic Party (LDP),
  69, 144, 156–59

Lill, Albert, 129
Lincoln, Abraham, 126
Los Angeles riots (1992), 189
Luddites, 67, 248

MacArthur, Douglas, 117–18
McDonnell-Douglas, 237
Machiavelli, Niccolò, 11, 15–16,
  17, 65, 248
McLaughlin, Brian, 81
Malaysia, 178, 180
Manchester, William, 173, 174
manufacturing:
  automated, 25, 43, 55, 91–96
  continuous improvement (*ka-
    izen*) in, 38, 44, 91–96, 101–
    103, 107, 165, 168
  cost reduction in, 38, 43
  customized production in, 112
  flexible, 38, 111–13
  goals for, 101, 102, 107
  Japanese innovations in, 63, 65,
    66, 75, 91–96, 97, 142, 168,
    218, 246
  joint, 74
  "just-in-time," 112–13, 119
  layoffs in, 43, 68
  lean production in, 95, 101–2,
    134
  mass production in, 101–2, 112,
    113, 127
  process innovation in, 108–10,
    169
  production noise in, 92
  service sector vs., 135–36
  transplanting of, 43, 78
  U.S., 25, 43–44
market share, 29, 41, 57
  in auto industry, 38, 43, 96,
    201, 220
  in electronics industry, 38, 128
  Japanese concentration on, 72,
    132, 152, 153, 167–69
  quotas and, 80–81
Marshall Plan, 184, 191, 246
Martin, Jim, 57
Massachusetts Institute of Technology (MIT), 75, 101–2

Materials Research Corporation, 75–76
Matsudaira, Sadatomo, 152
Matsunaga, Nobuo, 245
Matsushita, 29, 35, 73, 168, 178, 180
Mazda, 95, 219
MCA, 29, 35
MCC, 66–67
Mercedes, 94, 95–96
Mexico, 88, 174–75, 183, 187, 233
micromachines, 114
microprocessors, 171
Micro Tech 2000 plan, 208
Mieno, Yasushi, 38, 40, 145–46, 147
Ministry of Finance, 39, 132, 139, 141, 143, 144, 145, 146
Ministry of International Trade and Industry (MITI), 32, 100, 114, 131, 132, 170, 179, 181, 222, 243
Mitsubishi, 30, 34, 95, 117, 118
Mitsui, 117, 118
Miyazawa, Kiichi, 32, 71–72, 79, 100, 155, 157, 197, 198, 229–230
Miyazawa Plan, 180–81
Miyoshi, Masaya, 155
Morgan, James C., 86
Morgan, J. Jeffrey, 86
Morita, Akio, 36, 152–55, 215–16
Morrison-Knudsen, 78–79
Mosbacher, Robert, 198
Motorola, 42, 104, 207
Muncy, John, 176

Nagano, Takeshi, 154
Nagasaki bombing, 69
Nakagama, Sam, 70–71
Nakajima, Michio, 36
Nakasone, Yasuhiro, 201
National Advisory Committee on Semiconductors, 207–8
NEC, 74, 154, 219
New York Stock Exchange, 29, 209
New York Times, 43, 59–60, 75, 177–78

Nihon Keizai Shimbun, 147
Nikkei Index, 26–27, 33–34, 37, 142, 145
Nintendo, 81
Nishi, Kazuhiko, 147
Nissan, 94, 95, 109–10, 112, 166
Nixon, Richard M., 13, 157, 201
Noguchi, Yukio, 150
Nomura Securities, 38–39, 157
Nonaka, Ikujiro, 103
North American Free Trade Area (NAFTA), 88, 179, 230, 233, 247

Oda, Toshio, 177
Ohmae, Kenichi, 158
Ohmi, Tadahiro, 108
Ohta, Takeshi, 145
oil crisis, 13, 143, 151, 152
Omi, Naoto, 165
Onoue, Mrs. Nui, 34
Outnation, The (Rauch), 243

Paine Webber, 29
patents, 52, 115–16, 117, 131, 239
Pearl Harbor, 68–70, 86, 177
perestroika, 57, 247
Perot, H. Ross, 83–84, 209–10
Perry, Matthew Calbraith, 243
Persian Gulf War, 196, 209
  Japan's role in, 156, 180, 182, 197–98, 223
Peterson, Peter G., 193
Plaza Agreement (1985), 139
Postindustrial Revolution, 67
Potter, Robert B., 78
Prahalad, C. K., 110
presidential campaign (1992), 30, 54, 69, 77, 82–84, 209–10
Prestowitz, Clyde V., Jr., 57
Prince, The (Machiavelli), 11, 15–16, 17
products, 92
  development of, 106–10, 221
  domestic content of, 73, 78, 214–15
  "dumping" of, 167, 232

"hardware" vs. "software," 127–28, 129
high-value-added parts for, 73, 75
innovations in, 108, 109
"leaping" of, 107
pricing of, 169, 220–21
quality of, 51, 54, 95, 96, 103–105, 112, 168
testing of, 93
profit margins, 72, 96, 99, 167–169, 176
protectionism, 13, 32, 71
employment and, 64, 68
ineffectiveness of, 16, 80–81
Japanese, 14, 45–46, 49, 85–86, 131, 165, 193, 203, 217
political impact of, 82–83, 229–230
U.S., 48, 49, 176, 234, 242, 243

Quality Function Deployment (QFD), 104
Quayle, Dan, 204

Rauch, Jonathan, 243
RCA, 54
Reagan, Ronald:
economic policies of, 14, 16, 21–22, 24, 26, 28, 30, 56, 60, 62–63, 65, 98, 148, 199, 201, 205, 206, 207, 209
government as viewed by, 12, 199, 205, 207, 210
Reaganomics, 24, 28, 148, 209
Recruit affair, 144, 156, 157
Reich, Robert B., 76–77, 78, 225–26
Reilly, Edmund J., 85
Rengo Sangiin, 158
research and development (R&D):
civilian, 25, 55, 105, 106, 107–108
costs of, 66
failure in, 173
government support for, 54
investment in, 41, 45, 63–64, 106, 114

in Japan, 25, 28, 105–8, 218, 219, 246
military, 105, 106
product development and, 106–107
tax credits for, 223
in U.S., 103, 106, 107–8, 193, 219, 246
rice, 52, 163–64
Rio summit (1992), 181
Rise and Fall of the Great Powers, The (Kennedy), 24
robots, 25, 43, 55, 92, 110–11, 165, 166
Rockefeller Center, 30
Rodgers, T. J., 127–28
Roosevelt, Franklin D., 69, 160
Ross, Ian, 208
Russia:
economy of, 137, 175, 181, 183, 241
foreign aid for, 181, 191, 224
Japanese economic relations with, 30, 47, 181

Saba, Shoichi, 118
Saison Group, 29
Sakura, 34
Sakurauchi, Yoshio, 32
Salomon Brothers, 48
Sanders, W. J., III, 66
S&L crisis, 30, 65, 191
San Jose Mercury News, 246
Sanwa, 34
Sasaki, Takeshi, 158
savings rate, 25, 29, 53, 122, 138, 150, 162, 163, 242
Saxonhouse, Gary, 74
Schumpeter, Joseph, 192
Seattle Mariners, 81–82
Seikatsusha, 158
Sekimoto, Tadahiro, 154
Sematech, 66, 67, 206–7, 217
semiconductor industry, 42, 45, 58, 66
competitiveness in, 66, 127–28
corporate acquisitions in, 75–76
government policy on, 206–8
process innovation in, 108

service sector, 54, 128, 135–36
*Seven Fat Years and How to Do It
   Again, The* (Bartley), 24–26
Shilling, A. Gary, 23–24
Shima, Keiji, 42
Siemens, 219
Silicon Valley, 42, 70, 128
60 Minutes, 14
Smith, Adam, 56, 98
socialism, 98–99, 156
sogo-shosha, 117
Solarz, Stephen J., 244
Sony, 28–29, 30, 35, 70, 73, 75–
   76, 109–10, 111
South Sea Bubble (1720), 33
Soviet Union, 22, 98–99, 209
   see also Cold War; Russia
Spencer, William J., 67
Srisirichanya, Paisal, 177
Stahlman, Mark, 42
steel industry, 43, 74
stockholders, 72, 99, 123, 167
stock market:
   Japanese, 13, 33–34, 37, 38, 40,
      48, 122, 138, 141–44, 146,
      147
   U.S., 29, 37, 209
Structural Impediments Initiative
   (SII), 98, 241–42, 244
Subaru, 35
Sumita, Satoshi, 145
Sumitomo, 78–79, 115, 117
Sumitomo Bank, 29, 143
superconductors, 115
"Sushi Boy" case, 163

Tahara assembly plant, 91–93
Taiwan, 237
Takeshita, Noboru, 157
Tanahashi, Yuji, 215
taxes, 54, 62, 64, 65
   credits for, 73, 74, 223
   gasoline, 62, 192
Taylor, William, 214
technology:
   commercialization of, 38, 169,
      173
   copy-cat, 117
   creative, 42, 169–74
   critical, 113–17, 172

digital, 216
Japanese innovation in, 113–17,
   227, 234
"leap-frogging" in, 172
transfer of, 74, 215, 246
U.S. innovation in, 103, 114,
   116, 127, 172, 216–17
U.S. leadership in, 41–43, 115–
   117, 193–95, 205, 227
teleports, 54
television industry, 168
Terasawa, Yoshio, 157
Thailand, 177
Thatcher, Margaret, 98
Thinking Machines, 194
Thornburgh, Dick, 197
Thurow, Lester, 130
Tiananmen Square massacre, 175
tobacco industry, 82
Tokyo, 33, 164
Tokyo Stock Exchange, 29, 117,
   144
Toshiba, 30, 35, 70, 80, 109–10,
   118, 219, 231
Total Quality Management
   (TQM), 107
Toyoda, Keichiro, 93
Toyoda, Shoichiro, 96, 155
Toyota, 37, 75, 91–96, 102, 143,
   180, 220, 222
Toys R Us, 166
trade:
   balance of, 11, 23, 27, 39, 71,
      162, 201, 223, 247
   cross-border, 59, 66, 74, 240
   fair, 14–15, 31
   "free," 11, 56, 77, 98, 233,
      234, 244–45
   joint ventures in, 219
   managed, 58–59, 60, 61, 131,
      199
   as political issue, 82–83, 187
   quotas for, 80–81
   voluntary restraint in, 80–81,
      132, 200–201
Trans-Pacific Community (TPC),
   17, 230–48
   "G-2" approach for, 245–46
   as postindustrial organization,
      232–35

U.S.-Japanese relationship in, 230, 233–34, 235–48
transportation, public, 55, 78–79, 242
Treasury bonds, 29, 70
TRW, 122
Tsongas, Paul, 30, 69, 209
Tsukimura, Tetsuo, 147
Tsurumi, Yoshio, 121–22

Union Bank, 29
United Nations (UN), 156, 241
United States:
  agriculture in, 136, 205–6
  antitrust laws of, 118, 121
  budget deficit of, 53, 57, 61, 64, 138, 192, 193, 208, 210, 244
  as consumer society, 56, 93, 98, 166–67
  decline of, 12–13, 24, 26, 28, 49–50
  democratic traditions of, 98, 190, 192
  dysfunctionalism in, 191–93
  economy of, *see* economy, U.S.
  energy policy of, 151, 152, 191–92
  foreign investment by, 233, 236
  global role of, 40, 52, 133–34, 192, 196
  GNP of, 130
  Japan as perceived in, 14–15, 30–31, 49–55, 68–70, 86–87, 133
  Japanese investment in, 28, 44, 51, 55, 60–61, 63–64, 65, 67, 70–71, 72–77, 84–85, 133, 176, 177, 237
  Japanese political influence in, 83, 84–85
  literacy rate in, 126, 189
  living standards in, 12, 30, 45, 53, 77, 135, 138, 157, 188–89
  as market, 232–33, 236
  middle class of, 12, 25, 187, 188, 189
  as military power, 52, 178, 179, 182, 223–25, 235, 240

national debt of, 13, 27, 29, 149, 166, 191
  optimism in, 25–26, 53
  pessimism in, 26, 30, 189
  as pluralistic society, 227
  polarization in, 99, 187, 189, 190, 191
  productivity in, 25, 26, 27–28, 44, 53, 55, 63, 98, 135, 137–138, 191, 192, 239
  real estate market of, 33, 70
  "reinvention" of, 45, 208–10
  social transformation of, 160, 186–210
  special interests in, 51, 61
  as superpower, 32, 71
  trade deficit of, 13, 27, 28, 40, 49, 57, 62, 68, 79, 82, 95, 116, 136, 192, 201, 208, 218, 223, 235
  underclass in, 12, 25, 61
  wages in, 46, 71, 187, 189
  workforce of, 48, 93, 124–30
U.S.-Japanese relations:
  in Cold War, 12, 30, 48, 56, 202–3, 228, 236, 241, 245
  conventional wisdom on, 16, 22–28
  detente in, 49, 69, 88, 183
  interdependence in, 227–30
  "level playing field" for, 57
  Machiavellianism in, 11, 15–16, 17, 248
  media coverage of, 14, 23, 29–30
  as military conflict, 47–50
  new perspectives on, 70–88
  New Wisdom on, 22–28
  "paradigm shift" in, 136
  as political issue, 82–84, 195–202
  as power relationship, 11, 213–248
  practical proposals on, 213–25
  reciprocity in, 11, 58, 180–81, 185
  revisionist critique of, 56–63, 97
  strategic gap in, 195–210
  symbiosis in, 65, 246, 247

U.S.-Japanese relations (*cont.*)
  as synergistic relationship, 229,
    239
  in Trans-Pacific Community
    (TPC), 230, 233–34, 235–48
  trends in, 11–17, 213–49
Utsumi, Makoto, 180–81

video camcorders, 106, 111, 117
videophones, 42, 129
Vietnam, 177
Vietnam War, 53
Vincent, Fay, 81
virtù, 15, 17
"Visionary Factory," 166
Vogel, Ezra, 176
von Kuenheim, Eberhard, 96

Wall Street Journal, 66, 186
Washington Post, 47
wealth, 62, 65, 98, 99, 125, 137,
    157
Weinig, Sheldon, 75–76
welfare, 61, 62, 167, 191
Westin, 29

Wilder, Doug, 82
Wofford, Harris, 196–97
Womack, James P., 101, 103
Wong, Stephen, 177
working hours, 72, 152, 165–66
World Bank, 241

Yamashita, Yoshimichi, 174
Yamauchi, Horoshi, 81
Yankelovich, Daniel, 48, 189–90
Yardeni, Ed, 71
Yasuda Life, 29
yen:
  dollar vs., 56–57, 149, 151, 239
  revaluation of, 132, 139–40
  strength of, 13, 29, 46, 147,
    152, 169, 178
YEN! (Burstein), 15, 47
Yew, Lee Kuan, 180
Young, John, 116–17

zaibatsu, 117–18
zaitek, 142
Zenith, 54, 76
Zuckerman, Mortimer B., 40